PROBLEM SOLUTIONS MANUAL
for the text

Economic Evaluation and Investment Decision Methods

Ninth Edition

D1408746

Franklin J. Stermole
and
John M. Stermole

Copyright © 1996

Investment Evaluations Corporation
2000 Goldenvue Drive
Golden, Colorado 80401

Copyright © 1974, 1977, 1980, 1982, 1984, 1987, 1990, and 1993
by Investment Evaluations Corporation

All rights reserved. No part of this manual may be reproduced in any form
without permission in writing from the publisher.

ISBN 1-878740-07-5
Library of Congress Catalog Card Number 96-75182

Printed in the U.S.A.

CHAPTER 2 PROBLEM SOLUTIONS

2-1 Solution: All Values in Millions

```
P=?     –        –     .................  – $70
─────────────────────────────────────────────
0       1        2    ................  19  20  years
```

Calculating P given F:

$$P = 70\,(\overset{0.2584}{P/F_{7.0\%,20}}) = \$18.088$$

P is the bond cost today to cover the reclamation cost of $70, 20 years from today at 7.0% per year.

Calculating A Given F: **Calculating A Given P:**

$$A = 70\,(\overset{0.02439}{A/F_{7.0\%,20}}) = \$1.707 \qquad A = 18.088\,(\overset{0.09439}{A/P_{7.0\%,20}}) = \$1.707$$

2-2 Solution:

```
P=?      $15,000      $15,000      $15,000
─────────────────────────────────────────────
0          1            2            3
```

$$P = 15{,}000\,(\overset{0.8696}{P/F_{15\%,1}}) + 15{,}000\,(\overset{0.7561}{P/F_{15\%,2}}) + 15{,}000\,(\overset{0.6575}{P/F_{15\%,3}}) = \$34{,}248$$

Or,

$$P = 15{,}000\,(\overset{2.2832}{P/A_{15\%,3}}) = \$34{,}248$$

2-3 Solution:

```
  –      $15,000      $15,000      $15,000
─────────────────────────────────────────  F=?
0          1            2            3
```

$$F = 15{,}000\,(\overset{1.3225}{F/P_{15\%,2}}) + 15{,}000\,(\overset{1.1500}{F/P_{15\%,1}}) + 15{,}000 = \$52{,}087.5$$

Or,

$$F = 15{,}000\,(\overset{3.4725}{F/A_{15\%,3}}) = \$52{,}087.5$$

Or, using the present value, P, from Problem 2-2:

$$F = 34{,}248\,(\overset{1.5209}{F/P_{15\%,3}}) = \$52{,}087.8$$

The difference of .3 is due to round-off error.

2-4 Solution:

Case A, Annual Payments

$15,000	A=?	A=?	A=?	A=?

0	1	2	3	4 years

$$A = 15,000 \overset{0.35027}{(A/P_{15\%,4})} = \$5,254.05 \text{ per year}$$

Case B, Monthly Payments

$15,000	A=?	A=?	A=?	. . . . . .	A=?

0	1	2	3	. . . . . .	48 months

Period "i" equals 15.0% / 12 = 1.25% per month.

$$A = 15,000 \overset{0.02783}{(A/P_{15\%/12,48})} = \$417.46 \text{ per month}$$

2-5 Solution: Values in Thousands

–	–	–	. . . .	–	$30	$30	$30	$30

0	1	2	. . . .	17	18	19	20	21

Case A, Calculating P at Yr 17, given A

$$P = 30 \overset{3.1699}{(P/A_{10.0\%,4})} = \$95.097$$

Case B, Calculating P at time zero, given F or A

$$P = 30 \overset{3.1699}{(P/A_{10.0\%,4})} \overset{0.1978}{(P/F_{10.0\%,17})} = \$18.810$$

Or, $P = 95.097 \overset{0.1978}{(P/F_{10.0\%,17})} = \$18.810$

Or, by taking the uniform series forward first:

$$P = 30 \overset{4.6410}{(F/A_{10.0\%,4})} \overset{0.1351}{(P/F_{10.0\%,21})} = \$18.810$$

Case C, Calculating A

$$A_{1-17} = 95.097 \overset{0.0247}{(A/F_{10.0,17})} = 2.345$$

Or, $A_{1-17} = 18.810 \overset{0.1247}{(A/P_{10.0,17})} = \$2.345$

2-6 Solution:

Loan A - Nominal Flat Interest Rate of 6.5%

Down Payment = $20,000(0.20) = $4,000
Total Interest Paid (Eq 2-14) = $16,000(0.065)(3 years) = $3,120

Total Cost of the Loan = $16,000 principal + $3,120 interest = $19,120

> Nominal 6.5% Flat Interest, Loan Payment Per Month
> A = $19,120 / 36 = $531.11

Loan B - Nominal Interest Rate of 9.0% Compounded Monthly

Down Payment = $20,000(0.20) = $4,000

> Nominal 9.0% Compound Interest, Loan Payment Per Month
> Period Interest Rate = 0.090 / 12 = 0.0075 or 0.75% per month.
>
> $$A = 16,000(A/P\ 9.0\%/12,\ 36) = \$508.80 \quad \text{Least Monthly Cost}$$
> (0.03180)

Since the down payment and loan life are the same, the monthly loan payments can be compared, concluding the least cost approach is to select Loan Option B. Often times however, loan terms vary and this may require consolidating the sum of all costs at the same point in time, or over the same number of compounding periods. Comparing the alternatives by calculating the present cost of each follows:

Loan A: C=$4,000   C=$532.11 .... C=$532.11

0   1   10

Present Worth Cost = P = 4,000 + 532.11(P/A $_{0.83,36}$) = $20,490.75

Loan B: C=$4,000   C=$508.80 .... C=$508.80

0   1   10

Present Worth Cost = P = 4,000 + 508.80(P/A $_{0.83,36}$) = $19,768.34

The least present worth cost is Loan Option B.

2-7   Solution:

```
$1,000                    $2,000
————————————————————————————————————— F=?
0 .............. 10 ............... 20 semi-annual periods
```

The nominal interest rate of 6% compounded semi-annually gives semi-annual period interest, i = 3% per semi-annual period.

$$F = 1,000 \overset{1.806}{(F/P_{3,20})} + 2,000 \overset{1.344}{(F/P_{3,10})} = \$4,494$$

For annual periods, use an effective interest rate/yr:

$$E = (1+0.03)^2 - 1 = 0.0609$$

$$F = 1,000(F/P_{6.09,10}) + 2,000(F/P_{6.09,5}) = \$4,494$$

2-8   Solution:

The $500 payments may be considered to be either investments or incomes depending on whether you are the borrower or lender of money. The solution is the same for either case.

```
              A=$500    A=$500 . . .   A=$500
P = ? —————————————————————————————————————————
        0       1         2 . . . . . . 20 semi-annual periods
```

i = 4% per semi-annual period for a nominal interest rate of 8% compounded semi-annually.

$$P = 500 \overset{13.590}{(P/A_{4,20})} = \$6,795$$

2-9   Solution:

```
P=$5,000  A              A ........................... A
————————————————————————————————————————————————————————— F=$10,000
0         1              2 ........................... 6
```

$$A = 5,000 \overset{0.20336}{(A/P_{6,6})} + 10,000 \overset{0.14336}{(A/F_{6,6})} = \$2,450$$

$$A = [5,000 + 10,000 \overset{0.7050}{(P/F_{6,6})}] \overset{0.20336}{(A/P_{6,6})} = \$2,450$$

$$A = [5,000 \overset{1.4185}{(F/P_{6,6})} + 10,000] \overset{0.14336}{(A/F_{6,6})} = \$2,450$$

2-10 Solution:

```
P=$3,000      A         A .......................... A
_____
   0          1         2 ...................... 36 months
```

Nominal interest rate, r = 12% is compounded monthly, therefore, the period interest rate i = 12%/12, or 1% per month.

Mathematically, $A/P_{1,36} = \dfrac{0.01(1 + 0.01)^{36}}{(1 + 0.01)^{36} - 1} = 0.03321$

$A = 3,000(A/P_{1,36}) = \$99.63$

By interpolation:

$A/P_{1,35} = 0.03400$

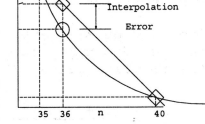

A/P 1,n

$A/P_{1,40} = 0.03046$

$A/P_{1,36} = 0.03400 - [(0.03400 - .03046)/5]$

$A/P_{1,36} = 0.03329$

$$A = 3,000(A/P_{1,36}) = \$99.87$$

2-11 Solution:

```
 -       A         A ................... A
_____  F = $10,000
 0       1         2 ................ 20 quarterly periods
```

i = 1.5% per period

$A/F_{1,20} = 0.04542$

$A/F_{2,20} = 0.04116$

Interpolating: (0.04542 - 0.04116)/2 = 0.00213

$A/F_{1.5,20} = 0.04542 - 0.00213 = 0.04329$

$$A = 10,000(A/F_{1.5,20}) = \$432.90$$

2-12 Solution:

```
P=?        $1,000     $1,000 ......... $1,000
─────────────────────────────────────────────
0           1          2 .............. 10 years
0    1      2     3     4 ............. 20 semi-annual periods
```

r=8% compounded semi-annually, so i=4% per semi-annual period.

$$A = 1,000 \overset{0.49020}{(A/F_{4,2})} = \$490.20$$

An equivalent time diagram:

```
P=?          $490.20 $490.20 $490.20 $490.20 .. $490.20
───────────────────────────────────────────────────────
0       1        2       3        4 . . . . . . .  20
```

$$P = (1,000 \overset{0.4902}{(A/F_{4,2})}) \overset{13.590}{(P/A_{4,20})} = \$6,661.82$$

Or find the effective interest rate, E, per year:

$$P = 1,000(P/A_{E,10})$$

$$E = (1 + 0.04)^2 - 1 = 0.0816 = 8.16\%$$

Interpolating between the 8% and 9% table values, E = 8.16%:

$$P/A_{8.16,10} = 6.710 - (6.710-6.418)(\frac{8.16-8.00}{9.00 - 8.00}) = 6.710 - 0.0467$$

$$= 6.6633$$

Therefore, $P = 1,000 \overset{6.6633}{(P/A_{E,10})} = \$6,663.30$

Interpolation error in determining $P/A_{E,10}$ accounts for the slight difference in results.

Explicitly solving for the factor given E = 8.16% yields:

$$P/A_{8.16\%,10} = \frac{(1.0816)^{10}-1}{0.0816(1.0816)^{10}} = 6.6619$$

$$P = 1,000(6.6619) = \$6,661.92$$

Alternately, $P=1,000[\overset{0.9246}{P/F_{4,2}} + \overset{0.8548}{P/F_{4,4}} + \overset{0.7903}{P/F_{4,6}} + ... + \overset{0.4564}{P/F_{4,20}}]= \$6,662$

2-13 Solution:

$3,000	$6,000	$7,000	$7,000	$4,000
0	1	2	3	4

$$P = 3{,}000 + 6{,}000\overset{0.8929}{(P/F_{12,1})} + 7{,}000\overset{0.7972}{(P/F_{12,2})} + 7{,}000\overset{0.7118}{(P/F_{12,3})}$$

$$+ 4{,}000\overset{0.6355}{(P/F_{12,4})} = \$21{,}462$$

Or,

$$P = 3{,}000 + 6{,}000\overset{0.8929}{(P/F_{12,1})} + 7{,}000\overset{1.690}{(P/A_{12,2})}\overset{0.8929}{(P/F_{12,1})}$$

$$+ 4{,}000\overset{0.6355}{(P/F_{12,4})} = \$21{,}462$$

$$F = 3{,}000\overset{1.574}{(F/P_{12,4})} + 6{,}000\overset{1.405}{(F/P_{12,3})} + 7{,}000\overset{1.254}{(F/P_{12,2})}$$

$$+ 7{,}000\overset{1.120}{(F/P_{12,1})} + 4{,}000 = \$33{,}770$$

$$7{,}000(F/P_{12,2}) + 7{,}000(F/P_{12,1}) = 7{,}000(F/A_{12,2})(F/P_{12,1})$$

$$A = 21{,}462\overset{0.32923}{(A/P_{12,4})} = \$7{,}066 = 33{,}770\overset{0.20923}{(A/F_{12,4})}$$

2-14 Solution:

P=?	$1,000	$1,000	$1,000	
0	1	2	20	F=?

$$F = 1{,}000\overset{57.275}{(F/A_{10,20})} = \$57{,}275$$

$$P = 1{,}000\overset{8.514}{(P/A_{10,20})} = \$8{,}514$$

Or,

$$P = 57{,}275\overset{0.1486}{(P/F_{10,20})} = \$8{,}511$$

The *difference of $3.00 is due to round off error.*

To check the answer: $\quad 8{,}514\overset{6.727}{(F/P_{10,20})} = \$57{,}274$

2-15 Solution:

$2,000	$1,000	$1,000	....	$1,000

0   1   2 5

i = 20% per year

A) Calculate the Future Value "F" of the Payments

$$F = 2,000 \overset{2.488}{(F/P_{20,5})} + 1,000 \overset{7.442}{(F/A_{20,5})} = \$12,418$$

B) Calculate the Future Value Based on Semi-Annual Compounding:

Period i = 20%/2 = 10% per semi-annual period

Effective Interest Rate, $E = (1 + 0.1)^2 - 1 = 0.21$ or, 21%

$$F = 2,000 \overset{2.5937}{(F/P_{21,5})} + 1,000 \overset{7.58925}{(F/A_{21,5})} = \$12,777$$

C) Equivalent Semi-Annual Payments for Semi-Annual Compounding:

–	$A=F(A/F_{10,2})$	A

                                              $F=\$1,000$

0   1   2

i = 10%   (semi-annual compound interest)

$A = 1,000(A/F_{10,2}) = \$476.19$

$2,000	$476.19	$476.19	....	$476.19

                                                        $F=?$

0   1   2 10
            (semi-annual periods)

$$F = 2,000 \overset{2.594}{(F/P_{10,10})} + 476.19 \overset{15.937}{(F/A_{10,10})} = \$12,777$$

2-16 Solution:

$(1 + 0.05) - 1 = (F/P_{5,4}) - 1 = 1.2155 - 1 = 0.2155$

Effective interest rate: E = 21.55%

2-17 Solution:

$(1 + i)^4 - 1 = 0.20$
$(1 + i)^4 = 1.20$
$i = (1.20)^{0.25} - 1 = 0.0466$ or, 4.66% per quarterly period
Nominal rate $r = (4.66\%/\text{period})(4 \text{ periods}) = 18.64\%$

2-18 Solution:

A)

```
   --      $1,000      $1,000 ............. 1,000
 _____ F=?
   0          1           2 . . . . . . . . 40 years
```

$i = 15\%$ per year

$$F = 1,000(F/A_{15,40}) \overset{1779.09}{=} \$1,779,090$$

B)

```
   --      $1,000      $1,100   gradient + $100/yr ...
 _____ F=?
   0          1           2 ................. 40 years
```

$$F = (1,000 + 100(A/G_{15,40}))(F/A_{15,40}) \overset{6.517 \quad 1779.09}{=} \$2,938,523$$

The A\G Factor gives the following time diagram with an equivalent uniform series of values in years 1-40:

$$A = 1,000 + 100(A/G_{15,40}) \overset{6.517}{=} \$1,651.70$$

```
   --     $1,651.70   $1,651.70 ........... $1,651.70
 _____ F=?
   0          1           2 ................. 40 years
```

$$F = 1,651.7(F/A_{15,40}) \overset{1779.09}{=} \$2,938,523$$

C)

$$P = 1,779,090(P/F_{15,40}) \overset{0.003733}{=} \$6,642$$

Or,

$$P = 1,000(P/A_{15,40}) \overset{6.642}{=} \$6,642$$

2-19 Solution: Values in Tons

P=?	20,000	19,500	19,000	16,000	15,500 .. 10,500
0	1	2	3 9		10 20

P = present worth of year 1-9 production @ $6/ton,
   plus present worth of year 10-20 production @ $8/ton

For i = 8%:

$$P = (120{,}000 - 3{,}000(\overset{3.491}{A/G_{8,9}}))(\overset{6.247}{P/A_{8,9}})$$

$$+ (124{,}000 - 4{,}000(\overset{4.240}{A/G_{8,11}}))(\overset{7.139}{P/A_{8,11}})(\overset{0.5002}{P/F_{8,9}})$$

$$P = 684{,}200 + 382{,}200 = \$1{,}066{,}400$$

Equivalent Profit Diagram using A/G$_{8\%,n}$:

P=?	$109,527 .... $109,527	$107,040 107,040
0	1 9	10 20

Alternate Solution:

P = present worth of 20 years of production @ $8/ton,
   less the present worth of $2/ton for year 1-9 production

$$P = (160{,}000 - 4{,}000(\overset{7.037}{A/G_{8,20}}))(\overset{9.818}{P/A_{8,20}})$$

$$- (40{,}000 - 1{,}000(\overset{3.491}{A/G_{8,9}}))(\overset{6.247}{P/A_{8,9}})$$

$$P = 1{,}294{,}500 - 228{,}100 = \$1{,}066{,}400$$

For i = 20%:

$$P = (160{,}000 - 4{,}000(\overset{4.464}{A/G_{20,20}}))(\overset{4.870}{P/A_{20,20}})$$

$$- (40{,}000 - 1{,}000(\overset{2.836}{A/G_{20,9}}))(\overset{4.031}{P/A_{20,9}}) = \$542{,}433$$

2-20 Solution:

```
P=? $6,000      $6,000 $8,000      $8,000 $10,000        $10,000
```
```
0       1 ...... 5     6 ....... 9     10 ........ 15
```

$$P=6,000\underset{3.791}{(P/A_{10,5})} + 8,000\underset{3.170}{(P/A_{10,4})}\underset{0.6209}{(P/F_{10,5})} + 10,000\underset{4.355}{(P/A_{10,6})}\underset{0.4241}{(P/F_{10,9})}$$

$$P=22,746 + 15,746 + 18,469 = \$56,961$$

$56,961 is less than $70,000, so accept the offer of $70,000 now to maximize profit.

Alternately:

$$P=6,000\underset{3.791}{(P/A_{10,5})} + 8,000(\underset{5.759}{(P/A_{10,9})}-\underset{3.791}{(P/A_{10,5})})$$

$$+10,000(\underset{7.606}{(P/A_{10,15})}-\underset{5.759}{(P/A_{10,9})}) = \$56,960$$

Or,

$$P=10,000(P/A_{10,15}) - 2,000(P/A_{10,9}) - 2,000(P/A_{10,5}) = \$56,960$$

Another alternate solution by comparing future values:

$$F=70,000\underset{4.177}{(F/P_{10,15})} = \$292,390$$

$$F=6,000\underset{31.772}{(F/A_{10,15})} + 2,000\underset{15.94}{(F/A_{10,10})} + 2,000\underset{7.716}{(F/A_{10,6})} = \$237,944$$

Or,

$$F=6,000\underset{6.105}{(F/A_{10,5})}\underset{2.594}{(F/P_{10,10})} + 8,000\underset{4.641}{(F/A_{10,4})}\underset{1.772}{(F/P_{10,6})}$$

$$+ 10,000\underset{7.716}{(F/A_{10,6})} = \$237,969$$

To maximize future value, accept $70,000 now.

2-21 Solution:

$$\overset{0.13147}{\text{Equivalent Annual Payments} = A = 56,961(A/P_{10,15}) = \$7,488}$$

Alternate Solution:

$$\overset{0.03147}{A = 237,969(A/F_{10,15}) = \$7,488}$$

2-22 Solution:

```
$11,000    $500      $550      $600 ........ $950
_____ Salvage=$2,000
   0        1         2        3 ........... 10
```

$$\text{Equivalent} \quad \overset{0.14903}{} \quad \overset{3.871}{} \quad \overset{0.06903}{}$$
$$\text{Annual Cost} = 11,000(A/P_{8,10}) + 500 + 50(A/G_{8,10}) - 2,000(A/F_{8,10})$$

$$= 1,639.33 + 500 + 193.55 - 138.06 = \$2,194.82$$

2-23 Solution:

```
  -       -       - ........ -      $100     $100 ..... $100
_____
  0       1       2 ...... 30       31       32 ....... 48
```

A) Monthly - Discrete Interest, Discrete Dollars:

A nominal interest rate of 15.0%, compounded monthly yields a period interest rate, i :

$$i = 0.15/12 = 0.0125 = 1.25\%$$

$$(P/A_{i,n}) = [(1+i)^n - 1]/i(1+i)^n$$
$$(P/F_{i,n}) = 1/(1+i)^n$$

$$(P/A_{1.25,18}) = 16.0295$$
$$(P/F_{1.25,30}) = 0.6889$$

$$\overset{16.0295}{} \quad \overset{0.6889}{}$$
$$P = 100(P/A_{1.25,18})(P/F_{1.25,30}) = \$1,104$$

2-23 Solution: *Continued*

B) *Yearly - Discrete Interest, Discrete Dollars:*

–	–	–	$1,200	$600
0	1	2	3	4

$$\begin{array}{cc} 0.6575 & 0.5718 \\ P = 1,200\,(P/F_{15,3}) + 600\,(P/F_{15,4}) = \$1,132 \end{array}$$

The $1,132 result is incorrect because it should be based on the annual effective discrete interest for a 15% nominal interest rate compounded monthly. Using Eq. 2-9 to calculate the effective interest rate (E):

$$E = (1.0125)^{12} - 1 = 0.16075 \text{ or } 16.07\%$$

$$\begin{array}{cc} 0.6395 & 0.55096 \\ P = 1,200\,(P/F_{16.07,3}) + 600\,(P/F_{16.07,4}) = \$1,098 \end{array}$$

Note that this result is very close to the $1,104 result from Case A.

C) *Yearly - Effective Continuous Interest, Discrete Dollars:*

The continuous interest rate (r) that is equivalent to the effective discrete interest rate of 16.07% is calculated using Eq. 2-10:

$$E = e^r - 1 = 0.1607, \quad \text{rearranging gives} \quad e^r = 1.1607$$

$$r = \ln(1.1607) = 0.1490 \text{ or } 14.9\%$$

$$\begin{array}{cc} 0.6395 & 0.5510 \\ P = 1,200\,(P/F_{14.9,3}) + 600\,(P/F_{14.9,4}) = \$1,098 \end{array}$$

This result is identical to the Case B result.

Appendix B gives continuous interest with discrete dollar values:

e = the natural log base
r = 14.9%
n = 3 and 4 respectively

$$P/F_{r,n} = 1/e^{rn}$$

2-23 Solution: *Continued*

D) Yearly - Continuous Interest, Continuous Flowing Dollars:

```
    -           -        ← $1,200 →← $600 →
  _____
    0           1           2           3           4
```

Working with the same continuous interest calculated in Case C, assume the dollars are realized uniformly over years 3 and 4 as illustrated on the time diagram. Appendix C gives:

$$P/F^*_{r,n} = [(e^r-1)/r]/e^{rn}, \text{ which is also equivalent to } (e^r-1)/(re^{rn})$$

$$
\begin{array}{cc}
0.6896 & 0.5942 \\
\end{array}
$$
$$P = 1,200(P/F^*_{14.9,3}) + 600(P/F^*_{14.9,4}) = \$1,184$$

2-24 Solution: *Answers are Rounded Up*

```
   P=?   $600     $700 .. gradient ..$1,200  $1,200  $1,200   $1,200
  _____
                                                                    F=?
    0      1        2 ............... 7        8       9       10
```

$$
\begin{array}{cccc}
2.552 & 4.564 & 2.402 & 0.4523
\end{array}
$$
A) $P = [600+100(A/G_{12,7})](P/A_{12,7})+1,200(P/A_{12,3})(P/F_{12,7}) = \$5,207$

$$
\begin{array}{cccc}
2.172 & 4.111 & 3.037 & 0.5066
\end{array}
$$
Or, $P = [600+100(A/G_{12,6})](P/A_{12,6})+1,200(P/A_{12,4})(P/F_{12,6}) = \$5,207$

$$3.106$$
B) $F = 5,206.84(F/P_{12,10}) = \$16,172$

Or,

$$
\begin{array}{cccc}
2.552 & 10.089 & 1.405 & 3.374
\end{array}
$$
$F = [600+100(A/G_{12,7})](F/A_{12,7})(F/P_{12,3})+1,200(F/A_{12,3}) = \$16,171$

2-25 Solution:

```
          -  ............  -        $5,000 .............. $5,000
   P=?  _____
    0          1 ........... 4        5 .................. 14
```

$$
\begin{array}{cc}
6.418 & 0.7084
\end{array}
$$
$$P = 5,000(P/A_{9,10})(P/F_{9,4}) = \$22,733$$

If the payments start at the end of year 1 instead of at the end of year 5, the time zero cost is: $5,000(P/A_{9,10}) = \$32,090.$

2-26 Solution:

```
  $6,000      A=?          A=?          A=? . . . . . . . . . . . A=?
  ─────────────────────────────────────────────────────────────────
    0          1            2            3 . . . . . . . . . . . . . . . . . . 36
```

A) 10% annual simple interest:

principal = 6,000/36 = $166.67
interest = 6,000(0.10)/(12) = $50.00

End-of month payments (A) = 166.67 + 50.00 = $216.67

B) 10% annual interest compounded monthly:

Using the mathematical definition of $A/P_{i,n}$, where $i = 10\%/12$:

$i = 0.10/12 = 0.00833$, $n = 36$

$A/P_{i,n} = i(1+i)^n/[(1+i)^n-1]$

$= 0.00833(1.00833)^{36}/[(1.00833)^{36}-1] = 0.032265$

$$\overset{0.032265}{\text{End-of-month payments (A)} = 6,000(A/P_{0.833\%,36}) = \$193.59}$$

If payments are made at the beginning of the month:

$$A = 193.59\overset{0.9917}{(P/F_{0.833\%,1})} = \$191.98$$

2-27 Solution:

APR of 11.5% compounded monthly is a period interest rate (i) of
$0.115/12 = 0.009583$ or 0.9583% per month.

End of Month Payments (A_{End}):

$$A_{End} = 15,000\overset{0.026094}{(A/P_{0.9583\%,48})} = \$391.42 \text{ per month.}$$

Beginning of Month Payments (A_{Beg}):

$$A_{Beg} = 391.32\overset{0.9905}{(P/F_{0.9583\%,1})} = \$387.61$$

An alternate beginning-of-month solution, where X = A:

$$\$15,000 = X + X\overset{37.6979}{(P/A_{0.9583\%,47})}$$

$$\$15,000 = X(1 + 37.6979)$$

$$X = \$387.62$$

2-28 Solution:

$$C=\$1,500 \qquad OC=\$400 \qquad OC=\$500 \qquad OC=\$600$$

$$L=\$300$$

$$0 \qquad\qquad 1 \qquad\qquad 2 \qquad\qquad 3$$

Present Worth Cost at 15%:

$$
\begin{array}{cccc}
 & 0.8696 & 0.7561 & 0.6575 \\
\end{array}
$$
$$P = 1,500 + 400(P/F_{15,1}) + 500(P/F_{15,2}) + (600-300)(P/F_{15,3}) = \$2,423$$

Or,

$$
\begin{array}{ccc}
 & 0.907 \quad 2.283 & 0.6575 \\
\end{array}
$$
$$P = 1,500 + [400 + 100(A/G_{15,3})](P/A_{15,3}) - 300(P/F_{15,3})$$

$$P = 1,500 + 1,120.27 - 197.25 = \$2,423$$

Future Worth Cost at 15%:

$$
\begin{array}{ccc}
1.521 & 1.322 & 1.150 \\
\end{array}
$$
$$F = 1,500(F/P_{15,3}) + 400(F/P_{15,2}) + 500(F/P_{15,1}) + (600-300) = \$3,685$$

Or,

$$
\begin{array}{ccc}
1.521 & 0.907 & 3.472 \\
\end{array}
$$
$$F = 1,500(F/P_{15,3}) + [400 + 100(A/G_{15,3})](F/A_{15,3}) - 300$$

$$F = 2,281.50 + 1,703.71 - 300 = \$3,685$$

Or,

$$
\begin{array}{c}
1.521 \\
\end{array}
$$
$$F = 2,423(F/P_{15,3}) = \$3,685$$

Equivalent Annual Cost at 15%:

$$
\begin{array}{c}
0.43798 \\
\end{array}
$$
$$A = 2,423(A/P_{15,3}) = \$1,061$$

Or,

$$
\begin{array}{c}
0.28798 \\
\end{array}
$$
$$A = 3,685(A/F_{15,3}) = \$1,061$$

2-29 Solution:

A)

	←\$300→	←\$400→	←\$400→	←\$400→	←\$500→
0	1	2	3	4	5

From Appendix C: $P/F^*_{r,n} = [(e^r-1)/r](1/e^{rn})$

$$P/A^*_{r,n} = [(e^{rn}-1)/r](1/e^{rn})$$

From Appendix B: $P/F_{r,n} = 1/e^{rn}$

$$\overset{0.9563}{P = 300(P/F^*_{9,1})} + \overset{0.8740}{400(P/F^*_{9,2})} + \overset{0.7988}{400(P/F^*_{9,3})} + \overset{0.7300}{400(P/F^*_{9,4})} + \overset{0.6672}{500(P/F^*_{9,5})}$$

$$P = \$1,581.61$$

Or,

$$\overset{0.9563}{P = 300(P/F^*_{9,1})} + \overset{2.6291 \quad 0.9139}{400(P/A^*_{9,3})(P/F_{9,1})} + \overset{0.6672}{500(P/F^*_{9,5})} = \$1,581.58$$

Note that since $400(P/A^*_{9,3})$ is a discrete year 1 sum, the continuous interest single payment present worth factor $(P/F_{9,1})$ from Appendix B, is needed to bring the year 1 sum to time 0. The continuous interest, continuous flow of money factor $(P/F^*_{9,1})$ is NOT valid for this calculation.

Continuously Flowing Yearly Payments:

From Appendix C: $A/P^*_{r,n} = re^{rn}/(e^{rn}-1)$

$$\overset{0.24836}{A = 1,581.61(A/P^*_{9,5})} = \$392.81$$

$$\overset{1.5683}{F = 1,581.61(F/P_{9,5})} = 1,581.61(e^{0.09(5)}) = \$2,480.46$$

2-29 Solution: *Continued*

B)

	(150+200)	(200+200)	(200+200)	(200+250)	
←$150→	←$350→	←$400→	←$400→	←$450→	←$250→
0	1	2	3	4	5	6

From Eq 2-10: Effective discrete interest rate (E) = 0.09 = e^r-1

so, r = ln(1.09) = 0.0862 or 8.62%

$$
\begin{array}{cccc}
0.9581 & 0.8790 & 0.8064 & 0.7398
\end{array}
$$

P = 150(P/F$^*_{8.62,1}$)+350(P/F$^*_{8.62,2}$)+400(P/F$^*_{8.62,3}$)+400(P/F$^*_{8.62,4}$)

$$
\begin{array}{cc}
0.6787 & 0.6226
\end{array}
$$

+ 450(P/F$^*_{8.62,5}$) + 250(P/F$^*_{8.62,6}$) = $1,530.91

This result is very similar to the $1,529 discrete compounding,
discrete value result from text Example 2-8.

$$
0.24619
$$

A = 1,530.91(A/P$^*_{8.62,5}$) = $376.89

$$
1.5388
$$

F = 1,530.91(F/P$_{8.62,5}$)

F = 1,530.91($e^{0.0862(5)}$) = $2,355.76

C)

	$300	$400	$400	$400	$500
0	0.5	1.5	2.5	3.5	4.5

Effective discrete interest rate equivalent to a 9% continuous rate:

E = e^r-1 = $e^{0.09}-1$ = 0.0942 = 9.42%

$$
\begin{array}{cccc}
0.9560 & 2.5125 \quad 0.9560 & & 0.6669
\end{array}
$$

P = 300(P/F$_{9.42,0.5}$) + 400(P/A$_{9.42,3}$)(P/F$_{9.42,0.5}$) + 500(P/F$_{9.42,4.5}$)

P = $1,581.03

This result is nearly equal to the result in (A).

2-30 Solution:

A)   *End of Period Values*

$$
\begin{array}{ccccc}
 & \$120 & \$120 & \$120 \\
P=? & \rule{6cm}{0.4pt} \\
0 & 1 & 2 & 3
\end{array}
$$

$$
\overset{2.4081}{P = 120(P/A_{12,3})} = \$288.22
$$

B)   *Beginning of Period Values*

$$
\begin{array}{ccccc}
\$120 & \$120 & \$120 & - \\
P=? \\
0 & 1 & 2 & 3
\end{array}
$$

$$
\overset{1.6901}{P = 120 + 120(P/A_{12,2})} = \$322.81
$$

Or,

$$
\overset{2.40181.1200}{P = 120(P/A_{12,3})(F/P_{12,1})} = \$322.81
$$

C)   *Mid-Period Values*

$$
\begin{array}{cccccc}
- & \$120 & \$120 & \$120 & - \\
P=? \\
0 & 0.5 & 1.5 & 2.5 & 3\ \text{yrs}
\end{array}
$$

$$
\overset{0.944910.843670.75328}{P = 120(P/F_{12,0.5}) + 120(P/F_{12,1.5}) + 120(P/F_{12,2.5})} = \$305.02
$$

$$
P = 120[1/(1+.12)]^{0.5} + 120[1/(1+.12)]^{1.5} + 120[1/(1+.12)]^{2.5} = \$305.02
$$

Also,

$$
P = 120(P/A_{12,3})(F/P_{12,\frac{1}{2}}) = 120(2.4018)(1.0583) = \$305.02
$$

D)   *End of Period Timing Variation*

$$
\begin{array}{ccccc}
\$60 & \$120 & \$120 & \$60 \\
P=? \\
0 & 1 & 2 & 3
\end{array}
$$

$$
\overset{1.69010.71178}{P = 60 + 120\ (P/A_{12,2}) + 60\ (P/F_{12,3})} = \$305.52
$$

2-31 Solution:

Annual Revenue = $2,400,000/yr, computed as follows:

$$10,000,000 \text{ watts} \times \frac{1 \text{kw}}{1,000 \text{ watts}} \times 6,000 \text{hrs/yr} \times \$.04/\text{kwh}$$

A)   *End of Period Values (000's)*

```
        -      $2,400 ...................... $2,400
P=?  ───────────────────────────────────────────────
        0          1 ......................... 10
```

$$P = 2,400 \overset{6.1446}{(P/A_{10,10})} = \$14,747$$

B)   *Beginning of Period Values (000's)*

```
     $2,400    $2,400 ............... $2,400    -
P=?  ───────────────────────────────────────────────
        0          1 ................... 9      10
```

$$P = 2,400 + 2,400 \overset{5.7590}{(P/A_{10,9})} = \$16,222$$

$$Or, \quad P = 2,400 \overset{6.1446}{(P/A_{10,10})} \overset{1.1000}{(F/P_{10,1})} = \$16,222$$

Round-off error on factors accounts for small difference in results.

C)   *Mid-Period Values (000's)*

```
       $2,400  $2,400 ............ $2,400     -
P=?  ───────────────────────────────────────────────
       0   0.5    1.5 ............. 9.5      10
```

$$P = 2,400 \overset{0.95346}{(P/F_{10,0.5})} + 2,400 \overset{0.86678}{(P/F_{10,1.5})} + \ . \ . \ + 2,400 \overset{0.40436}{(P/F_{10,9.5})}$$

$$\qquad\qquad [1/(1.1)]^{0.5} \qquad\qquad [1/(1.1)]^{1.5} \qquad\qquad [1/(1.1)]^{9.5}$$

$$P = \$15,467$$

$$Or, \quad P = 2,400 \overset{6.1446}{(P/A_{10,10})} \overset{1.04881}{(F/P_{10,0.5})} = \$15,467$$

The case C result is halfway between the case A and case B results.

2-31 Solution: *Continued*

D) *End of Period Timing Variation to Approximate Mid-Period Discounting (000's)*

```
   $1,200        $2,400 ............... $2,400      $1,200
P=? ───────────────────────────────────────────────────
   0              1 .................... 9           10
```

$$
\begin{array}{cc}
5.5790 & 0.3855 \\
P = 1,200 + 2,400(P/A_{10,9}) + 1,200(P/F_{10,10}) = \$15,484
\end{array}
$$

This case D result very closely approximates the Mid-Period Case C result.

2-32 Solution: All Values in Thousands

```
Payments   P=?     1,100     1,100     1,100     700       700
          ──────────────────────────────────────────────────────
           0        1         2         3         4         5
Annual
Interest   6.5%     6.5%      7.0%      7.5%      7.5%
```

To determine the present value of the loan, each payment must be discounted at the corresponding interest rate for each compounding period, (years) as follows:

$$
\begin{array}{ccc}
1.8206 & 0.93458 & 0.88166 \\
P = 1,100(P/A_{6.5,2}) + 1,100(P/F_{7.0,1})(P/F_{6.5,2})
\end{array}
$$

$$
\begin{array}{ccc}
1.7956 & 0.93458 & 0.88166 \\
+ 700(P/A_{7.5,2})(P/F_{7.0,1})(P/F_{6.5,2}) = \$3,944.72
\end{array}
$$

Year	Loan Balance	Payment	Interest	Principal	Loan Balance
1	3,944.72	1,100.00	256.41	843.59	3,101.13
2	3,101.13	1,100.00	201.57	898.43	2,202.70
3	2,202.70	1,100.00	154.19	945.81	1,256.89
4	1,256.89	700.00	94.27	605.73	651.15
5	651.15	700.00	48.85	651.15	0.00

CHAPTER 3 PROBLEM SOLUTIONS

3-1 Solution:

Time Purchase:

C=$5,500	C=$5,000	C=$5,000	C=$5,000	C=$5,000
0	1	2	3	4

Cash Purchase:

C=$22,500	-	-	-	-
0	1	2	3	4

Present Worth Equation:

$$\$22,500 = 5,500 + 5,000(P/A_{i,4})$$

$$P/A_{i,4} = \frac{22,500 - 5,500}{5,000} = \frac{17,000}{5,000} = 3.400$$

$$P/A_{6\%,4} = 3.465$$
$$P/A_{7\%,4} = 3.387$$

$$i = 6\% + 1\% \left(\frac{3.465 - 3.400}{3.465 - 3.387}\right) = 6.83\% \text{ compounded annually}$$

The meaning of the 6.83% is that it is the percentage return on unamortized incremental investment each year as follows:

Incremental Time Diagram (Cash-Time):

C=$17,000	I=$5,000	I=$5,000	I=$5,000	I=$5,000
0	1	2	3	4

If cash is paid, an extra $17,000 is spent at time zero to save making $5,000 payments in years 1-4, saving an effective interest cost of 6.83% per year on unamortized incremental investment.

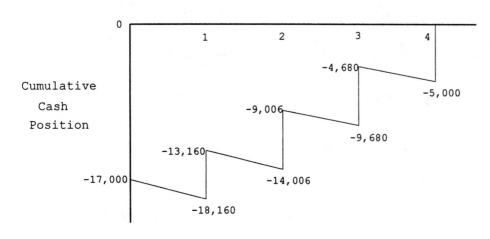

3-2 Solution:

```
P=?  $3,000 ..... $3,000   $5,000 ..... $5,000   $6,000 ... $6,000
```
```
0     1 ......... 5         6 .......... 13        14 ....... 16
```

$$P = 3{,}000 \overset{3.993}{(P/A_{8,5})} + 5{,}000 \overset{5.747}{(P/A_{8,8})} \overset{0.6806}{(P/F_{8,5})} + 6{,}000 \overset{2.577}{(P/A_{8,3})} \overset{0.3677}{(P/F_{8,13})}$$

$$P = 11{,}979 + 19{,}557 + 5{,}685 = \$37{,}221 \text{ at year } 0$$

Value at the end of the 3rd year $= (37{,}221) \overset{1.260}{(F/P_{8,3})} = \$46{,}900$

Alternate Solution:

Value at year 3:

$$[6{,}000 \overset{8.851}{(P/A_{8,16})} - 1{,}000 \overset{7.904}{(P/A_{8,13})} - 2{,}000 \overset{3.993}{(P/A_{8,5})}] \overset{1.260}{(F/P_{8,3})} = \$46{,}900$$

3-3 Solution:

Machine A

```
                              $10,000
  $50,000     $5,000  $5,000 ... $5,000  $5,000 ... $5,000
                                                         L=$10,000
    0          1       2 ...... 5        6 ....... 10
```

Using Text Eq.3-1 for Equivalent Annual Cost:

$$AC_A = 50{,}000 \overset{0.16275}{(A/P_{10,10})} - 10{,}000 \overset{0.06275}{(A/F_{10,10})} + 10{,}000 \overset{0.6209}{(P/F_{10,5})} \overset{0.16275}{(A/P_{10,10})}$$
$$+ 5{,}000 = \$13{,}520$$

Using Text Eq. 3-2:

$$AC_A = (50{,}000 - 10{,}000)(A/P_{10,10}) + 10{,}000(0.10) + 10{,}000(P/F_{10,5})(A/P_{10,10})$$
$$+ 5{,}000 = \$13{,}520$$

Or, $AC_A = (\text{PW Cost A})(A/P_{10,10}) = (83{,}067)(0.16275) = \$13{,}520$

Machine B

```
  $40,000      $8,000   $8,500 ........ grad=$500 ... $12,500
    0          1         2 ......................... 10
```

Annual Cost Equation for Machine B:

$$AC_B = 40{,}000 \overset{0.16275}{(A/P_{10,10})} + 8{,}000 + 500 \overset{3.276}{(A/G_{10,10})} = \$16{,}373$$

Or, $AC_B = (\text{PW Cost B})(A/P_{10,10}) = (100{,}598)(0.16275) = \$16{,}373$

To maximize profit, select Machine A with smaller annual cost.

3-4 Solution: *Profit/Year: $25,000 - $15,000 = $10,000*

$120,000 $10,000 $10,000 .... $10,000

L=$70,000
_____

0   1   2 15

PW Eq: $0 = -120,000 + 10,000(P/A_{i,15}) + 70,000(P/F_{i,15})$

For investment lives of 10 years or more it is desirable to start with an i value equal to average profit/initial investment; 10/120 = 8.33% in this case.

i = 8%: $120,000 = 10,000(8.559) + 70,000(0.3152) = \$107,654$
i = 7%: $120,000 = 10,000(9.108) + 70,000(0.3624) = \$116,448$
i = 6%: $120,000 = 10,000(9.712) + 70,000(0.4173) = \$126,331$

$$i = 6\% + 1\% \left(\frac{126,331 - 120,000}{126,331 - 116,448} \right) = 6.64\%$$

3-5 Solution:

Purchase Costs:

$400 $400
$200 $200
$50,000 $900 .... $900

L=?
_____

0   1 10

Rental Costs:

$4,800 .... $4,800

L=0
_____

0   1 10

Annual Cost Equation: Rental Cost = Purchase Cost

$$\overset{0.1359}{} \qquad \overset{0.07587}{}$$
$4,800 = (50,000)(A/P_{6,10}) + 1,500 - L(A/F_{6,10})$

$3,300 = 50,000(0.1359) - L(0.07587)$

$L(0.07587) = 6,795 - 3,300 = \$3,495$

$L = 3,495/0.0758 = \$46,066$

Present Worth Cost Equation:

$$\overset{7.360}{} \qquad\qquad \overset{7.360}{} \quad \overset{0.5584}{}$$
$4,800(P/A_{6,10}) = 50,000 + 1,500(P/A_{6,10}) - L(P/F_{6,10})$

L = $46,046 with difference due to factor round-off error.

Future Worth Cost Equation:

$$\overset{13.181}{} \qquad\qquad \overset{1.791}{} \qquad \overset{13.181}{}$$
$4,800(F/A_{6,10}) = 50,000(F/P_{6,10}) + 1,500(F/A_{6,10}) - L$

L = $46,053 with difference due to factor round-off error.

3-6 Solution:

```
C=$800       I=$40 . . . . . . . . . . . . . .     I=$40
                                                          L=$1,000
_____
  0              1 . . . . . . . . . . . . . . 40 semi-annual periods
```

Present Worth Equation: $0 = -800 + 40(P/A_{i,40}) + 1,000(P/F_{i,40})$
By trial and error, i = 5.197% semi-annual period ROR by calculator.

The nominal or annual bond ROR, commonly referred to as "yield to maturity," is 10.394% compounded semi-annually.

If the bond is callable in 8 years (16 semi-annual periods):

```
  C=?          I=$40 . . . . . . . . . I=$40
                                              L=$1,000
_____
  0              1 . . . . . . . . . 16 semi-annual periods to call date
```

Present Worth Cost Equation:

$$C = 40(P/A_{3,16}) + 1,000(P/F_{3,16}) = \$1,125.64$$

An investor can pay $1,125.64 for this old bond to realize a 6% ROR compounded semi-annually to the call date on this bond investment.

3-7 Solution:

```
  C=?          I=$40 . . . . . . . . .   I=$40
                                              L=$1,000
_____
  0              1 . . . . . . . . . . 40 semi-annual periods to maturity
```

Present Worth Equation:

$$\overset{17.159}{C = 40(P/A_{5,40})} + \overset{0.1420}{1,000(P/F_{5,40})} = \$828.36$$

3-8 Solution:

```
 C=$5,000        C=$200        C=$200 . . . . . . . . C=$200
                                                          L=$13,000
_____
   0              1             2 . . . . . . . . . 10
```

Present Worth Equation:

$$\$5,000 = -200(P/A_{i,10}) + 13,000(P/F_{i,10})$$

i = 7%: $-200(7.024) + 13,000(0.5083) = \$5,203$
i = 8%: $-200(6.710) + 13,000(0.4632) = \$4,680$

$$i = 7\% + 1\%\left(\frac{5,203 - 5,000}{5,203 - 4,680}\right) = 7.39\%.$$

Alternate Future Worth Analysis:

$$\overset{1.967}{5,000(F/P_{7,10})} + \overset{13.816}{200(F/A_{7,10})} = \$12,598 < \$13,000 \text{ so select "land."}$$

3-9 Solution:

		C=$100			
C=$60	I=$40	I=$40	I=$40	I=$70 . . .	I=$70

0	1	2	3	4 10

Year 0 Present Worth Equation:

$60 = -100(P/F_{i,2}) + 40(P/A_{i,3}) + 70(P/A_{i,7})(P/F_{i,3})$

$i=40\% = -100(0.5102) + 40(1.589) + 70(2.263)(0.3644) = +\$70.26$

$i=50\% = -100(0.4444) + 40(1.407) + 70(1.883)(0.2963) = +\$50.90$

$$i = ROR = 40\% + (50\%-40\%)\left(\frac{70.26 - 60.00}{70.26 - 50.90}\right) = 45.3\%$$

3-10 Solution: *Values Are In Thousands*

Lease Option:

C=$500	C=$500	C=$500	C=$750	C=$750	C=$750	C=$750	–
0	1	2	3	4	5	6	7

Purchase Option:

C=$2,000	–	–	–	C=$600	–	–	–
0	1	2	3	4	5	6	7

$$PC_{Lease} = 500 + 500\underset{1.528}{(P/A_{20,2})} + 750\underset{2.589}{(P/A_{20,4})}\underset{0.6944}{(P/F_{20,2})} = \$2,612$$

$$PC_{Purchase} = 2,000 + 600\underset{0.4823}{(P/F_{20,4})} = \$2,289$$

Note that using the "replacement-in-kind" assumption for the lease at the end of year 3 would make the year 3, 4, 5 and 6 lease costs $500 instead of $750, making the present worth cost of leasing $2,162 instead of $2,612. This would make leasing look economically better than purchasing, which is not correct if you think the year 3 to 6 lease costs will actually be $750. Replacement-in-kind often leads to incorrect economic conclusions, and so should not be used.

3-10 Continued, *Incremental ROR Analysis, Purchase - Lease:*

```
C=$1,500    I=$500   I=$500  I=$750   I=$150   I=$750   I=$750      -
─────────────────────────────────────────────────────────────────────
   0          1         2       3        4        5        6        7
```

Present Worth Equation:

$$0 = -1{,}500 + 500(P/A_{i,2}) + 750(P/F_{i,3}) + 150(P/F_{i,4})$$

$$+ 750(P/A_{i,2})(P/F_{i,4})$$

By trial and error,

i = *Incremental ROR* = 28.0% > 20.0%, *so accept purchase*

$$
\begin{array}{ccc}
1.528 & 0.5787 & 0.4823
\end{array}
$$
NPV = $-1{,}500 + 500(P/A_{20,2}) + 750(P/F_{20,3}) + 150(P/F_{20,4})$

$$
\begin{array}{cc}
1.528 & 0.4823
\end{array}
$$
$+ 750(P/A_{20,2})(P/F_{20,4}) = +323.0 > 0$ *So, accept purchase*

3-11 Solution: *All Values in Thousands*

```
 C=$100        C=$200            I=$90 ............... I=$90
─────────────────────────────────────────────────────────── L=150
   0             1              2 ................. 10
```

A) *Discrete Interest, Discrete Dollar Values*
Present Worth Equation:

$$0 = -100 - 200(P/F_{i,1}) + 90(P/A_{i,9})(P/F_{i,1}) + 150(P/F_{i,10})$$

Approximate i = 90 / (100+200) = 0.30 or 30%

i=30% = $-100-200(0.7692)+90(3.019)(0.7692)+150(0.0725)$ = $-$33.96
i=25% = $-100-200(0.8000)+90(3.463)(0.8000)+150(0.1074)$ = $+$5.45

i = ROR = 25% + (30%-25%)[(5.45-0)/(5.45+33.96)] = 25.69%

Due to interpolation error, the 25.69% result is a little high. The true interpolation error-free ROR is 25.60% which is illustrated on the following page. The PW equation is a non-linear function of "i" represented by the curve on the following graph.

3-11 Solution: *Continued, Interpolation*

$$\frac{a}{b} = \frac{c}{d}$$

Therefore, $a = b * \dfrac{c}{d}$

Substitution gives:

$$a = (30\% - 25\%) * \frac{(5.45 - 0)}{(5.45 - (-33.96))}$$

ROR $= 25\% + a = 25.69\%$

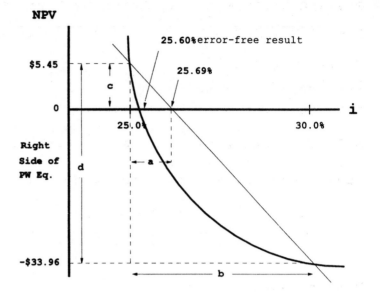

3-11 Case A, *Cumulative Cash Position at i = 25.6%:*

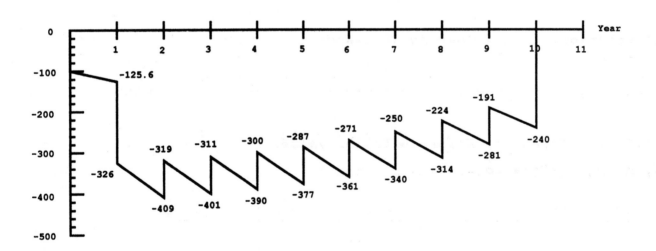

3-11 B) Continuous Interest, Discrete Dollar Values (Appendix B)

Present Worth Equation Based on Discrete End of Period Values:

$$0 = -100 - 200(P/F_{r,1}) + 90(P/A_{r,9})(P/F_{r,1}) + 150(P/F_{r,10})$$

r=25%: -100-200(0.7788)+90(3.1497)(0.7788)+150(0.0821) = -$22.68
r=20%: -100-200(0.8187)+90(3.7701)(0.8187)+150(0.1353) = +$34.35

r = ROR = 20% + (25%-20%)(34.35-0)/(34.35+22.68) = 23.01%

3-11 C) Continuous Interest, Continuous Flowing Dollars (Appendix C)

Year 0 cost flows from time 0 to the end of year 1.

```
      ←C=$100→  ←C=$200→  ←I=$90→  . . . . .   ←I=$90→   ←L=$150→
      ─────────────────────────────────────────────────────────────
         0         1        2       3 . . . 10      11        12
```

Present Worth Equation:

$$0 = -100(P/F^*_{r,1}) - 200(P/F^*_{r,2}) + 90(P/A^*_{r,9})(P/F_{r,2}) + 150(P/F^*_{r,12})$$

Note that $P/F_{r,2}$ is a continuous interest, discrete value factor. It is used because $P/A^*_{r,9}$ converts the income stream of $90 to a discrete sum at the beginning of year 3 (the end of year 2).

r=25%=-100(0.8848)-200(0.6891)+90(3.5784)(0.6065)+150(0.0566)= -$22.48
r=20%=-100(0.9064)-200(0.7421)+90(4.1735)(0.6703)+150(0.1004)= +$27.77

r = ROR = 20% + (25%-20%)[(27.77-0)/(27.77+22.48)] = 22.76%

3-11 D) Continuous Interest, Continuous Flowing Dollars

Year 0 cost is a discrete sum at time 0.

```
   C=$100  ←C=$200→  ←I=$90→  .......   ←I=$90→  ←L=$150→
   ──────────────────────────────────────────────────────
     0        1        2 ...... 9        10        11
```

Present Worth Equation:

$$0 = -100-200(P/F^*_{r,1})+90(P/A^*_{r,9})(P/F_{r,1})+150(P/F^*_{r,11})$$

Note that $P/F_{r,1}$ is a continuous interest, discrete value factor. It is used because $P/A^*_{r,9}$ converts the income stream of $90 to a discrete sum at the beginning of year 2 (the end of year 1).

r=25% = -100-200(0.8848)+90(3.5784)(0.7788)+150(0.0726) = -$15.25
r=20% = -100-200(0.9064)+90(4.1735)(0.8187)+150(0.1227) = +$44.64

r = ROR = 20% + (25%-20%)(44.64-0)/(44.64+15.25) = 23.73%

3-11 E) *Mid-Period Discrete Dollars, Discrete Compounding Interest*

	C=$100	C=$200	I=$90	. . . . .	I=$90	I=$90
						L=$150
Years	0	1	2		9	10
Discount Periods	0	0.5	1.5		8.5	9.5

PW Eq: $0 = -100 - 200(P/F_{i,0.5}) + 90(P/F_{i,1.5}) + \cdots$

$\qquad\qquad + 90(P/F_{i,8.5}) + 240(P/F_{i,9.5})$

Or, $\quad 0 = -100 - 200(P/F_{i,0.5}) + 90(P/A_{i,8})(P/F_{i,0.5}) + 240(P/F_{i,9.5})$

Trial and Error:

$\quad i=30\% = -100-200(0.8771)+90(2.9247)(0.8771)+240(0.08271) = -24.697$
$\quad i=25\% = -100-200(0.8944)+90(3.3289)(0.8944)+240(0.12005) = 17.895$

Interpolating:

$\qquad i = 25\% + 5\%[(17.895-0)/(17.895+24.697)] = 27.1\%$

An alternate method for calculating mid-period discrete ROR using a financial calculator is to take the mid-period discrete diagram based on annual periods and convert it to a semi-annual period diagram as follows:

-100	-200	0	90	0	90	. . . . .	0	90	0	240
0	1	2	3	4	5		16	17	18	19 semi-annual

Using a financial calculator that will handle twenty uneven cash flows or more, the semi-annual period i = 12.663%.

Now, using text Equation 2-9, $E = (1+i)^n - 1$ to convert the semi-annual period ROR, i, to the equivalent effective interest rate per year, $E = (1 + 0.12663)^2 - 1 = 0.2693$ or 26.93%. The difference in this result and the 27.1% result initially calculated with the time value of money factors is due to interpolation error. The 26.93% result is the correct annual ROR.

3-12 Solution: *All Values in Thousands*

Purchase Option:

```
C=$240
OC=$20       OC=$40       OC=$50       OC=$30
————————————————————————————————— L=$100
   0            1            2            3
```

Lease Option:

```
OC=$10       OC=$20       OC=$20       OC=$10
OC=$60       OC=$120      OC=$120      OC=$60
————————————————————————————————
   0            1            2            3
```

PW Cost Purchase:

$$260 + 40(P/F_{15,1}) + 50(P/F_{15,2}) + (30-100)(P/F_{15,3}) = \$286.6$$

PW Cost Lease:

$$70 + 140(P/F_{15,1}) + 140(P/F_{15,2}) + 70(P/F_{15,3}) = \$343.6$$

Select Purchasing with the smallest present worth cost.

Incremental Analysis, Purchase-Lease:

```
C=$190      Savings=$100  Savings=$90   Savings=$40
————————————————————————————————————— L=$100
   0            1             2             3
```

Incremental NPV = $-190 + 100(P/F_{15,1}) + 90(P/F_{15,2}) + 140(P/F_{15,3})$

$$= +\$57.0 > 0, \text{So accept the purchase option.}$$

Incremental ROR = 31.4% is the "i" that makes incremental NPV equal 0.

31.4% > 15.0% *so accept the purchase option.*

Incremental PVR = 57.0 / 190 = 0.30 > 0, *so, accept purchase.*

3-13 Solution:

Purchase Option:

```
-        OC=$120,000 ................................ OC=$120,000
    ─────────────────────────────────────────────────────────
    0              1 .........................................    5
```

Produce Option:

```
                                    C= $10,000
C=$40,000 OC=$100,000 OC=$100,000 OC=$100,000 OC=$100,000 OC=$100,000
    ───────────────────────────────────────────────────────────
    0         1         2         3         4         5
```

Incremental Timeline, Produce - Purchase:

Negative incremental operating costs give positive savings
each year = ($0.04/lb)(500,000 lb) = $20,000 as shown below.

```
                             C=$10,000
C=$40,000 -OC$20,000 -OC$20,000 -OC$20,000 -OC$20,000 -OC$20,000
    ───────────────────────────────────────────────────────────
    0         1         2         3         4         5
```

A) ROR, NPV, and PVR Analysis:

$$40,000 + 10,000(P/F_{i,3}) = 20,000(P/A_{i,5})$$

Re-arranging:

$$40,000 = 20,000(P/A_{i,5}) - 10,000(P/F_{i,3})$$

i=30%: 20,000(2.436) - 10,000(0.4552) = $44,168
i=40%: 20,000(2.035) - 10,000(0.3644) = $37,056

$$i = 30\% + 10\%\left(\frac{44,168 - 40,000}{44,168 - 37,056}\right) = 35.87\% > 30\% \text{ satisfactory economics.}$$

$$NPV = 20,000\underset{2.436}{(P/A_{30,5})} - 10,000\underset{0.4552}{(P/F_{30,3})} - 40,000 = +\$4,168$$

Positive NPV shows more than enough savings to cover costs at 30% ROR.

PVR = 4,168/40,000 = 0.1042 > 0 *so accept internal production.*

3-13 B) PW Cost Analysis:

Present Worth Cost of Purchase:

$$120,000 \, \overset{2.436}{(P/A_{30,5})} = \$292,320$$

Present Worth Cost of Internal Production:

$$40,000 + 100,000 \, \overset{2.436}{(P/A_{30,5})} + 10,000 \, \overset{0.4552}{(P/F_{30,3})} = \$288,152 < \$292,320$$

Therefore, to minimize cost, choose internal production.

3-14 Solution:

Stock Investment: F_1 = Stock Sale Value

```
 C=$30        Div=$2 ....Div=$2  Div=$4 ..... Div=$4
_____  F₁ = $93
 0           1 ........ 5       6 ......... 10
```

Present Worth Equation:

$$0 = -30 + 2(P/A_{i,5}) + 4(P/A_{i,5})(P/F_{i,5}) + 93(P/F_{i,10})$$

By trial and error, i = ROR = 17.75%

Dividend Reinvestment at 8% Per Year: F_2 = Stock Sale Value

Reinvestment i = ROR = 8.0%

```
   -         C=$2 ..... C=$2    C=$4 ...... C=$4
_____  F₂ = $40.71
 0           1 ........ 5       6 ........ 10
```

$$\underset{5.867}{} \quad \underset{1.469}{} \quad \underset{5.867}{}$$

$$\text{Where: } F_2 = 2 \, \overset{5.867}{(F/A_{8\%,5})} \, \overset{1.469}{(F/P_{8\%,5})} + 4 \, \overset{5.867}{(F/A_{8\%,5})} = \$40.71$$

Stock Investment and Dividend Reinvestment Combined:

```
 C=$30            - ......................... -
_____  F₁ + F₂ = $133.71
 0           1 ........................... 10
```

Present Worth Equation:

$$0 = -30 + 133.71(P/F_{i,10})$$

By trial and error, i = Growth ROR = 16.12%

3-15 Solution:

Initial Investment:

C=$250,000   I=$100,000 .... I=$100,000

$$\overline{\hspace{8cm}}$$ L=$150,000   **ROR$_A$=36.1%**

　0   1 5

Reinvestment of Profits:

                                    C=$150,000

-            C=$100,000 .... C=$100,000   F=$2,000,000

$$\overline{\hspace{8cm}}$$ **ROR$_B$=45.8%**

　0   1 5   6

Investment and Reinvestment Combined:

C=$250,000   - .... -   F=$2,000,000

$$\overline{\hspace{8cm}}$$

　0   1 5   6

Present Worth Equation:

$250,000 = 2,000,000(P/F_{i,6})$

Therefore, $P/F_{i,6} = 0.125,$
Or by interpolation, $i = 41.73\%$ = *Growth ROR*

3-16 Solution: *X = Monthly Payment*

Value=$100,000
Payments = X   X   X X   -

$$\overline{\hspace{8cm}}$$ Balloon=$25,000

　　　0   1   2 29   30

Present Worth Equation:

$$\overset{25.066}{} \qquad \overset{0.7419}{}$$
$$100,000 = X + X(P/A_{1,29}) + 25,000(P/F_{1,30})$$

$$X = \frac{100,000 - 25,000(0.7419)}{1 + 25.066} = \$3,124.86 \text{ or } \$3,125$$

Payment	Month	Interest	Unpaid Principal
1	0	-	96,875
2	1	969	94,719
3	2	947	92,541 principal owed during 3rd month
4	3	925	90,341

3-16 Solution: *Continued*

An alternative calculation of remaining unpaid mortgage principal after the fourth payment equals the present worth at end-of-month 3 remaining payments to be made with calculations at the mortgage interest rate:

Present Worth Equation:

$$\overset{22.795}{\$3,124.86(P/A_{1,26})} + \overset{0.7644}{\$25,000(P/F_{1,27})} = \$90,341$$

3-17 Solution:

Period i = 8%/4 = 2%

$$A = 50,000\overset{0.02516}{(A/P_{2,80})} = \$1,258 \text{ per quarter}$$

```
   -$1,000
   $50,000    A       A ..................... A
   _____
      0       1       2 .................... 80 quarters
```

Present Worth Equation:

$$50,000 - 1,000 = (50,000\overset{0.02516}{(A/P_{2,80})})(P/A_{i,80})$$

$$49,000 = 1,258(P/A_{i,80})$$

$$38.951 = P/A_{i,80}$$

i=2%: $P/A_{2,80}$ = 39.745

i=3%: $P/A_{3,80}$ = 30.201

$$i = 2\% + 1\%\left(\frac{39.745 - 38.951}{39.745 - 30.201}\right) = 2\% + 1\%\left(\frac{0.794}{9.544}\right) = 2.083\% \text{ per quarter}$$

Nominal Annual Rate = 8.332%

3-18 Solution: *All Values in Millions*

Development A:

```
               C=$2.0
               I=$1.8        I=$1.8                              I=$1.8
     C=$1.0    OC=$0.7       OC=$0.7 ...................... OC=$0.7
     ─────────────────────────────────────────────────────────────
       0          1            2 ........................... 10
```

Development B:

```
                            I=$2.0                              I=$2.0
     C=$1.0    C=$0.9       OC=$0.9 ...................... OC=$0.9
     ─────────────────────────────────────────────────────────────
       0          1            2 ........................... 10
```

Incremental Time Line For B - A:

```
     C=0        C=0          I=0 ......................... I=0
     ─────────────────────────────────────────────────────────────
       0          1            2 ........................... 10
```

ROR Analysis:

ROR_A PW Eq: $1.0 = 1.1(P/A_{i,10}) - 2.0(P/F_{i,1})$ $i = 45.1\%$

ROR_B PW Eq: $1.0 = [1.1(P/A_{i,9}) - 0.9](P/F_{i,1})$ $i = 45.1\%$

ROR_{B-A} PW Eq: $0 = 0$ *There is no economic difference with A & B.*

NPV Analysis:

$$NPV_A = 1.1\overset{5.019}{(P/A_{15,10})} - 2.0\overset{0.8696}{(P/F_{15,1})} - 1.0 = \$2.782$$

$$NPV_B = [1.1\overset{4.772}{(P/A_{15,9})} - 0.9]\overset{0.8696}{(P/F_{15,1})} - 1.0 = \$2.782$$

$NPV_{B-A} = 0$, *so A and B are economically equivalent.*

PVR Analysis:

$$PVR_A \text{ Denominator} = 1.0 + [2.0-(1.8-0.7)]\overset{0.8696}{(P/F_{15,1})} = 1.783$$

$$PVR_A = \frac{2.782}{1.783} = 1.56 > 0$$

$$PVR_B \text{ Denominator} = 1.0 + 0.9\overset{0.8696}{(P/F_{15,1})} = 1.783$$

$$PVR_B = \frac{2.782}{1.783} = 1.56 > 0$$

3-18 Solution Continued:

Note that if you do not net the year 1 costs and revenues for A before calculating the present worth cost denominator for PVR_A, you do not get the equivalence of A and B shown with both ROR and NPV.

$$Incorrect\ PVR_A = \frac{2.782}{1 + 2(P / F_{15,1})} = 1.01$$

3-19 Solution: *All Values in Thousands*

Investment A:

```
        Sunk Costs
      ┌──────────────┐
  C=$100    C=$200      -      I=$120   I=$120 . . . . . . . I=$120
 ─────────────────────────────────────────────────────────────────
    -2        -1        0       1        2  . . . . . . . . . 12
```

Investment B:

```
                     -      C=$350    I=$150 . . .  I=$150
                ──────────────────────────────────────────
                     0        1         2  . . . . .  10
```

$$\text{Time 0 } NPV_A = 120 \overset{4.439}{(P/A_{20,12})} = \$532.7$$

$$\text{Time 0 } NPV_B = [-350 + 150 \overset{4.031}{(P/A_{20,9})}] \overset{0.8333}{(P/F_{20,1})} = \$212.2$$

Cumulative NPV = 532.7 + 212.2 = \$744.9

\$744.9 is the maximum value of the company @ i*=20%

3-20 Solution: *Before-tax Cash Flows in 000's*

Year	0	1	2	3	4	5
Revenues		1,612.0	1,378.0	910.0	655.2	487.9
-Royalties		-225.7	-192.9	-127.4	-91.7	-68.3
-Operating Cost		-175.0	-193.0	-212.0	-233.0	-256.0
-Research & Dev.	-750.0	-250.0				
-Equipment		-670.0				
-Patent Rights	-100.0					
Before-Tax CF	-850.0	291.3	992.1	570.6	330.5	163.6

NPV Analysis:

$$\text{NPV @ 15\%} = -850 + 291.3 \overset{0.8696}{(P/F_{15,1})} + 992.1 \overset{0.7561}{(P/F_{15,2})} + 570.6 \overset{0.6575}{(P/F_{15,3})}$$

$$+ 330.5 \overset{0.5718}{(P/F_{15,4})} + 163.6 \overset{0.4972}{(P/F_{15,5})} = +\$798.9 > 0, \text{ accept}$$

ROR Analysis:

$$\text{PW Eq: } 0 = -850 + 291.3(P/F_{i,1}) + 992.1(P/F_{i,2}) + 570.6(P/F_{i,3})$$

$$+ 330.5(P/F_{i,4}) + 163.6(P/F_{i,5})$$

NPV @ 50% = +$41
NPV @ 70% = -$168   ROR = i = 50% + 20%(41/209) = 53.9% > i*=15%

By Financial Calculator, i = ROR = 53.276% > i* = 15%, accept

Ratio Analysis:

PVR = 798.9/850 = 0.94 > 0   *B/C Ratio = PVR + 1 = 1.94 > 1.0*

Break-even Uniform Selling Price Per Unit:

Year	0	1	2	3	4	5
Revenues		62X	53X	35X	24X	17X
-Royalties		-8.68X	-7.42X	-4.90X	-3.36X	-2.38X
-Operating Cost		-175.0	-193.0	-212.0	-233.0	-256.0
-Research & Dev.	-750.0	-250.0				
-Equipment Cost		-670.0				
-Patent Rights	-100.0					
Before-Tax CF	-850.0	53.32X	45.58X	30.10X	20.64X	14.62X
		-1,095	-193	-212	-233	-256

$$\text{PW Eq: } 0 = -850 + (53.32X-1,095)\overset{0.8696}{(P/F_{15,1})} + (45.58X-193)\overset{0.7561}{(P/F_{15,2})}$$

$$+ (30.10X-212)\overset{0.6575}{(P/F_{15,3})} + (20.64X-233)\overset{0.5718}{(P/F_{15,4})} + (14.62X-256)\overset{0.4972}{(P/F_{15,5})}$$

$$0 = -2,348.0 + 119.69X \qquad \textit{Break-even Price, X = \$19.62 per unit}$$

3-21 Solution: *Before-tax Cash Flows in 000's*

Year	0	1	2	3	4	5
Revenues		1,612.0	1,378.0	910.0	655.2	487.9
-Royalties		-225.7	-192.9	-127.4	-91.7	-68.3
-Operating Cost		-175.0	-193.0	-212.0	-233.0	-256.0
-Intangible	-750.0	-250.0				
-Tangible		-670.0				
-Min Rights Acq.	-100.0					
Before-Tax CF	-850.0	291.3	992.1	570.6	330.5	163.6

NPV Analysis:

$$\text{NPV @ 15\%} = -850 + 291.3\underset{0.8696}{(P/F_{15,1})} + 992.1\underset{0.7561}{(P/F_{15,2})} + 570.6\underset{0.6575}{(P/F_{15,3})}$$

$$+ 330.5\underset{0.5718}{(P/F_{15,4})} + 163.6\underset{0.4972}{(P/F_{15,5})} = +\$798.9 > 0, \text{ accept}$$

ROR Analysis:

PW Eq: $0 = -850 + 291.3(P/F_{i,1}) + 992.1(P/F_{i,2}) + 570.6(P/F_{i,3})$

$$+ 330.5(P/F_{i,4}) + 163.6(P/F_{i,5})$$

NPV @ 50% = +$41
NPV @ 70% = -$168   ROR = i = 50% + 20%(41/209) = 53.9% > i* = 15%

By financial calculator, i = ROR = 53.276% > i* = 15%, accept

PVR Analysis:

PVR = 798.9/850 = 0.94 > 0,   *B/C Ratio = PVR + 1 = 1.94 > 1.0*

Break-even Uniform Selling Price Per Unit:

Year	0	1	2	3	4	5
Revenues		62X	53X	35X	24X	17X
-Royalties		-8.68X	-7.42X	-4.90X	-3.36X	-2.38X
-Operating Cost		-175.0	-193.0	-212.0	-233.0	-256.0
-Intangible	-750.0	-250.0				
-Tangible		-670.0				
-Min Rights Acq	-100.0					
Before-Tax CF	-850.0	53.32X	45.58X	30.10X	20.64X	14.62X
		-1,095	-193	-212	-233	-256

PW Eq: $0 = -850 + (53.32X-1,095)\underset{0.8696}{(P/F_{15,1})} + (45.58X-193)\underset{0.7561}{(P/F_{15,2})}$

$$+ (30.10X-212)\underset{0.6575}{(P/F_{15,3})} + (20.64X-233)\underset{0.5718}{(P/F_{15,4})} + (14.62X-256)\underset{0.4972}{(P/F_{15,5})}$$

$0 = -2,348.0 + 119.69X$ *Break-even Price, X = $19.62 per bbl*

3-22 Solution: *Before-tax Cash Flows in 000's*

Year	0	1	2	3	4	5
Revenues		1,612.0	1,378.0	910.0	655.2	487.9
-Royalties		-225.7	-192.9	-127.4	-91.7	-68.3
-Operating Cost		-175.0	-193.0	-212.0	-233.0	-256.0
-Mine Dev	-750.0	-250.0				
-Mine Equipment		-670.0				
-Min Rights Acq	-100.0					
Before-Tax CF	-850.0	291.3	992.1	570.6	330.5	163.6

NPV Analysis:

$$\text{NPV @ 15\%} = -850 + 291.3\underset{0.8696}{(P/F_{15,1})} + 992.1\underset{0.7561}{(P/F_{15,2})} + 570.6\underset{0.6575}{(P/F_{15,3})}$$

$$+ 330.5\underset{0.5718}{(P/F_{15,4})} + 163.6\underset{0.4972}{(P/F_{15,5})} = +\$798.9 \quad \text{accept}$$

ROR Analysis:

$$\text{PW Eq:} \quad 0 = -850 + 291.3(P/F_{i,1}) + 992.1(P/F_{i,2}) + 570.6(P/F_{i,3})$$

$$+ 330.5(P/F_{i,4}) + 163.6(P/F_{i,5})$$

NPV @ 50% = +$41
NPV @ 70% = -$168   ROR = i = 50% + 20%(41/209) = 53.9% > i*=15%

By financial calculator, i = ROR = 53.276% > i* = 15%, accept

Ratio Analysis:

PVR = 798.9/850 = 0.94 > 0   *B/C Ratio = PVR + 1 = 1.94 > 1.0*

Break-even Uniform Selling Price Per Unit:

Year	0	1	2	3	4	5
Revenues		62X	53X	35X	24X	17X
-Royalties		-8.68X	-7.42X	-4.90X	-3.36X	-2.38X
-Operating Cost		-175.0	-193.0	-212.0	-233.0	-256.0
-Mine Dev	-750.0	-250.0				
-Mine Equipment		-670.0				
-Min Rights Acq	-100.0					
Before-Tax CF	-850.0	53.32X	45.58X	30.10X	20.64X	14.62X
		-1,095	-193	-212	-233	-256

$$\text{PW Eq:} \ 0 = -850 + (53.32X-1,095)\underset{0.8696}{(P/F_{15,1})} + (45.58X-193)\underset{0.7561}{(P/F_{15,2})}$$

$$+ (30.10X-212)\underset{0.6575}{(P/F_{15,3})} + (20.64X-233)\underset{0.5718}{(P/F_{15,4})} + (14.62X-256)\underset{0.4972}{(P/F_{15,5})}$$

0 = -2,348.0 + 119.69X   *Break-even Price, X = $19.62 per ton*

3-23 Solution:

Existing Machine (A):

$$C=\$25,000$$

$C=0$ $OC=\$4,500$ $OC=\$5,500$ $OC=\$2,500$ $OC=\$3,000$ $OC=\$3,500$ $OC=\$4,000$

$$L=\$7,000$$

0	1	2	3	4	5	6

Present Worth Cost of Existing Machine (PWC$_A$):

$$\begin{array}{ccc} 0.8333 & 0.6944 & 0.3349 \end{array}$$

$PWC_A 4,500(P/F_{20,1}) + (25,000 + 5,500)(P/F_{20,2}) - 7,000(P/F_{20,6})$

$$\begin{array}{ccc} 1.274 & 2.589 & 0.6944 \end{array}$$

$+ [2,500 + 500(A/G_{20,4})](P/A_{20,4})(P/F_{20,2}) = \$28,224$

Annual Cost of Existing Machine (AC$_A$):

$$0.30071$$

$AC_A: (28,224)(A/P_{20,6}) = \$8,487$

Replacement Machine (B):

$C=\$21,000$ $OC=\$2,000$ $OC=\$2,500$ $OC=\$3,000$ $OC=\$3,500$ $OC=\$4,000$ $OC=\$4,500$

$$L=\$4,000$$

0	1	2	3	4	5	6

Present Worth Cost of Replacement Machine (PWC$_B$):

$$\begin{array}{ccc} 1.979 & 3.326 & 0.3349 \end{array}$$

$21,000 + [2,000 + 500(A/G_{20,6})](P/A_{20,6}) - 4,000(P/F_{20,6}) = \$29,603$

Annual Cost of Replacement (AC$_B$):

$$0.30071$$

$AC_B: (29,603)(A/P_{20,6}) = \$8,902$

Incremental Analysis (A-B):

$$C=-\$25,000$$

$C=\$21,000$ $OC=-\$2,500$ $OC=-\$3,000$ $C=\$500$ $C=\$500$ $C=\$500$ $C=\$500$

$$L=-\$3,000$$

0	1	2	3	4	5	6

Incremental NPV:

$$\begin{array}{cccc} 0.8333 & 0.6944 & 2.589 & 0.6944 \end{array}$$

$-21,000 + 2,500(P/F_{20,1}) + 28,000(P/F_{20,2}) - 500(P/A_{20,4})(P/F_{20,2})$

$$0.3349$$

$- 3,000(P/F_{20,6}) = -\$1,377$ *so, reject replacement machine B,*
and select existing machine A.

3-24 Solution:

The specified discount rates on Treasury Bills are annual rates, so half of 15% or 7.5% is the interest on this six month T-Bill. The interest is paid within 10 days of the T-Bill purchase date, so assume the purchase cost and interest occur at the same time.

```
  Int=$750
C=$10,000    Net=$9,250                        Terminal Value=$10,000
  ────────────────────────────────────────────────────────────────
     0                                            1 six month period
```

Present Worth Equation: $\$9,250 = 10,000(P/F_{i,1})$

i = 6 month period interest rate = 8.1%
So, nominal annual rate of return = 16.2% compounded semi-annually.

3-25 Solution: *All Values in Millions*

```
                   C=$4
     C=$1.5        C=$5        I=$4 ................ I=$4
     ──────────────────────────────────────────────────
                                                       L=$6
       0            1          2 ................. 9
```

Present Worth Equation:

$$0 = -1.5 - 9(P/F_{i,1}) + 4(P/A_{i,8})(P/F_{i,1}) + 6(P/F_{i,9})$$

$i=40\%$: = $-\$0.979$
$i=30\%$: = $+\$1.142$ *Using a calculator, i = ROR = 34.6%*

Project growth ROR:

Reinvestment Income @i* = 15%

```
       -            -          C=$4 .............. C=$4
     ──────────────────────────────────────────────────
                                                  C=$6   F=$60.91
       0            1          2 ................ 9
                 13.727
```
Where: $F = 4(F/A_{15,8}) + 6 = \$60.91$

Initial Investment plus Reinvestment Income:

```
                   C=$4
     C=$1.5        C=$5        - ................. -
     ──────────────────────────────────────────────────
                                                  F=$60.91
       0            1          2 ................ 9
```

Present Worth Equation:

$$0 = -1.5 - 9.0(P/F_{i,1}) + 60.91(P/F_{i,9})$$

$i = 20\%$: $-1.5 - 9.0(0.8333) + 60.91(0.1938) = +\$2.805$
$i = 25\%$: $-1.5 - 9.0(0.8000) + 60.91(0.1342) = -\$0.526$

i = Growth ROR = 20% + (25%-20%)[(2.805-0)/(2.805+0.526)] = 24.2%

3-25 Solution: *Continued*

NPV Analysis:

$$
\underset{0.8696}{-1.5 - 9.0(P/F_{15,1})} + \underset{4.487 \quad 0.8696}{4.0(P/A_{15,8})(P/F_{15,1})} + \underset{0.2843}{6(P/F_{15,9})} = +\$7.99
$$

Calculating NPV from the values used to determine growth ROR gives the same NPV result. Reinvestment of revenues at the minimum ROR is implicitly built into all net value calculations.

$$
NPV = -1.5 - 9.0(P/F_{15,1}) + 60.91(P/F_{15,9}) = +\$7.99
$$

PVR Calculation:

$$
PVR = 7.99 \ / \ [1.5 + 9.0(P/F_{15,1})] = 0.86
$$

3-26 Solution: *All Values in Millions*

```
C=?      C=$1.5    C=$2.0    I=$1.0    I=$1.0 ....... I=$1.0
                                                               L=$3.0
─────────────────────────────────────────────────────────────
0        1         2         3         4 ........... 10
```

On a before-tax basis, NPV represents the additional cost that could be incurred at year 0 to receive a 15% rate of return. In this problem, NPV equals the maximum year 0 development cost that can be incurred and still have the project return 15% on invested capital.

NPV Analysis at ROR of 15%:

$$
\underset{0.8696}{-1.5(P/F_{15,1})} - \underset{0.7561}{2.0(P/F_{15,2})} + \underset{4.487 \quad 0.7561}{1.0(P/A_{15,8})(P/F_{15,2})}
$$

$$
+ \underset{0.2472}{3.0(P/F_{15,10})} = +\$1.3176
$$

NPV Analysis at ROR of 10%:

$$
\underset{0.9091}{-1.5(P/F_{10,1})} - \underset{0.8264}{2.0(P/F_{10,2})} + \underset{5.335 \quad 0.8264}{1.0(P/A_{10,8})(P/F_{10,2})}
$$

$$
+ \underset{0.3855}{3.0(P/F_{10,10})} = +\$2.5489
$$

At the lower discount rate of 10% the project NPV increased by more than $1.2 million, nearly doubling the original value. Lower discount rates always lead to increased value from positive revenue streams.

3-27 Solution: *All Values in Millions*

C=X	–	–	C_{Dev}=$2.5	I=$1.5	I=$1.3 grad/yr=-$0.2 ...
0	1	2	3	4	5 11

In a before-tax analysis, the year 0 break-even property acquisition cost, X, equals the year 0 NPV for property.

Year 0 NPV Equation:

$$X = -2.5 \underset{0.5787}{(P/F_{20,3})} + [1.5-0.2 \underset{2.576}{(A/G_{20,8})}] \underset{3.837}{(P/A_{20,8})} \underset{0.5787}{(P/F_{20,3})}$$

$$X = \$0.74 \quad \text{to break-even with a 20\% ROR}$$

This represents the maximum price a buyer could pay to develop the property three years later to get a 20% ROR. The owner should make the same analysis. The minimum sales price for an owner who uses the same analysis numbers would be $0.740 million. Any amount over that price would make selling economically better than developing from the owner viewpoint.

3-28 Solution, *Summary of Input Data:*

Year	0	1	2	3	4
Intangible Drilling	$250,000				
Tangible Completion	$100,000				
Lease Cost	$0				
Production, bbls/yr		17,500	9,000	6,500	3,000
Selling Price, $/bbl		$20.00	$20.00	$21.00	$22.05
Operating Cost, $/bbl		$4.00	$4.00	$4.00	$4.00
Royalties(12.5%Gross,$/bbl)		$2.50	$2.50	$2.625	$2.756

Before-Tax Cash Flows Calculations:

Year	0	1	2	3	4
Gross Revenue		350,000	180,000	136,500	66,150
-Royalties		-43,750	-22,500	-17,063	-8,269
Net Revenue Interest		306,250	157,500	119,438	57,881
-Operating Expenses		-70,000	-36,000	-26,000	-12,000
-Capital Costs	-350,000				
Before-Tax CF	-350,000	236,250	121,500	93,438	45,881

Net Present Value Equation:

$$NPV @12\% = -350,000 + 236,250 \underset{0.8929}{(P/F_{12,1})} + 121,500 \underset{0.7972}{(P/F_{12,2})}$$

$$+ 93,438 \underset{0.7118}{(P/F_{12,3})} + 45,881 \underset{0.6355}{(P/F_{12,4})} = \$53,473$$

PVR Calculation: 53,473 / 350,000 = 0.15

3-28 Solution: *Continued*

Present Worth Equation:

$0 = -350{,}000 + 236{,}250(P/F_{i,1}) + 121{,}500(P/F_{i,2})$
$\quad + 93{,}438(P/F_{i,3}) + 45{,}881(P/F_{i,4})$

$i = 25\%: -\$16{,}607$
$i = 20\%: +\$7{,}438$

$i = ROR = 20\% + (25\%-20\%)(7{,}438-0)/(7{,}438+16{,}607) = 21.55\%$

Growth ROR Calculation:

$$\begin{array}{ccc} 1.4049 & 1.2544 & 1.1200 \end{array}$$
$F=236{,}250(F/P_{12,3})+121{,}500(F/P_{12,2})+93{,}438(F/P_{12,1})+45{,}881 = \$634{,}849$

Growth ROR Present Worth Equation:

$0 = -350{,}000 + 634{,}849(P/F_{i,4})$
$GROR = i = 16.05\%$

Break-even Uniform Price per Barrel: Let X = price/barrel each year

Due to royalties, only 87.5% of production is available to generate revenues to pay off the initial investment, and give a 12.0% ROR.

$$\begin{array}{cc} 0.8929 & 0.7972 \end{array}$$
$0 = -350{,}000 + (15{,}313X-70{,}000)(P/F_{12,1}) + (7{,}875X-36{,}000)(P/F_{12,2})$

$$\begin{array}{cc} 0.7118 & 0.6355 \end{array}$$
$\quad + (5{,}688X-26{,}000)(P/F_{12,3}) + (2{,}625X-12{,}000)(P/F_{12,4})$

$25{,}667X = 467{,}335$

$X = \$18.21/bbl$

3-29 Solution, *5.0% Caried Interest - Backing in for a 25.0% Working Interest & a 21.875% Net Revenue Interest after payout:*

Year	0	1	2	3	4
Intangible Drilling	$250,000				
Tangible Completion	$100,000				
Lease Cost	$0				
Production,bbls/yr		17,500	9,000	6,500	3,000
Selling Price,$/bbl		$20.00	$20.00	$21.00	$22.05
Operating Cost,$/bbl		$4.00	$4.00	$4.00	$4.00
Royalties(12.5%Gross,$/bbl)		$2.50	$2.50	$2.63	$2.76

Pay-out Calculation Using Production:

When the cumulative value of net revenue (defined here as production times the selling price less royalties and cash operating costs) gives revenue equal to the total dollars invested, the project is at pay-out. In this case, $350,000 has been spent, and the price in years 1 and 2 is constant at $20.00 per barrel. Due to the two royalties, the producer only gets 82.5% of each barrel to pay off the investment. Hence, pay-out in production is calculated as follows:

Yr 1 Pay-out Basis: $350,000-[17,500x($20.00(0.825)-$4.00)]=$131,250
Yr 2 Pay-out Basis: $131,250-[9,000x($20.00(0.825)-$4.00)]=$ 18,750
Yr 3 Pay-out: $ 18,750 = (X bbl)($21.00(0.825)-$4.00)   X = 1,407 bbl

So, in year 3, 1,407 barrels would be subject to the over-riding royalty interest of 5.0%, after which (the reversion point), 5,093 barrels would be subject to the 25.0% working interest and a 21.875% net revenue interest (25.0% adjusted for ¼ of the 12.5% royalty).

Year	0	1	2	3	4
Carried Interest Rev.(5%)		17,500	9,000	1,477	–
+N.R.I.*(25% After Reversion)		0	0	23,396	14,470
Total Net Revenue		17,500	9,000	24,873	14,470
-Operating Exp.(25% A.R.**)		0	0	-5,093	-3,000
Before-Tax CF	0	17,500	9,000	19,780	11,470

*   Net Revenue Interest
** After Reversion

NPV Analysis, i = 12%:

$$\begin{array}{cccc} 0.8929 & 0.7972 & 0.7118 & 0.6355 \end{array}$$
$$17,500(P/F_{12,1})+9,000(P/F_{12,2})+19,780(P/F_{12,3})+11,470(P/F_{12,4})=\$44,169$$

PVR and ROR are infinite (undefined) due to zero investment.

3-30 Solution: *All Values in Thousands*

$$\text{Period Interest Rate} = \frac{\text{Nominal Rate of 12.0\%}}{\text{12 Monthly Compounding Periods}} = 1\% \text{ per month}$$

Effective Annual Rate, E, $= [(1.01)^{12}-1] = 0.1268$ or 12.68%

Purchase Compressor:

Installation=$75
Acquisition =$1,000   –   –   C=$225   –

                                                          L=$300
Years   0   1   2   3   4   5
Months   0   12   24   36   48   60

Present Worth Cost Analysis of Purchase:

Using a monthly period interest rate, i:
$$\underset{0.6989}{1,075} + 225(P/F_{1,36}) - \underset{0.5504}{300}(P/F_{1,60}) = \$1,067.13$$

Annual Period Present Worth Cost Analysis of Purchase:

Using an effective annual interest rate, E:
$$\underset{0.6989}{1,075} + 225(P/F_{12.68,3}) - \underset{0.5504}{300}(P/F_{12.68,5}) = \$1,067.13$$

$$\text{Equivalent Monthly Cost: } (1-60) = 1,067.13\underset{0.02224}{(A/P_{1,60})} = \$23.73$$

Lease Compressor:

Installation = $75
Lease Payment = $24 ... $24 ..... $24 .... $24
Months   0 .... 12 ...... 24 59

Present Worth Cost Analysis of Leasing:

Using a monthly period interest rate, i:
$$99 + 24\underset{44.4046}{(P/A_{1,59})} = \$1,164.71$$

$$\text{Equivalent Monthly Cost: } (1-60) = 1,164.71\underset{0.02224}{(A/P_{1,60})} = \$25.90$$

Purchasing gives the smallest PW Cost and Equivalent Monthly Cost at 1% monthly, therefore the economic decision is to purchase the compressor.

Annual Period Present Worth Cost Analysis of Leasing:

75+6(24)=$219 12(24)=$288   12(24)=$288   12(24)=$288   12(24)=$288 6(24)=$144
Year 0   1   2   3   4   5

Using effective annual interest rate, E:
$$219 + 288\underset{2.99436}{(P/A_{12.68,4})} + 144\underset{0.5505}{(P/F_{12.68,5})} = \$1,160.64$$

3-31 Solution:

A) 10 Year Bond Analysis

```
Value(P)=?     I=$800 ............... I=$800
──────────────────────────────────────── Maturity Value = $10,000
   0            1 .................. 10 years
```

i=8%: P = $10,000

$$\text{i=6\%: P} = 800\underset{7.360}{(P/A_{6,10})} + 10,000\underset{0.5584}{(P/F_{6,10})} = \$11,472$$

$$\text{i=10\%: P} = 800\underset{6.144}{(P/A_{10,10})} + 10,000\underset{0.3855}{(P/F_{10,10})} = \$8,770$$

B) 30 Year Bond Analysis

```
Value(P)=?     I=$800 ............... I=$800
──────────────────────────────────────── Maturity Value = $10,000
   0            1 ..................... 30 years
```

i=8%: P = $10,000

$$\text{i=6\%: P} = 800\underset{13.765}{(P/A_{6,30})} + 10,000\underset{0.1741}{(P/F_{6,30})} = \$12,753$$

$$\text{i=10\%: P} = 800\underset{9.427}{(P/A_{10,30})} + 10,000\underset{0.05731}{(P/F_{10,30})} = \$8,115$$

C) 30 Year Zero Coupon Bond

```
Value(P)=?     -                         -
──────────────────────────────────────── Maturity Value = $10,000
   0            1 ..................... 30 years
```

$$\text{i=8\%: P} = 10,000\underset{0.099377}{(P/F_{8,30})} = \$994$$

$$\text{i=6\%: P} = 10,000\underset{0.17411}{(P/F_{6,30})} = \$1,741$$

$$\text{i=10\%: P} = 10,000\underset{0.05731}{(P/F_{10,30})} = \$573$$

3-32 Solution:

Current Remediation System:

```
      -$50,000    -$50,000 . . .  -$50,000    -$50,000    -$50,000
  ─────────────────────────────────────────────────────────────────
   0         1           2 . . . . . . 5          6          7
```

$$5.0330$$
PW Cost: $-50,000(P/A_{9,7}) = -\$251,650$

Upgraded Remediation System:

```
 -$75,000     -$35,000   -$35,000 . . . . . . -$35,000
 ─────────────────────────────────────────────────────
  0            1            2 . . . . . . . . . 5
```

$$3.8897$$
PW Cost: $-75,000 - 35,000(P/A_{9,5}) = -\$211,140$ least cost alternative.

Incremental Analysis (Upgrade - Current):

```
 -$75,000     $15,000    $15,000 . . . $15,000    $50,000    $50,000
 ──────────────────────────────────────────────────────────────────
  0            1            2  . . . . 5           6          7
```

Incremental NPV @ 9.0%:

$$1.7591 \quad 0.6499 \qquad\qquad 3.8897$$
$$50,000(P/A_{9,2})(P/F_{9,5}) + 15,000(P/A_{9,5}) - 75,000 = \$40,510$$

$40,510 > 0$, *so accept the upgrade investment.*

3-33 Solution:

Alternative 1

```
-$170,000  -$35,000    -$35,000 . . . . . . . . . . . . -$35,000
_____  $50,000
     0          1          2 . . . . . . . . . . . . . . 5
```

PW Cost Equation:

$$\begin{array}{cc} 3.8897 & 0.6499 \end{array}$$
$$-170{,}000 - 35{,}000(P/A_{9,5}) + 50{,}000(P/F_{9,5}) = -\$273{,}645 \text{ least cost}$$

Alternative 2

```
  -        -$50,000     -$50,000 . . .-$50,000    -$50,000 . . . -$50,000
_____
  0           1           2 . . . . . 5           6 . . . . . . 10
```

$$\begin{array}{c} 6.4177 \end{array}$$
PW Cost Equation: $-50{,}000(P/A_{9,10}) = -\$320{,}885$

Incremental Analysis (Alternative 1 - Alternative 2)

```
-$170,000   $15,000    $15,000 . . $15,000    $65,000        $50,000
_____
    0          1         2 . . . . 4             5             6-10
```

Incremental NPV @ 9.0%:

$$\begin{array}{ccccc} 0.6499 & & 3.8897\ 0.6499 & & 3.2397 \end{array}$$
$$65{,}000(P/F_{9,5}) + 50{,}000(P/A_{9,5})(P/F_{9,5}) + 15{,}000(P/A_{9,4}) - 170{,}000$$

$$= \$47{,}235$$

Or, Looking at the differences in the present worth costs will also give the incremental NPV result as follows:

Incremental NPV = PW Cost$_1$ - PW Cost$_2$

$$= -273{,}645 - -320{,}885 = +47{,}240$$

The difference in the two results is round-off error in the factors.

3-34 Solution:

Nominal Interest Rate = 10.0% Compounded Monthly
Period Interest Rate = 10.0%/12 = 0.833%
Effective Interest Rate, E = $(1.00833)^{12} - 1 = 10.47\%$

Option 1; Catalytic Converter

Equipment	-70,000					
O & M	- 6,000	-12,000	-12,000	-12,000	-12,000	-6,000
	0	1	2	3	4	5

$$\text{PW Cost}_1 = -76,000 - 12,000\,\overset{3.13788}{(P/A_{10.47\%,4})} - 6,000\,\overset{0.60782}{(P/F_{10.47\%,5})}$$

$$= -117,301 \quad \text{select the least cost, Alternative 1}$$

Option 2; Two 1,000 Pound Carbon Canisters

Carbon Replacement: 2 Canisters * 1,000 lbs ea * $4.00/lb = $8,000

Time Zero: Allocate 3 Replacements: 3 * $8,000 = $24,000

Year One: Allocate 6 Replacements: 6 * $8,000 = $48,000

Year Two: Allocate 3 Replacements: 3 * $8,000 = $24,000
Allocate 2 Replacements: 2 * $8,000 = $16,000 $40,000

Year Three: Allocate 2 Replacements: 2 * $8,000 = $16,000
Allocate 1 Replacement: 1 * $8,000 = $ 8,000 $24,000

Year Four: Allocate 1 Replacement: 1 * $8,000 = $ 8,000
Allocate 1/2 Replacement: 0.5 * $8,000 = $ 4,000 $12,000

Year Five: Allocate 1/2 Replacement: 0.5 * $8,000 = $ 4,000

Equipment	-15,000					
Can. Replace.	-24,000	-48,000	-40,000	-24,000	-12,000	-4,000
	0	1	2	3	4	5

$$\text{PW Cost}_2 = - 39,000 - 48,000\,\overset{0.90522}{(P/F_{10.47\%,1})} - 40,000\,\overset{0.81943}{(P/F_{10.47\%,2})}$$

$$- 24,000\,\overset{0.74177}{(P/F_{10.47\%,3})} - 12,000\,\overset{0.67146}{(P/F_{10.47\%,4})}$$

$$- 4,000\,\overset{0.60782}{(P/F_{10.47\%,5})} = -143,519$$

NPV = PW Cost$_1$ - PW Cost$_2$ -117,301 - -143,519 = 26,218 > 0 Accept 1

CHAPTER 4 PROBLEM SOLUTIONS

4-1 Solution: *All Values in Thousands*

Project A

C=$300	I=$450	I=$450	I=$450
0	1	2	10

Project B

C=$900	I=$550	I=$550	I=$550
0	1	2	10

Project C

	I=$750		
C=$1,200	C=$800	I=$850	I=$850
0	1	2	10

ROR Analysis:

"A" PW Eq: $0 = -300 + 450(P/A_{i,10})$, $i = ROR_A = 150\% > i^\star = 15\%$, *ok*

"B" PW Eq: $0 = -900 + 550(P/A_{i,10})$, $i = ROR_B = 60.6\% > i^\star = 15\%$, *ok*

"C" PW Eq: $0 = -1,200 - 50(P/F_{i,1}) + 850(P/A_{i,9})(P/F_{i,1})$,

$$i = ROR_C = 45.7\% > i^\star = 15\%, \ ok$$

Incremental Analysis, Project B - Project A

C=$600	I=$100	I=$100	I=$100
0	1	2	10

"B-A" PW Eq: $0 = -600 + 100(P/A_{i,10})$,

$$i = ROR_{B-A} = 10.5\% < 15\%, \ so \ reject \ B$$

Incremental Analysis, Project C - Project A

C=$900	C=$500	I=$400	I=$400
0	1	2	10

"C-A" PW Eq: $0 = -900 - 500(P/F_{i,1}) + 400(P/A_{i,9})(P/F_{i,1})$,

$$i = ROR_{C-A} = 20.5\% > i^\star = 15\%, \ so \ select \ C$$

4-1 Solution: *Continued*

NPV Analysis:

$NPV_A = -300 + 450(P/A_{15,10}) = +\$1,958$
$NPV_B = -900 + 550(P/A_{15,10}) = +\$1,860$
$NPV_C = -1,200 - 50(P/F_{15,1}) + 850(P/A_{15,9})(P/F_{15,1}) = +\$2,283$

Since $NPV_{B-A} = -98$ and $NPV_{C-A} = +\$325$, "C" is the economic choice.

Alternative "C" is the economic choice for $i^*=15\%$ since NPV_{C-A} and NPV_{C-B} are both positive. As always, the largest total investment NPV is the economic choice.

PVR Analysis:

$PVR_A = 1,958/300 = 6.5 > 0$, *so satisfactory*
$PVR_B = 1,860/900 = 2.1 > 0$, *so satisfactory*
$PVR_C = 2,283/[1,200+50(P/F_{15,1})] = 1.8 > 0$, *so satisfactory*

$PVR_{B-A} = (1,860-1,958)/600 = -0.2 < 0$, *unsatisfactory, select A over B*
$PVR_{C-A} = (2,283-1,958)/(900 + 500(P/F_{15,1})) = +0.2 > 0$ *select C over A*

NPV Analysis for $i^* = 25\%$:

$NPV_A = -300 + 450(P/A_{25,10}) = +\$1,307$ *Select the maximum NPV.*
$NPV_B = -900 + 550(P/A_{25,10}) = +\$1,064$
$NPV_C = -1,200 - 50(P/F_{25,1}) + 850(P/A_{25,9})(P/F_{25,1}) = +\$1,115$

The economic choice switches to alternative "A" for $i^* = 25\%$. Comparing the incremental ROR results to $i^* = 25\%$ verifies the NPV result.*

4-2 Solution: *All Values in Thousands*

```
 C=$ 80        I=$290              I=$290
 C=$200       OC=$160 . . . . . OC=$160     C=$360
─────────────────────────────────────────────────
 0             1 . . . . . . . 5          6
```

Net Present Value: $-280 + 130(P/A_{i,5}) - 360(P/F_{i,6})$

i	NPV	
0%	+ 10.0	
5%	+ 14.2	
10%	+ 9.6	
15%	+ 0.1	*Dual i = 15%.*
20%	- 11.8	*The other dual "i" is negative.*

Since NPV @ 20% is -\$11.8, reject the project for $i^* = 20\%$.

4-2 Continued - *PW Cost Modified ROR Analysis:*

$$280 + 360(P/F_{20,6}) \overset{0.3349}{=} 130(P/A_{i,5})$$

$$400.56 = 130(P/A_{i,5})$$

i = *PW Cost Modified ROR = 18.6% < i^* = 20% so reject.*

4-3 Solution: **Maximize Incremental NPV from Savings**

Incremental Insulation (inches)	Annual Savings From Insulation	Incremental NPV Analysis Equation	Incremental NPV
0	$ 0	(3.326)	$ 0.00
1-0	600	$600(P/A_{20,6}) - 1,200 =$	+795.60
2-0	800	$800(P/A_{20,6}) - 1,800 =$	+860.80*
3-0	900	$900(P/A_{20,6}) - 2,500 =$	+ 93.40
4-0	1,000	$1,000(P/A_{20,6}) - 3,500 =$	-174.00

* *Select the largest Incremental NPV of +$860.00 at 2 Inches.*

Alternate Solution: **Minimize Total PW Cost**

Insulation (inches)	PW Cost Calculation	PW Cost
0	$1,400 (P/A_{20,6})$ =	$4,656.40
1	$800 (P/A_{20,6}) + 1,200 =$	3,860.80
2	$600 (P/A_{20,6}) + 1,800 =$	3,795.60*
3	$500 (P/A_{20,6}) + 2,500 =$	4,163.30
4	$400 (P/A_{20,6}) + 3,500 =$	4,830.40

* *Select the minimum PW cost of $3,795.60 at 2 Inches.*

4-4 Solution: *All Values in Thousands of Dollars*

This is an income-cost-income analysis situation and involves the Dual ROR problem, as does the cost-income-cost problem.

		C=50	C=50	C=50	C=1,450		
	I=450	I=450	I=450	I=450	I=450	I=450	I=450
-	OC=310	OC=310	OC=310	OC=310	OC=310	OC=310	OC=310

L=300

0	1	2	3	4	5	6 10
CF -	140	90	90	90	-1,310	140 140+300

$$NPV = 140(P/F_{i},1) + 90(P/A_{i},3)(P/F_{i},1) - 1,310(P/F_{i},5)$$

$$+ 140(P/A_{i},5)(P/F_{i},5) + 300(P/F_{i},10)$$

i	NPV
0	+ 100.0
5	- 0.6
10	- 37.5
15	- 43.4
20	- 35.0
30	- 5.8
40	+ 21.9
50	+ 42.5

4.95%   *These are the project dual i values and are not valid for ROR economic decision making.*

32.90%

Although the Dual "i" values are not valid for ROR economic decision-making, the NPV results that were the basis for determining the dual "i" values are valid for economic decision making.

NPV @ i^* = 5% is similar to zero indicating break-even economics.
NPV @ i^* = 15% is negative indicating unsatisfactory economics.
NPV @ i^* = 50% is positive indicating satisfactory economics.

Increasing the minimum ROR to 50% from 15% improves the economics because of the strong rate of reinvestment meaning (as opposed to rate of return meaning) associated with i^* in this income-cost-income analysis.

4-4 Solution: *Continued*

Modified Present Worth Cost ROR Analysis for i* = 5%:

i* = 5%, Modified Year 0 PW Cost = $1,310(P/F_{5,5}) = \$1,026$

$1,026=140(P/F_{i,1})+90(P/A_{i,3})(P/F_{i,1})+140(P/A_{i,5})(P/F_{i,5})+300(P/F_{i,10})$

i = PW Cost Modified ROR = 5.0%=i* of 5% *Indicates break-even economics.*

Modified Present Worth Cost ROR Analysis for i* = 15%:

$$0.49718$$
i* = 15%, Modified Yr 0 PW Cost = $1,310(P/F_{15,5}) = \$651.3$

$651.3=140(P/F_{i,1})+90(P/A_{i,3})(P/F_{i,1})+140(P/A_{i,5})(P/F_{i,5})+300(P/F_{i,10})$

i = PW Cost Modified ROR = 13.5% < i* = 15%   *Unsatisfactory*

Modified Present Worth Cost ROR Analysis for i* = 50%:

$$0.13169$$
i* = 50%, Modified Yr 0 PW Cost = $1,310(P/F_{50,5}) = \$172.5$

$\$172.5=140(P/F_{i,1})+90(P/A_{i,3})(P/F_{i,1})+140(P/A_{i,5})(P/F_{i,5})+300(P/F_{i,10})$

i = PW Cost Modified ROR = 63.3% > i* = 50% *so satisfactory*

PW Cost Modified ROR analysis and NPV analysis give the same economic conclusion for the different minimum rates of return.

4-5 Solution:

Case A) Net Present Value Analysis

$NPV_1 = 80,000(P/A_{40,6}) - 150,000 = + \$23,440$ *Select the largest, NPV_1*
$NPV_2 = 115,000(P/A_{40,6}) - 230,000 = + \$19,320$
$NPV_2 - NPV_1 = -\$4,120$, *so select NPV_1*

Case B) Break-even Service Life

To determine break-even service, n, set NPV_1=NPV_2 for unknown life, n:
$80,000(P/A_{40,n})-150,000 = 115,000(P/A_{40,n}) - 230,000$
$P/A_{40,n} = 2.286$,
break-even service life n=7.34 yrs

For an evaluation life, n, less than 7.34 years, 1 is best.
For evaluation life, n, greater than 7.34 years, 2 is best.

4-6 Solution: *All Values in Dollars*

Alternative A)

```
                  C=200                 C=230
      C=100       I=110      I=110      I=110      I=110 ........ I=110
   ───────────────────────────────────────────────────────────────────
        0           1          2          3          4 ............ 8
```

$NPV_A = 110(P/A_{15,8}) - 230(P/F_{15,3}) - 200(P/F_{15,1}) - 100 = +\$68.4$

$PVR_A = 68.4 \, / \, [100 + (200-110)(P/F_{15,1})] = +0.38$

The year 3 cost of \$230 does not affect the PVR$_A$ denominator because it is offset by the combination of year 2 and 3 income as follows:

$[(-230+110)(P/F_{15,1}) + 110] = +\$5.65$ *which is year 2 net income, not a net cost, resulting from the year 2 and 3 incomes and cost.*

Alternative B)

```
                  C=200                 C=180
      C=100       I=110      I=20       I=110      I=110 ........ I=110
   ───────────────────────────────────────────────────────────────────
        0           1          2          3          4 ............ 8
```

$NPV_B = 110(P/A_{15,5})(P/F_{15,3}) - 70(P/F_{15,3}) + 20(P/F_{15,2}) - 90(P/F_{15,1})$

$\quad\quad - 100 = +\$33.3$

$PVR_B = 33.3/\{100+(200-110)(P/F_{15,1})+[(180-110)(P/F_{15,1})-20](P/F_{15,2})\}$

$\quad\quad = 33.3/209.2 = +0.16$

Project "A" with PVR of +0.38 ranks first, project "B" with PVR of +0.16 ranks second.

4-7 Solution:

Annual Worth equations for projects A & B give:

Project A ROR = 40%, Project B ROR = 40%

i) *Incremental Analysis for B-A:*

```
                                  L=+150,000              C=100,000
C=50,000      I=+20,000 ....... I= +20,000   C=40,000   C= 40,000
         ──────────────────────────────────────────────────────────
             0              1 .............   3           4           5
```

$50,000 = 20,000(P/A_{i,3}) + 150,000(P/F_{i,3}) - 40,000(P/F_{i,4})$

$\qquad - 140,000(P/F_{i,5})$

Two values of "i" exist that make the right side of the equation equal 50,000: i = 12%, and i = 40%.

No decision can be made from dual "i" values, except to establish the range of i* values for which the incremental NPV in this problem will be positive.

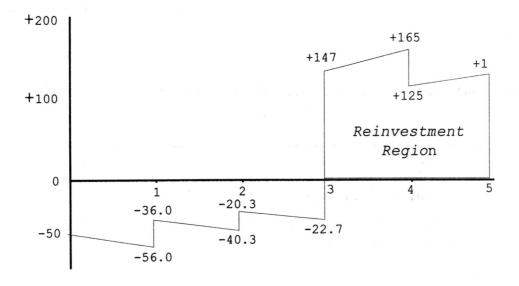

Cumulative Cash Position Diagram for i* = 12%
(Values in 000's)

4-7 ii) *NPV Analysis:*

$$NPV_A = 40,000\overset{2.991}{(P/A_{20,5})} + 100,000\overset{0.4019}{(P/F_{20,5})} - 100,000 = +\$59,830$$

$$NPV_B = 60,000\overset{2.106}{(P/A_{20,3})} + 150,000\overset{0.5787}{(P/F_{20,3})} - 150,000 = +\$63,165$$

Select project B with the greater NPV.

4-7 iii) *Incremental Growth ROR Analysis B-A:*

```
                              L=150,000
  C=50,000  I=20,000  I=20,000  I=20,000  C=40,000  C=140,000
  _____
      0        1         2         3         4         5
```

Reinvestment of Income @ 20%

```
                        C=150,000
   -      C=20,000 C=20,000 C=20,000     -         -
  _____    F=320,832
      0        1         2         3         4         5
```

$$\text{Where } F = [20,000\overset{3.640}{(F/A_{20,3})} + 150,000]\overset{1.440}{(F/P_{20,2})} = \$320,832$$

Alternative B - Alternative A + Income Reinvestment

```
  C=50,000    -         -         -      C=40,000     -
  _____    Net F=180,832
      0        1         2         3         4         5
```

PW Eq: $0 = -50,000 - 40,000(P/F_{i,4}) + 180,832(P/F_{i,5})$

By trial and error, Incremental Growth ROR, i, = 21.5% > i*=20% *indicating satisfactory economics, select B.*

4-7 iv) *Present Worth Cost Modified Incremental ROR Analysis:*

Present Worth Modified Cost:

$$50,000 + 40,000(P/F_{20,4}) + 140,000(P/F_{20,5}) = \$125,560$$

C=125,560	I=20,000	I=20,000	I=170,000	–	–
0	1	2	3	4	5

Present Worth Equation: $125,560 = 20,000(P/A_{i,2}) + 170,000(P/F_{i,3})$

By trial and error, i = PW Cost Modified ROR = 21.2% > i*=20%

4-7 v) *Reduce* i^* *to 10% from 20%:*

$$NPV_A = -100 + 40\overset{3.791}{(P/A_{10,5})} + 100\overset{0.6209}{(P/F_{10,5})} = +\$113.7$$

$$NPV_B = -150 + 60\overset{2.487}{(P/A_{10,3})} + 150\overset{0.7513}{(P/F_{10,3})} = +\$111.9$$

Select the greater NPV of \$113,000, alternative A.

4-8 Solution: *All Values in Dollars*

I=1,000	I=1,000	I=1,000	C=9,000	I=1,000 .... I=1,000
0	1	2	3	4 10

A) *Net Present Value Analysis:*

$$1,000+1,000\overset{1.528}{(P/A_{20,2})}-9,000\overset{0.5787}{(P/F_{20,3})}+1,000\overset{3.605}{(P/A_{20,7})}\overset{0.5787}{(P/F_{20,3})} = -\$595$$

The -\$595 indicates unsatisfactory economics, so reject the offer.

B) *PW Cost Modified ROR Analysis:*

Bring the year 3 cost back to year 0 at the minimum ROR:

$$9,000\overset{0.5787}{(P/F_{20,3})} = 1,000 + 1,000(P/A_{i,2}) + 1,000(P/A_{i,7})(P/F_{i,3})$$

Present Worth Cost Modified ROR, i, = 15.9%

15.9% < i^* *of 20%, again indicating unsatisfactory economics, so reject the offer.*

4-9 Solution: *All Values in Thousands*

Operation Level A)

```
C=100              Net I=40 .............. Net I=40
─────────────────────────────────────────────────
  0                  1 .................... 5
```

Operation Level B)

```
C=150              Net I=55 .............. Net I=55
─────────────────────────────────────────────────
  0                  1 .................... 5
```

NPV Analysis @ $i^* = 20\%$:

$NPV_A = -100 + 40(P/A_{20,5}) = +\$19.6$ *Select A, with the maximum NPV.*

$NPV_B = -150 + 55(P/A_{20,5}) = +\$14.5$

ROR Analysis:

"A" PW Eq: $0 = -100 + 40(P/A_{i,5})$, so $i = ROR_A = 28.6\% > i^* = 20\%$, *ok*

"B" PW Eq: $0 = -150 + 55(P/A_{i,5})$, so $i = ROR_B = 24.3\% > i^* = 20\%$, *ok*

Incremental Analysis B-A:

```
C=50               Net I=15 .............. Net I=15
─────────────────────────────────────────────────
  0                  1 .................... 5
```

"B-A" PW Eq: $0 = -50 + 15(P/A_{i,5})$, so $i = ROR_{B-A} = 15.2\% < i^* = 20\%$

The ROR_{B-A} is less than the minimum ROR of 20%; reject B, select A.

PVR Analysis:

$PVR_A = 19.6/100 = 0.196 > 0$, *satisfactory*

$PVR_B = 14.5/150 = 0.097 > 0$, *satisfactory*

$PVR_{B-A} = (14.5-19.6)/(150-100) = -0.10 < 0$, *unsatisfactory, select A*

Change the Minimum ROR to 12% from 20% over all 5 years:

The total investment and incremental investment ROR results are the same. Comparing them to $i^*=12\%$, however, gives a different economic conclusion, which is to select B.

$NPV_A = -100 + 40(P/A_{12,5}) = +\$44.4$

$NPV_B = -150 + 55(P/A_{12,5}) = +\$48.3$ *Select B, with the greatest NPV.*

Change the Min. ROR to 12% in years 1 & 2, and 20% for years 3, 4 & 5:

$NPV_A = -100 + 40(P/A_{20,3})(P/F_{12,2}) + 40(P/A_{12,2}) = +\$34.75$

$NPV_B = -150 + 55(P/A_{20,3})(P/F_{12,2}) + 55(P/A_{12,2}) = +\$35.28$

Results are effectively break-even since the NPV results are approximately equal. The slight advantage is to B with the greater NPV.

4-10 Mutually Exclusive Alternatives Solution:

Alternative A

```
-              I=450       I=450 ............ I=450
─────────────────────────────────────────────────────
0              1           2    ............. 10
```

Alternative B

```
C=800          I=700       I=700 ........... I=700
─────────────────────────────────────────────────────
0              1           2    ............. 10
```

Alternative C

```
               I=850
C=1,300        C=900       I=1,050 ........ I=1,050
─────────────────────────────────────────────────────
0              1           2    ............. 10
```

Net Present Value @ i* = 15%:

A) $\overset{5.019}{450(P/A_{15,10})}$ = +\$2,259

B) $\overset{5.019}{700(P/A_{15,10})}$ − 800 = +\$2,713

C) $[\overset{4.772}{1,050(P/A_{15,9})} - 50]\overset{0.8696}{(P/F_{15,1})}$ − 1,300 = +\$3,014   *Economic Choice*

Since NPV_{C-B} and NPV_{C-A} are positive, "C" with maximum NPV is the economic choice. The mutually exclusive alternative with maximum NPV on total investment always turns out to be the economic choice from incremental NPV analysis.

Present Value Ratio @ i* = 15%:

A)   2,259 / 0 = ∞ > 0, *so acceptable*
B)   2,713 / 800 = +3.39 > 0, *so acceptable*
C)   3,014 /(1,300+50$(P/F_{15,1})$)= 3,014/1,344 = +2.24 > 0, *so acceptable*

B-A) (2,713−2,259)/(800−0)=+0.57 > 0, *so acceptable*

Then, comparing alternative C to alternative B:

C-B) (3,014−2,713)/(500+652.2) = +0.26 > 0, (C is the economic choice)

Since B was preferred to A, there is no real value in comparing C to A. Comparing the next level of incremental investment (C-B), C is preferred to B since the incremental C-B PVR is positive indicating that the additional dollars invested in C over B earn a present worth profit of \$0.55 per present worth dollar invested. This exceeds the PVR of 0 obtained by investing elsewhere at the minimum rate of return and verifies that alternative C will provide the maximum return possible from available investment dollars.

4-10 Solution: *Continued*

Rate of Return Analysis for $i^* = 15.0\%$:

ROR_A: $\qquad 0 = 450(P/A_{i,10}) \qquad i = \infty\% > i^* = 15\%$

ROR_B: $\qquad 800 = 700(P/A_{i,10}) \qquad i = 87.34\% > i^* = 15\%$

ROR_C: $\quad 1,300 = 1,050(P/A_{i,9})(P/F_{i,1}) - 50(P/F_{i,1})$

$\qquad\qquad i = 50.9\% > i^* = 15\%$

ROR_{B-A}: $\quad 800 = 250(P/A_{i,10})$

$\qquad\qquad i = 28.8\% > 15\%,$ *Accept B over A*

ROR_{C-B}: $\quad 500 = \{350(P/A_{i,9}) - 750\}(P/F_{i,1})$

$\qquad\qquad i = 21.25\% > i^* = 15\%$ *"C" is the economic choice.*

Changing the Minimum Rate of Return to $i^* = 25\%$:

A) $\quad 450\overset{3.571}{(P/A_{25,10})} = +\$1,607$

B) $\quad 700\overset{3.571}{(P/A_{25,10})} - 800 = +\$1,700$ *"B" is now the economic choice.*

C) $\quad [1,050\overset{3.463}{(P/A_{25,9})} - 50]\overset{0.800}{(P/F_{25,1})} - 1,300 = +\$1,569$

For rate of return analysis, the only incremental alternative generating an incremental rate of return in excess of the new 25.0% minimum rate is (B-A) which indicates selecting alternative "B" is the economic choice, consistent with the NPV results. Incremental C-B is shown below to verify that "B" is preferred to "C." PVR would select "B" also.

ROR_{C-B} $\quad 500 = \{350(P/A_{i,9}) - 750\}(P/F_{i,1})$

$i = 21.25\% < i^* = 25\%$ $\quad$ *Accept B with the greater ROR.*

Changing the minimum rate of return to 25% for years 1 and 2, then back to 15% for years 3 through 10 causes rate of return to yield inconsistent conclusions, this forces you to a criteria like NPV:

$NPV_A = 450(P/A_{15,8})(P/F_{25,2}) + 450(P/A_{25,2}) = +\$1,940$

$NPV_B = 700(P/A_{15,8})(P/F_{25,2}) + 700(P/A_{25,2}) - 800 = +\$2,218$

$NPV_C = 1,050(P/A_{15,8})(P/F_{25,2}) + 1,050(P/F_{25,2}) - 50(P/F_{25,1}) - 1,300$

$\qquad = +\$2,347$ $\quad$ *Select "C" with the largest NPV.*

4-10 Solution: *Continued*

Changing the minimum ROR with time indicates alternative C as the economic choice. This same result is not achieved by changing the minimum ROR to 25% over the entire evaluation life. The minimum ROR is a very significant evaluation parameter and must represent other opportunities for investing capital both now and in the future over the evaluation life of projects. If the minimum ROR is projected to change with time, that change must be built into evaluation calculations as illustrated to achieve valid economic analysis results.

4-11 Solution: *Values in Millions of Dollars*

Alternative A:

```
   C=$32        I=$12        I=$12 .................... I=$12
 ──────────────────────────────────────────────────────────
      0            1            2 ....................... 5
```

Alternative B:

```
   C=$38        I=$13.5      I=$13.5 ................. I=$13.5
 ──────────────────────────────────────────────────────────
      0            1            2 ....................... 5
```

Incremental Analysis B-A:

```
   C=$6         I=$1.5       I=$1.5 ................... I=$1.5
 ──────────────────────────────────────────────────────────
      0            1            2 ....................... 5
```

ROR_A: $0 = -32 + 12(P/A_{i,5})$; $32/12 = (P/A_{i,5}) = 2.667$

$i = 25\% + 5\%[(2.689-2.667)/(2.689-2.436)] = 25.43\% > i^* = 15\%$, *so ok.*

ROR_B: $0 = -38 + 13.5(P/A_{i,5})$; $38/13.5 = (P/A_{i,5}) = 2.815$

$i = 20\% + 5\%[(2.991-2.815)/(2.991-2.689)] = 22.91\% > i^* = 15\%$, *so ok.*

ROR_{B-A}: $0 = -6 + 1.5(P/A_{i,5})$; $6/1.5 = (P/A_{i,5}) = 4.000$

$i = 7\% + 1\%[(4.100-4.000)/(4.000-3.993)] = 7.93\% < i^* = 15\%$ *Reject B, Select A*

$$3.352$$
$NPV_A = -32 + 12(P/A_{15,5}) = +\$8.22$ *Select A with largest NPV.*

$NPV_B = -38 + 13.5(P/A_{15,5}) = +\$7.25$

$NPV_{B-A} = -6 + 1.5(P/A_{15,5}) = -\$0.97 < 0$ *Reject B, Select A.*

4-12 Solution: *All Values in Thousands*

Project A:

```
  C=$240       I=$50 ................................. I=$50
  ─────────────────────────────────────────────────────────        L=$240
    0            1 ................................. 5
```

Using Text Equation 3-2, Annual Worth Equation:

$(240 - 240)(A/P_{i,5}) + 240(i) = \$50$

$i = ROR_A = 50/240 = 21\% > i^* = 10\%,$ *satisfactory*

Project B:

```
  C=$240       I=$98.5 ............................. I=$98.5
  ─────────────────────────────────────────────────────────        L=0
    0            1 ................................. 5
```

Present Worth Equation: $240 = 98.5(P/A_{i,5})$

By trial and error, $i = ROR_B = 30\% > i^* = 10\%,$ *satisfactory*

Incremental Analysis A-B creates cost followed by revenue:

```
  C=0         I=-$48.5 ........................... I=-$48.5
  ─────────────────────────────────────────────────────────        L=+$240
    0            1 ................................. 5
```

Annual Worth Equation: $48.5 = 240(A/F_{i,5})$

$i = ROR = -0.5\% < i^* = 10\%$ *Reject A, and Select B.*

$NPV_A = 50(P/A_{10,5}) + 240(P/F_{10,5}) - 240 = +\$98.57$

$NPV_B = 98.5(P/A_{10,5}) - 240 = +\$133.41$ *Select B.*

4-13 Solution:

$$NPV_A = \overset{3.326}{90,000(P/A_{20,6})} - 200,000 = +\$99,340$$

$$NPV_B = \overset{2.106}{300,000(P/A_{20,3})} - 500,000 = +\$131,800$$

$$NPV_C = \overset{2.991}{120,000(P/A_{20,5})} + \overset{0.4019}{100,000(P/F_{20,5})} - 300,000 = +\$99,110$$

Maximum Cumulative NPV from $500,000 = $NPV_A + NPV_C = \$198,450$

$PVR_A = 0.497,$ *1st Choice*

$PVR_B = 0.264,$ *3rd Choice*

$PVR_C = 0.330,$ *2nd Choice*

4-13 Solution: *Continued*

Growth ROR Analysis Using a 6 Year Evaluation Life:

$$\text{A) } [90,000 \overset{9.930}{(F/A_{20,6})}] P/F_{i,6} = \$200,000$$

$$893,700(P/F_{i,6}) = \$200,000$$

$$P/F_{i,6} = 0.2238; \quad i = \text{Growth ROR} = 28.5\%, \quad \textit{1st}$$

$$\text{B) } [300,000 \overset{3.640}{(F/A_{20,3})} \overset{1.728}{(F/P_{20,3})}] P/F_{i,6} = \$500,000$$

$$1,886,976(P/F_{i,6}) = \$500,000$$

$$P/F_{i,6} = 0.2650; \quad i = \text{Growth ROR} = 24.8\% \quad \textit{3rd}$$

$$\text{C) } [120,000 \overset{7.442}{(F/A_{20,5})} + 100,000] \overset{1.200}{(F/P_{20,1})} P/F_{i,6} = \$300,000$$

$$1,191,648(P/F_{i,6}) = 300,000$$

$$P/F_{i,6} = 0.25175; \quad i = \text{Growth ROR} = 25.9\%, \quad \textit{2nd}$$

4-14 Solution: *All Values in Thousands*

Alternative A:

```
  C=$20        I=$12 ................................... I=$12
                                                              L=$20
  ─────────────────────────────────────────────────────
   0            1 ................................... 12
```

Alternative B:

```
  C=$28        I=$14 ................................... I=$14
                                                              L=$28
  ─────────────────────────────────────────────────────
   0            1 ................................... 12
```

ROR Analysis:

"A" PW Eq: $0 = -20 + 12(P/A_{i,12}) + 20(P/F_{i,12}), \quad i = ROR_A = 60\% > i^* = 15\%$

"B" PW Eq: $0 = -28 + 14(P/A_{i,12}) + 28(P/F_{i,12}), \quad i = ROR_B = 50\% > i^* = 15\%$

Incremental Analysis B-A:

```
  C=$8          I=$2 ................................... I=$2
                                                              L=$8
  ─────────────────────────────────────────────────────
   0            1 ................................... 12
```

"B-A" PW Eq: $0 = -8 + 2(P/A_{i,12}) + 8(P/F_{i,12})$

$$i = ROR_{B-A} = 25\% > i^* = 15\%, \quad \textit{Satisfactory, select alternative B.}$$

4-14 Solution: *Continued*

NPV Analysis:

$$NPV_A = -20 + 12\overset{6.194}{(P/A_{15,12})} + 20\overset{0.2567}{(P/F_{15,12})} = +\$48.79 > 0, \text{ } Acceptable.$$

$$NPV_B = -28 + 14(P/A_{15,12}) + 28(P/F_{15,12}) = +\$53.13 > 0, \text{ } Select \text{ } B.$$

Note, the incremental NPV_{B-A} is positive: 53.13-48.79 = \$4.34, indicating that alternative B is the best alternative.

PVR Analysis:

$PVR_A = 48.79/20 = 2.44 > 0,$ *Satisfactory.*

$PVR_B = 53.13/28 = 1.90 > 0,$ *Satisfactory.*

$PVR_{B-A} = (53.13-48.79)/(28-20) = 0.54 > 0,$ *Satisfactory, select B.*

Change the minimum ROR to 30% from 15%:

$$NPV_A = -20 + 12\overset{3.190}{(P/A_{30,12})} + 20\overset{0.0429}{(P/F_{30,12})} = +\$19.1 > 0, \text{ } Select \text{ } A.$$

$$NPV_B = -28 + 14(P/A_{30,12}) + 28(P/F_{30,12}) = +\$17.8 > 0$$

Note incremental NPV_{B-A} is negative: 17.8-19.1 = -1.3, indicating that alternative A is the best selection. ROR and PVR give the same conclusion.

4-15 Solution: All Values in Thousands

$$NPV_A = 150\overset{2.991}{(P/A_{20,5})} + 50\overset{0.4019}{(P/F_{20,5})} - 160 = +\$308.75$$

$$NPV_B = 275\overset{2.589}{(P/A_{20,4})} + 70\overset{0.4823}{(P/F_{20,4})} - 320 = +\$425.74$$

$$NPV_C = 500\overset{2.106}{(P/A_{20,3})} + 100\overset{0.5787}{(P/F_{20,3})} - 480 = +\$630.87$$

If A, B, and C are mutually exclusive, select C with the largest NPV. If A, B, and C are non-mutually exclusive and the budget is \$480,000, select A+B to maximize cumulative NPV. Note this does not involve selecting C, even though it has the largest NPV.

$$PVR_A = \frac{308}{160} = 1.93; \quad PVR_B = \frac{425}{320} = 1.33; \quad PVR_C = \frac{630}{480} = 1.31$$

If A, B, and C are mutually exclusive, incremental PVR analysis must be made. The project with the largest PVR is not necessarily the choice.

4-15 Solution: *Continued*

$$PVR_{B-A} = \frac{425 - 308}{320 - 160} = +0.73 \succ 0 \quad Satisfactory, \; select \; B \; over \; A.$$

$$PVR_{C-B} = \frac{630 - 425}{480 - 320} = +1.28 \succ 0 \quad Satisfactory, \; select \; C \; over \; B.$$

C is selected even though it has the smallest PVR on total investment if the alternatives are mutually exclusive.

If the alternatives are non-mutually exclusive, select the projects in order of decreasing PVR: "A" first, "B" second, "C" third. Growth ROR analysis of A, B, and C would rank the projects the same as PVR. To make ROR analysis of mutually exclusive alternatives A, B, and C, incremental ROR analysis must be made:

Alternative A:

```
 C=$160      I=$150 ......................... I=$150     I=$150
                                                                L=$50
 _____

   0             1 ........................... 4          5
```

PW Eq: $0 = -160 + 150(P/A_{i,5}) + 50(P/F_{i,5}), \; i = ROR_A = 91\% > i^* = 20\%$

Alternative B:

```
 C=$320      I=$275 ....................... I=$275
                                                   L=$70
 _____

   0             1 ........................... 4
```

PW Eq: $0 = -320 + 275(P/A_{i,4}) + 70(P/F_{i,4}), \; i = ROR_B = 79\% > i^* = 20\%$

Incremental Analysis B-A:

```
 C=$160      I=$125 ...................... I=$125+$70    C=$200
 _____

   0             1 ........................... 4          5
```

$$0.4019$$

PW Cost Modified ROR: $160 + 200(P/F_{20,5}) = 125(P/A_{i,4}) + 70(P/F_{i,4})$

$i =$ PW Modified Incremental ROR $= 42.4\% > i^* = 20\%$, *Select B.*

Incremental C-B analysis would also give an acceptable C-B ROR indicating accept C, which is the mutually exclusive alternative choice consistent with NPV and PVR analysis.

4-16 Solution, i* = 20.0%, Budget = $500 at time zero:

Yr	0	1	2	3	4	5
A)	-200	60	100	-200	300	300
B)	-300	-90	100	200	300	400
C)	-300	250	250	250	250	-600
D)	-300	100	150	-350	400	400

$$NPV_A = -200 + 60(P/F_{20,1}) + 100(P/F_{20,2}) - 200(P/F_{20,3})$$
$$+ 300(P/A_{20,2})(P/F_{20,3}) = +68.9$$

$$NPV_B = -300 - 90(P/F_{20,1}) + 100 + 100(A/G_{20,4})(P/A_{20,4})(P/F_{20,1})$$
$$= +115.6$$

$$NPV_C = -300 + 250(P/A_{20,4}) - 600(P/F_{20,1}) = +106.1$$

$$NPV_D = -300 + 100(P/F_{20,1}) + 150(P/F_{20,2}) - 350(P/F_{20,3})$$
$$+ 400(P/A_{20,2})(P/F_{20,3}) = +38.6$$

$$PVR_A = 68.9 / 200 = 0.3445$$
$$PVR_B = 115.6 / \{300 + 90(P/F_{20,1})\} = 115.6 / 375 = 0.3083$$
$$PVR_C = 106.1 / 300 = 0.3537$$
$$PVR_D = 38.6 / \{[(350(P/F_{20,1})-150)(P/F_{20,1})-100](P/F_{20,1}) + 300\}$$
$$= 38.6 / 315 = 0.1225$$

Ranking Order: C, A, B, D
For a $500 Time Zero Budget, Select Alternatives C & A.

Alt. D Cumulative NPV Diagram @ i* = 20%

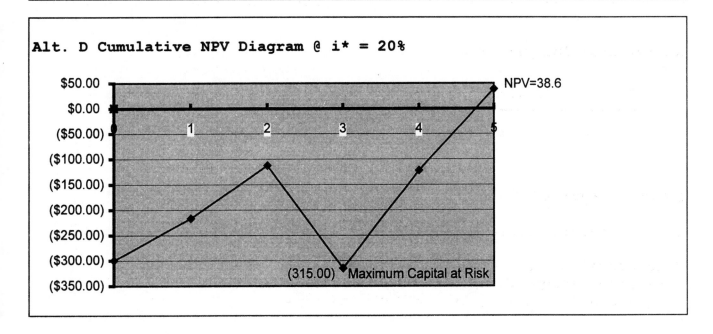

4-17 Solution: *Values in Thousands*

Existing Haul Road Alternative A:

Production	2,000 tons	2,000 tons
Profit	$20/ton	$20/ton
Revenue	$40,000	$40,000

      0   1 7

$ROR_A = \infty$, *so ok*

                4.1604

NPV_A @ **15%** $= 40,000(P/A_{15\%,7}) = \$166,416 > 0$, *so ok*

Improved Haul Road Alternative B:

Production	2,500 tons ...	2,500 tons	1,500 tons	–
Profit	$20/ton	$20/ton	$20/ton	–
Revenue	$50,000	$50,000	$30,000	–
Cost C=$6,000	–		–	–

      0   1 5   6   7

ROR_B **PW Eq:** $0 = -6,000 + 50,000(P/A_{i,5}) + 30,000(P/F_{i,6})$

ROR_B, $i = 833\% > i^* = 15\%$, *so ok*

NPV_B @ **15%** $= \$174,578 > 0$, *so ok*

Incremental Analysis A-B:

C=$6,000   I=$10,000   I=$10,000   C=$10,000   C=$40,000

      0   1 5   6   7

PW Eq: $0 = -6,000 + 10,000(P/A_{i,5}) - 10,000(P/F_{i,6}) - 40,000(P/F_{i,7})$

Dual "i" values are 3.83% and 163.3%. Neither of these results are valid for evaluation purposes because of the combination rate of return and rate of reinvestment meaning included in each. They do however establish the range over which our incremental net present value will be positive.

Use Modified PW Cost Eq:

                 0.4323   0.3759

$0 = -6,000 - 10,000(P/F_{15,6}) - 40,000(P/F_{15,7}) + 10,000(P/A_{i,5})$

$0 = -25,359 + 10,000(P/A_{i,5})$

@15%, NPV =   8,161 > 0, *Accept "B"*
@25%, NPV =   1,534
@30%, NPV = -1,003

$ROR = 25\% + 5\%[(1,534-0)/(1,534+1,003)] = 28.0\% > 15.0\%$, *Accept "B"*

4-18 Solution: Values in Thousands of Units or Dollars

Alternative A, Existing Haul Road:

Year	0	1-5	6	7
Production (Tons)		2,000	2,000	2,000
Production (oz)		153	153	153
Revenue ($350/oz gold)x(oz)		53,550	53,550	53,550
-Oper. Costs ($190/oz)x(oz)		29,070	29,070	29,070
Net Revenue		24,480	24,480	24,480
-Capital Costs	-	-	-	-
Cash Flow	0	24,480	24,480	24,480

PW Eq: $0 = 24,480(P/A_{i},7)$; ROR is infinite (no costs).

$$\text{NPV} = 24,480 \underset{4.1604}{(P/A_{15},7)} = \$101,847.$$

Alternative B, Improved Haul Road:

Year	0	1-5	6	7
Production (Tons)		2,500	1,500	0
Production (oz)		191.25	114.75	0
Revenue		66,937	40,162	0
-Operating Costs		-36,337	-21,802	0
Net Revenue		30,600	18,360	0
-Capital Costs	-6,000	-	-	-
Cash Flow	-6,000	30,600	18,360	0

PW Eq: $0 = -6,000 + 30,600(P/A_{i},5) + 18,360(P/F_{i},6)$; ROR = 510%

$$\text{NPV} = -6,000 + 30,600 \underset{3.3522}{(P/A_{15},5)} + 18,360 \underset{0.4323}{(P/F_{15},6)} = \$104,514 \text{ Accept}$$

Incremental Analysis B-A:

Year	0	1-5	6	7
Proposed Cash Flow	-6,000	30,600	18,360	0
-Existing Cash Flow	0	24,480	24,480	24,480
Incremental Cash Flow	-6,000	6,120	-6,120	-24,480

Incremental ROR leads to dual rates, unless cash flows are modified:

Mod. Yr 0 Cost: $-6,000 - 6,120 \underset{0.4323}{(P/F_{15},6)} - 24,480 \underset{0.3759}{(P/F_{15},7)} = -\$17,848$

Mod. PW Eq. $= -17,848 + 6,120(P/A_{i},5)$

ROR = 21.15% > i* = 15%, *Accept B, The Haul Road Improvement*

4-19 Solution: All Values in 000's

A)
```
-250      115.32      115.32 ............... 115.32
_____  L=0
0          1           2                      6
```

B)
```
-250        -           - ..................   -
_____  L=1,206.7
0          1           2                      6
```

B-A)
```
 -        -115.32     -115.32 ............... -115.32
_____  L=1,206.7
0          1           2                      6
```

Rate of Return Analysis:

PW Eq$_A$: $0 = -250 + 115.32(P/F_{i,6})$ $i = 30\% > i^* = 15\%$, acceptable
PW Eq$_B$: $0 = -250 + 1,206.7(P/A_{i,6})$ $i = 40\% > i^* = 15\%$, acceptable

PW Eq$_{B-A}$: $0 = -115.32(P/A_{i,6}) + 1,206.7(P/F_{i,6})$

$i = 22.1\% > i^* = 15\%$, Select "B"

Net Present Value Analysis:

$$NPV_A = -250 + 115.32\overset{3.7845}{(P/A_{15,6})} = 186.4$$

$$NPV_B = -250 + 1,206.7\overset{0.4323}{(P/A_{15,6})} = 271.7 \quad \text{Select "B", Largest NPV}$$

PVR Analysis:

PVR$_A$ = 186.4/250 = 0.746
PVR$_B$ = 271.7/250 = 1.087

$$PVR_{B-A} = (271.7-186.4)/115.32\overset{3.3522}{(P/A_{15,5})}$$
$$= 0.22 > 0, \text{ Select "B"}$$

Growth Rate of Return Analysis, Case A:

Reinvest
"A" +CF's
```
 -        -115.32     -115.32 ................ -115.32
_____  F=1,009.5
0          1           2 ......................... 6
```

$$\text{Where } F = 115.32\overset{8.7537}{(F/A_{15,6})} = 1,009.5$$

A+Reinvest
```
-250        -           -                      -
_____  F=1,009.5
0          1           2 ......................... 6
```

Growth ROR$_A$: $0 = -250 + 1,009.5(P/F_{i,6})$ $i = 26.2\%$

Growth ROR$_B$ is 30% on identical investment, so select B.

FW Profit$_A$ = 1,009.5, FW Profit$_B$ = 1,206.7 Largest FW Profit is B.

4-20 Solution, All Values in (000's):

Net CF's	-1,470	1,705	897	103	-617	-559	-294
Year	0	1	2	3	4	5	6

Dual "i" values exist for this cost-income-cost situation as follows:

NPV EQ: $-1,470 + 1,705(P/F_{i,1}) + 897(P/F_{i,2}) + 103(P/F_{i,3})$

$- 617(P/F_{12,4}) - 559(P/F_{12,5}) - 294(P/F_{12,6})$

Solving this equation yields dual "i" values of 14.83% and 27.78%. Even though both solutions exceed the minimum rate of return of 12.0%, neither "i" value is valid for economic evaluation purposes because both contain a combination of rate of return and rate of reinvestment meaning. An investor must modify the cost-income-cost cash flow stream to eliminate cost following revenue and obtain cost (negative cash flow) generating revenue (positive cash flow) in order to get valid rate of return meaning in the results.

Present Worth Cost Modification:

$$\begin{array}{ccc} 0.6355 & 0.5674 & 0.5066 \end{array}$$

PW Mod. Cost $= -1,470 - 617(P/F_{12,4}) - 559(P/F_{12,5}) - 294(P/F_{12,6})$

$= -2,328$

Mod. PW EQ: $0 = -2,328 + 1,705(P/F_{i,1}) + 897(P/F_{i,2}) + 103(P/F_{i,3})$

Modified ROR, i = 11.4% < i* = 12.0% so reject the investment.

Although not asked for, note that the NPV for this project at 12.0% is -17.5 indicating not enough present worth positive cash flow exists to cover all of the years of present worth negative cash flow. This is a slightly unsatisfactory situation leading to rejecting the project.

4-21 Solution, All Values in (000's):

Present Worth Cost Analysis

100,000 Mcf of lost gas at $2.00 per Mcf = $200,000 per year cost.

(1) Present

$$\underline{\quad - \qquad -200,000 \quad -200,000 \quad \ldots \ldots \quad -200,000\quad}$$
$$0 \qquad 1 \qquad\quad 2 \quad \ldots \ldots \ldots \quad 10$$

$$\overset{5.0188}{}$$

PW Cost at 15%: $-200,000(P/A_{15,10}) = -1,003,760$

(2) Replace

$$\underline{\quad -1,000,000 \qquad - \qquad\qquad - \quad \ldots \ldots \ldots \quad -\quad}$$
$$0 \qquad 1 \qquad\quad 2 \quad \ldots \ldots \ldots \quad 10$$

PW Cost at 15% = -1,000,000

(3) Repair

$$\underline{\quad -400,000 \quad -50,000 \quad -62,000 \quad \ldots \quad \text{gradient series}\quad}$$
$$0 \qquad 1 \qquad\quad 2 \quad \ldots \ldots \ldots \quad 10$$

$$\overset{3.3832 \qquad\quad 5.0188}{}$$

PW Cost at 15% $= -400,000 - [-50,000 - 12,000(A/G_{15,10})](P/A_{15,10})$

$\qquad\qquad = -400,000 - 90,598.4(5.0188)$

$\qquad\qquad = -854,695$ Select Repair to Minimize PW Cost.

Incremental Net Present Value Analysis:

(2-1)

$$\underline{\quad -1,000,000 \quad 200,000 \qquad 200,000 \quad \ldots \ldots \quad 200,000\quad}$$
$$0 \qquad 1 \qquad\quad 2 \quad \ldots \ldots \ldots \quad 10$$

$$\overset{5.0188}{}$$

NPV @ 15% $-1,000,000 + 200,000(P/A_{15,10}) = -3,760$ Reject Replace

(3-1)

$$\underline{\quad -400,000 \quad 150,000 \qquad 138,000 \quad \ldots \ldots \quad 32,000\quad}$$
$$0 \qquad 1 \qquad\quad 2 \quad \ldots \ldots \ldots \quad 10$$

$$\overset{3.3832 \qquad\quad 5.0188}{}$$

NPV @ 15% $-400,000 + [150,000 - 12,000(A/G_{15,10})](P/A_{15,10})$

$\qquad\qquad = +149,065$ Select repair to maximize incremental NPV

CHAPTER 5 PROBLEM SOLUTIONS

5-1 Solution:

Today's Dollar Diagram:

```
                              R=600
  C=100          C=200        OC=100
  ───────────────────────────────────
  0              1            2
```

(A) Escalated Dollar Diagram:

```
                                              1.210
                                     R=600(F/P_{10%,2})=726.0
                                              1.1236
  C=100          C=200(F/P6%,1)=212.0  OC=100(F/P_{6%,2})=112.36
  ─────────────────────────────────────────────────────────────
  0              1                    2
```

Escalated $ NPV

$$
\begin{array}{cc}
0.8696 & 0.7561
\end{array}
$$

$= -100 - 212(P/F_{15,1}) + (726-112.36)(P/F_{15,2}) = +\$179.6$

(B) Constant Dollar Diagram:

```
                      0.9524                   0.9070
  C=100      C=212(P/F5%,1)=201.9    I=613.64(P/F_{5%,2})=556.57
  ───────────────────────────────────────────────────────────────
  0              1                    2
```

Using Text Eq 5-1: $i^{*\prime} = (1.15)/(1.05) - 1 = .0952$ **or 9.52%**

Constant Dollar NPV

$$
\begin{array}{cc}
0.91304 & 0.83365
\end{array}
$$

$= -100 - 201.9(P/F_{9.52,1}) + (556.75)(P/F_{9.52,2}) = +\$179.6$

(C) Today's Dollars Equal Escalated Dollars

This assumes an escalation rate of 0% on costs and revenues each year or that a washout of operating cost and revenue escalation occurs in the revenue producing years.

$$
\begin{array}{cc}
0.8696 & 0.7561
\end{array}
$$

NPV @ 15% $= -100 - 200(P/F_{15,1}) + 500(P/F_{15,2}) = +\$104.1$

(D) Today's Dollars Equal Constant Dollars

This assumes both revenues and costs escalate at the rate of inflation This is a constant dollar analysis so the 9.52% constant dollar equivalent discount rate calculated in "B" must be used.

$$
\begin{array}{cc}
0.91304 & 0.83365
\end{array}
$$

NPV @ 9.52% $= -100 - 200(P/F_{9.52,1}) + 500(P/F_{9.52,2}) = +\$134.2$

5-2 Solution: *All Values in Trillions*

Escalated (Current or Nominal) Dollars:

$4.54 $4.90

| 1987 | 1988 |

Current (nominal) dollar % gain = $[(4.90-4.54)/4.54](100) = 7.95\%$

Constant (Real) Dollars With 4% Inflation:

$4.54 4.90(P/F_{4,1}) = \$4.71$

| 1987 | 1988 |

Constant (real) dollar % gain: $[(4.71-4.54)/4.54](100) = 3.79\%$

5-3 Solution: *Values in Thousands*

A) Escalated Dollar Analysis

$$I=200(F/P_{10,2})=\$242.0$$

$C_0=\$50 \qquad C_1=150(F/P_{15,1})=\$172.5 \qquad OC=100(F/P_{15,2})=\$132.2$

Net=$109.8

| 0 | 1 | 2 |

$I=200(F/P_{10,3})=\$266.2 \quad I=200(F/P_{10,4})=\$292.8 \quad I=200(F/P_{10,5})=\$322.2$
$OC=100(F/P_{15,3})=\$152.1 \quad OC=100(F/P_{15,4})=\$174.9 \quad OC=100(F/P_{15,5})=\$201.1$

Net=$114.1   Net=$117.9   Net=$121.1

| 3 | 4 | 5 |

PW Eq: $0 = -50 - 172.5(P/F_{i,1}) + 109.8(P/F_{i,2}) + 114.1(P/F_{i,3})$
$+ 117.9(P/F_{i,4}) + 121.1(P/F_{i,5})$

ROR $= i = 32.29\%$ *using a financial calculator*

5-3 Solution: *Continued*

B) *Constant Dollar Analysis of Case A*

Net Escalated Dollar Time Diagram From Case A:

C_0=\$50 C_1=\$172.5 Net_2=\$109.8 Net_3=\$114.1 Net_4=\$117.9 Net_5=\$121.1

| 0 | 1 | 2 | 3 | 4 | 5 |

Constant Dollar Equivalent Time Diagram for Inflation of 10% per Year:

                156.82   90.74   85.72
C_0=50 C_1=172.5$(P/F_{10,1})$ 109.8$(P/F_{10,2})$ 114.1$(P/F_{10,3})$ . . . .

| 0 | 1 | 2 | 3 . . . . |

PW Eq: $0 = -50 - 156.82(P/F_{i',1}) + 90.74(P/F_{i',2}) + 85.72(P/F_{i',3})$

$+ 80.53(P/F_{i',4}) + 75.19(P/F_{i',5})$

Constant Dollar ROR = i' = 20.26%

An alternate solution would be to utilize Equation 5-1 as follows:
$1+i = (1+f)(1+i')$ *and* $i = 32.29\%$ *from Case A and* $f = 10\%$ *as given, so
the constant dollar ROR =* i' = (1.3229)/(1.10) − 1 = 0.2026 *or* 20.26%.

C) *Escalated Dollar Analysis Using the Washout Assumption*

*The "washout" assumption assumes that the dollar (not percent)
escalation of operating costs is offset by the same dollar escalation
of revenue, therefore, profit margins remain constant at what they
would be today.*

C_0=\$50 C_1=\$172.5 Net_2=\$100.0 Net_3=\$100.0 Net_4=\$100.0 Net_5=\$100.0

| 0 | 1 | 2 | 3 | 4 | 5 |

PW Eq: $0 = -50 - 172.5(P/F_{i,1}) + 100(P/A_{i,4})(P/F_{i,1})$

Escalated Dollar ROR = i = 25.25%

5-4 Solution:

Escalated and Constant Dollar Selling Price

Price = $100/Unit   Escalated $ Price = ?

    Year 0   1   2   3
Escalation Rates |-- 6.0% ---|-- 8.0% ---|-- 10.0% --|

Yr 3 Escalated Dollar Price = $100 $(F/P_{6,1})(F/P_{8,1})(F/P_{10,1})$ = $125.93

                                        Constant $ Price = ?

    Year 0   1   2   3
 Inflation Rates |-- 5.0% ---|-- 9.0% ---|-- 12.0% --|

Yr 3 Constant $ Price = ($125.93)$(P/F_{12,1})(P/F_{9,1})(P/F_{5,1})$ = $98.24

5-5 Solution:

C=$100,000   Escalated $ Sale Price = X

0   1   2
                                    Constant $ Sale Price = X$(P/F_{10,2})$

Constant $ PW Eq:

$100,000 = X$(P/F_{10,2})(P/F_{25,2})$

    X = $100,000 / [(0.82645)(0.6400)]

    X = $189,062

$1+i = (1+f)(1+i')$ where f = 0.10 and i' = 0.25 or 25%

Escalated $ Growth Rate = $i = (1+f)(1+i') - 1$

                    $i = (1.10)(1.25) - 1 = 0.375$ or 37.5%

To prove the equivalence of the 37.5% escalated dollar Growth Rate:

Escalated $ PW Eq:

$100,000 = $189,062$(P/F_{37.5,2})$ so proof is complete

5-6 Solution:

	Year 1	Year 2
Escalated $ Sales	$1,000X(F/P_{10,1})=1,100X$	$1,000X(F/P_{10,2})=1,210X$
Escalated $ OC	$50,000(F/P_{15,1})=57,500$	$50,000(F/P_{15,2})=66,130$
Escalated Profit	$1,100X - 57,500$	$1,210X - 66,130$
Const. $ Profit	$(1,100X-57,500)(P/F_{12,1})$	$(1,210X-66,130)(P/F_{12,2})$

Constant Dollar PW Eq: Constant $ minimum ROR = $i^{*'}$ = 15%

$$100,000 = (1,100X - 57,500)\overset{0.8929}{(P/F_{12,1})}\overset{0.8696}{(P/F_{15,1})}$$

$$+ (1,210X - 66,130)\overset{0.7972}{(P/F_{12,2})}\overset{0.7561}{(P/F_{15,2})}$$

X = $116.55 per unit in today's dollar value

Escalated Dollar PW Eq:

$1+i^* = (1+f)(1+i^{*'})$, where f = 12.0%, $i^{*'}$ = 15.0%,

i^* = 28.8%

$$100,000 = (1,100X - 57,500)(P/F_{28.8,1}) + (1,210X - 66,130)(P/F_{28.8,2})$$

X = $116.55/unit in today's dollar value.

Escalated $ year 1 sales price = $116.55(F/P_{10,1})$ = $128.21/unit

Escalated $ year 2 sales price = $116.55(F/P_{10,2})$ = $141.03/unit

5-7 Solution: *Values in Thousands*

Today's Dollar Time Diagram

			Rev=$150	Rev=$150	Rev=$150
C_{Acq}=?	–	C=$200	OC=$50	OC=$50	OC=$50
0	1	2	3	4	5

Case 1 (Today's Dollars Equal Escalated Dollar Values):

C_{acq} = NPV_{time0}

$$= 100\overset{2.283}{(P/A_{15\%,3})}\overset{0.7561}{(P/F_{15\%,2})}-200\overset{0.7561}{(P/F_{15\%,2})} = +\$21.4$$

5-7 Solution: *Continued*

Case 2: For constant dollar NPV analysis a constant dollar minimum rate of return obtained from equation 5-1 must be used:

Eq. 5-1: $1+i = (1+f)(1+i')$ or rearranged, $i' = [(1+i)/(1+f)] - 1$

Constant $ Minimum ROR i*' $= [(1.15)/(1.07)] - 1 = 0.07477$ or 7.477%

$C_{Acq} = NPV_{time0} = 100(P/A_{7.47\%,3})(P/F_{7.47\%,2}) - 200(P/F_{7.47\%,2}) = +\$52.1$

The Case 2 solution assumes that the escalation rate for costs and revenues equals the rate of inflation, as illustrated below:

Escalated Dollar Time Diagram:

```
                                                    1.2250
                          1.1449            Rev=150(F/P7,3)=$183.76
C_acq=?          -      C=200(F/P7,2)=$228.98   OC= 50(F/P7,3)=$ 61.25
                                                   Net=$122.51
────────────────────────────────────────────────────────────────────
0               1                 2                          3

        1.3108                          1.4025
  Rev=150(F/P7,4)=$196.62        Rev=150(F/P7,5)=$210.38
  OC= 50(F/P7,4)=$ 65.54         OC= 50(F/P7,5)=$ 70.12
          Net=$131.08                    Net=$140.26

            4                               5
```

$$\text{Escalated \$ NPV} = -228.98(P/F_{15,2}) + 122.51(P/F_{15,3}) + 131.08(P/F_{15,4})$$
(with factors 0.7561, 0.6575, 0.5718)

$$+140.26(P/F_{15,5}) = +\$52.1$$
(with factor 0.4972)

Constant Dollar Time Diagram:

```
                                                    0.81630
                          0.87344           Rev=183.76(P/F7,3)=$150
C_acq=?          -      C=228.98(P/F7,2)=$200   OC= 61.25(P/F7,3)=$50
                                                   Net=$100
────────────────────────────────────────────────────────────────────
0               1                 2                          3

          0.76289                        0.7129
  Rev=210.38(P/F7,5)=$150        Rev=196.62(P/F7,4)=$150
  OC= 65.54(P/F7,4)=$ 50         OC= 70.12(P/F7,5)=$ 50
          Net=$100                       Net=$100

            4                               5
```

5-7 Solution: *Case 2 Continued*

From Text Eq 5-1, $1+i = (1+f)(1+i')$

Constant $ Minimum ROR Equivalent to 15% Escalated $ Minimum ROR

$= i^{*'} = [(1+i^*)/(1+f)]-1 = [(1+0.15)/(1+0.07)]-1 = 0.07477$ *or* 7.477%

$$\text{Constant \$ NPV} = -200\underset{0.86570}{(P/F_{7.477},2)} + 100\underset{0.80548}{(P/F_{7.477},3)} + 100\underset{0.74944}{(P/F_{7.477},4)}$$

$$+ 100\underset{0.69730}{(P/F_{7.477},5)} = +\$52.1$$

Case 3) Escalated Dollar Diagram

```
                        1.254                  1.331
                     200(F/P12,2)        (150-50)(F/P10,3)
   CAcq      -         C=$250.8             Net R=$133.1
  _____
    0         1            2                    3
```

```
              1.464                1.611
         (150-50)(F/P10,4)    (150-50)(F/P10,5)
          Net R=$146.4          Net R=$161.1
        _____
              4                    5
```

$$C_{Acq} = \text{NPV}_{time\ 0} = 133.1\underset{0.6575}{(P/F_{15},3)} + 146.4\underset{0.5718}{(P/F_{15},4)}$$

$$+ 161.1\underset{0.4972}{(P/F_{15},5)} - 250.8\underset{0.7561}{(P/F_{15},2)}$$

$$= +\$61.69$$

Case 4) Constant Dollar Diagram:

```
          C'=$250.8X   Net R'=$133.1X   Net R'=$146.4   Net R'=$161.1X
  CAcq   -  (P/F7,2)       (P/F7,3)        (P/F7,4)         (P/F7,5)
 _____
    0    1      2             3               4                5
```

Constant Dollar NPV must be made using $i^{*'} = 7.477\%$:

$$C_{Acq} = \text{NPV}_{time0} = 133.1\overbrace{(P/F_{7},3)(P/F_{7.477},3)}^{P/F_{15,3}} + 146.4\overbrace{(P/F_{7},4)(P/F_{7.477},4)}^{P/F_{15,4}}$$

$$+ 161.1\overbrace{(P/F_{7},5)(P/F_{7.477},5)}^{P/F_{15,5}} - 250.8\overbrace{(P/F_{7},2)(P/F_{7.477},2)}^{P/F_{15,2}}$$

$$= +\$61.69, \textit{Identical to Case 3 escalated dollar results.}$$

5-7 Solution, *Case 5 - Washout Assumption (Escalated Dollars)*:

$$200(F/P_{12,2})$$

C_{Acq}	-	C=\$250.8	Net R=\$100	Net R=\$100	Net R=\$100
0	1	2	3	4	5

$$\text{2.283} \qquad \text{0.7561} \qquad\qquad \text{0.7561}$$
$$\boldsymbol{C_{Acq}} = NPV_{time0} = 100(P/A_{15,3})(P/F_{15,2}) - 250.8(P/F_{15,2}) = -\$17.0$$

5-8 Solution: *Values in Thousands of Dollars*

Break-even Sales Price Analysis

C=\$100	R=\$5X OC=\$8	R=5X(F/P_{10,1})=\$5.5X OC=8(F/P_{15,1})=\$9.2	R=5X(F/P_{10,1})(F/P_{6,1})=\$5.83X OC=8(F/P_{15,1})(F/P_{8,1})=\$9.94
0	1	2	3

Constant Dollar Present Worth Equation for i' = 12%*:

$$0 = -100 + (5X-8)(P/F_{7,1})(P/F_{12,1}) + (5.5X-9.2)(P/F_{7,2})(P/F_{12,2})$$
$$+ (5.83X-9.94)(P/F_{7,3})(P/F_{12,3})$$

To work in escalated dollars, calculate i* equivalent to i*':

$$(1+i) = (1+f)(1+i') \text{ so } i^* = \{(1.07)(1.12) - 1\} = 0.1984 \text{ or } 19.84\%$$

i* = 19.84% is equivalent to i*' = 12% for inflation of 7% per year.

Escalated \$ PW Eq for equivalent i = 19.84%*:

$$\text{0.83445} \qquad\qquad\qquad \text{0.69630}$$
$$0 = -100 + (5X-8)(P/F_{19.84,1}) + (5.5X-9.2)(P/F_{19.84,2})$$
$$\text{0.58102}$$
$$+ (5.83X-9.94)(P/F_{19.84,3})$$

Both the constant dollar or escalated dollar present worth equation simplify as follows:

$$0 = -100 + 11.389X - 18.8569; \qquad 118.8569 = 11.389X$$

Escalated Dollar Selling Price X = \$10.44 per unit in year 1.

$$X = \$10.44 \text{ per unit in year 1.}$$
$$X(1.1) = \$11.48 \text{ per unit in year 2}$$
$$X(1.1)(1.06) = \$12.17 \text{ per unit in year 3.}$$

5-9 Solution: *All Values in Thousands*

Reclamation Cost, Escrow Fund Analysis:

Let X equal the annual reclamation costs in years 27 through 56:

$$1,000 = X \underset{15.372}{(P/A_{5\%,30})} \underset{0.2812}{(P/F_{5\%,26})}$$

$$1,000 = X(4.3226), \quad \text{therefore,} \quad X = \$231.34$$

Since the problem statement indicated that the dollars in escrow today are to be invested in 9.0% U.S. Treasury Bonds, the future reclamation costs need to be discounted at the 9.0% rate in order to determine the dollars to be invested today.

$$231.34 \underset{10.274}{(P/A_{9\%,30})} \underset{0.1064}{(P/F_{9\%,26})} = \$252.89$$

$252,890 is the total amount of 9.0% bonds to be purchased today, to cover anticipated reclamation costs over 30 years, beginning 27 years from today.

CHAPTER 6 PROBLEM SOLUTIONS

6-1 Solution:

a) *Expected Value(EV)* = (1/38)($35)-(37/38)($1) = -$0.0526
b) EV = (2/38)($17)-(36/38)($1) = -$0.0526
c) EV = (4/38)($8)-(34/38)($1) = -$0.0526
d) EV = (18/38)($1)-(20/38)($1) = -$0.0526

6-2 Solution:

Expected Cost = 0.10(5,000)+0.30(8,000)+0.40(10,000)+0.20(14,000)
              = 500 + 2,400 + 4,000 + 2,800 = $9,700

6-3 Solution:

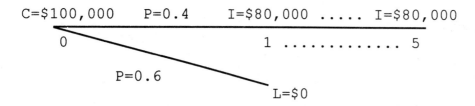

$$\text{Expected NPV} = \$80,000(P/A_{20,5})(0.4) - \$100,000 = -\$4,288, \textit{ Reject.}$$

(2.991)

Alternative Solution:

$$\text{Expected NPV} = [\$80,000(P/A_{20,5}) - \$100,000](0.4) - \$100,000(0.6)$$

$$= -\$4,288, \textit{ Reject.}$$

Expected ROR is the "i" value that makes Expected NPV = 0

Expected PW Equation: $0 = \$80,000(P/A_{i,5})(0.4) - \$100,000$

By trial and error, i = Expected ROR = 18.3% < i of 20%, Reject.*

6-4 Solution:

There are 8 possible combinations of winning and losing teams for 3 games. The bettor wins on only 1 of these outcomes.

Expected Value = (1/8)($25-$5)-(7/8)($5) = -$1.875

Over the long run, for many repeated bets of this type the bettor would lose an average of $1.875 for each $5 bet placed.

6-5 Solution: *All Values in Thousands*

Expected Cash Flow Year 1 = 0.4(25) + 0.6(18) = $20.80
Expected Cash Flow Year 2 = 0.5(30) + 0.5(20) = $25.00
Expected Cash Flow Year 3 = 0.7(35) + 0.3(25) = $32.00

ENPV = 20.80(P/F_{15,1}) + 25.00(P/F_{15,2}) + 32.00(P/F_{15,3}) - 50 = +$8.03

(0.8696)   (0.7561)   (0.6575)

6-6 Solution:

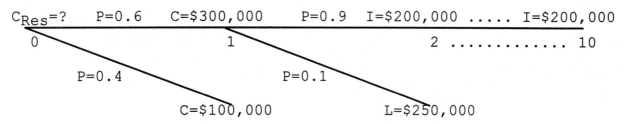

$$ENPV = \overset{3.4631}{200,000(P/A_{25,9})}(0.9)\overset{0.8000}{(P/F_{25,1})}(0.6) - 300,000\overset{0.8000}{(P/F_{25,1})}(0.6)$$

$$+ 250,000\overset{0.6400}{(P/F_{25,2})}(0.1)(0.6) - 100,000\overset{0.8000}{(P/F_{25,1})}(0.4)$$

$$= +\$132,812 = \textit{Maximum acceptable time zero research cost.}$$

Expected Value Approach:

$$\{200,000\overset{3.4631}{(P/A_{25,9})}\overset{0.8000}{(P/F_{25,1})} - 300,000\overset{0.8000}{(P/F_{25,1})}\}(0.54) = 169,612$$

$$\{250,000(P/F_{25,2}) - 300,000(P/F_{25,1})\}(0.06) \qquad = \quad -4,800$$

$$\underline{\{-100,000(P/F_{25,1})\}(0.40) \qquad\qquad\qquad\qquad = -32,000}$$

Expected Value $= 132,812$

Alternate Time Diagram: All Values in Dollars

Risk-Adjusted Net Cost and Net Income

This approach builds all risk into the cash flows before applying time value of money considerations:

$C_{Res}=?$	C=300,000(.6) C=100,000(.4) Net C=220,000	I=200,000(.6)(.9) L=250,000(.6)(.1) Net I=123,000	I=200,000(.6)(.9) ... Net I=108,000 .. Net I=108,000
0	1	2	3 10

$$ENPV = 108,000((P/A_{25,8})(P/F_{25,2})) + 123,000(P/F_{25,2}) - 220,000(P/F_{25,1})$$

$$= +\$132,812 = \textit{Maximum acceptable time zero research cost.}$$

Neglecting risk of failure gives the following risk free NPV:

The risk-free analysis is based on assuming 100% certainty that the project will be successful and follow the top branch of the time diagram (decision tree) through year 10.

$$NPV = [200,000\overset{3.463}{(P/A_{25,9})} - 300,000]\overset{0.8000}{(P/F_{25,1})} = \$314,080$$

This $314,080 is the risk free maximum time zero research cost.

6-7 Solution: *Expected Net Present Value*

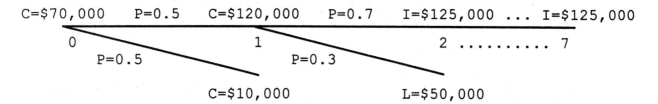

C=\$70,000   P=0.5   C=\$120,000   P=0.7   I=\$125,000 ... I=\$125,000

ENPV @ 20%

$$= [125,000(P/A_{20,6})(0.7) - 120,000](P/F_{20,1})(0.5)$$

with 3.3255 above $(P/A_{20,6})$ and 0.8333 above $(P/F_{20,1})$

$$+ 50,000(P/F_{20,2})(0.3)(0.5) - 10,000(P/F_{20,1})(0.5) - 70,000$$

with 0.6944 above $(P/F_{20,2})$ and 0.8333 above $(P/F_{20,1})$

$$= +\ 2,281 > 0, \text{ acceptable}$$

Expected Value Approach:

$$\{[125,000(P/A_{20,6}) - 120,000](P/F_{20,1}) - 70,000\}(0.35) = \ 61,739$$
$$\{[50,000(P/F_{20,1}) - 120,000](P/F_{20,1}) - 70,000\}(0.15) = -20,291$$
$$\{-10,000(P/F_{20,1}) - 70,000\}(0.50) \qquad\qquad\quad = -39,167$$

Expected Value	= +2,281

$$\textbf{EPVR} = 2,281\ /\ [70,000+(0.5)(120,000)(P/F_{20,1})+(0.5)10,000(P/F_{20,1})]$$

with 0.8333 above each $(P/F_{20,1})$

$$= 2,281\ /\ 124,164 = +0.018 > 0, \text{ acceptable}$$

Alternate Time Diagram, Risk-Adjusted Net Cost and Net Income

This approach builds all risk into the cash flows before applying time value of money considerations as follows:

	C=120,000(.5)	I=125,000(.7)(.5)	
	C=10,000(.5)	I=50,000(.3)(.5)	I=125,000(.7)(.5) . . .
C=70,000	Net C=65,000	Net I=51,250	Net I=43,750 .. Net I=43,750
0	1	2	3 7

$$\textbf{ENPV} = -70,000 - 65,000(P/F_{20,1}) + 51,250(P/F_{20,2})$$
$$+ 43,750(P/A_{20,5})(P/F_{20,2}) = +\$2,281$$

Risk Free Analysis:

The risk free analysis is based on assuming 100% certainty that the project will be successful and follow the top branch of the time diagram (decision tree) through year 7.

$$\textbf{Risk Free NPV @ 20\%} = [125,000(P/A_{20,6}) - 120,000](P/F_{20,1}) - 70,000$$

with 3.3255 above $(P/A_{20,6})$ and 0.8333 above $(P/F_{20,1})$

$$= +\$176,397$$

Risk Free Rate of Return = 50.7% *Using a financial calculator.*

6-8 Solution: *All Values in Thousands*

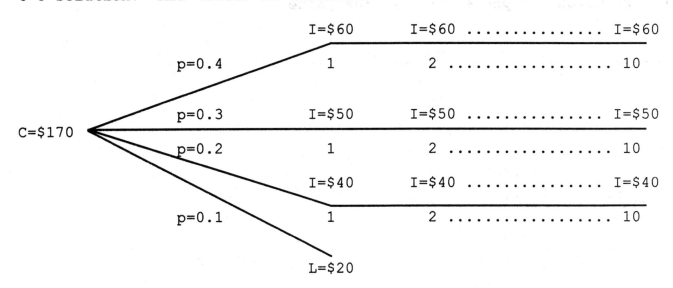

$$ENPV = 60(P/A_{20,10})(0.4) + 50(P/A_{20,10})(0.3) + 40(P/A_{20,10})(0.20)$$

$$+ 20(P/F_{20,1})(0.1) - 170$$

$$= [60(0.4) + 50(0.3) + 40(0.2)](P/A_{20,10}) + 20(P/F_{20,1})(0.1) - 170$$

$$\overset{4.192}{=} [24+15+8](P/A_{20,10}) + 20\overset{0.8333}{(P/F_{20,1})}(0.1) - 170$$

$$= \underline{+\$28.69} > 0, \textit{ So satisfactory.}$$

Expected ROR is the i value that makes the ENPV Equation = 0.
By trial and error, EROR = <u>24.9%</u> *> i* = 20%, so satisfactory.*

6-9 Solution: *All Values in Millions*

Sale value today of $1.0 = CF_{Sell} = NPV_{Sell}$. The develop analysis follows:

$$\begin{array}{ccccccc} CF=-\$1.5 & P=0.6 & \$1.0 & \$1.8 & \$1.2 & \$0.8 & \$0.4 \\ \text{Develop} & & & & & & \\ 0 & & 1 & 2 & 3 & 4 & 5 \\ & P=0.4 & & & & & \\ & & 0 & & & & \end{array}$$

$$ENPV_{Develop} = -1.5 + [1.0\overset{0.8333}{(P/F_{20,1})} + 1.8\overset{0.6944}{(P/F_{20,2})} + 1.2\overset{0.5787}{(P/F_{20,3})}$$

$$+ (0.8)\overset{0.4823}{(P/F_{20,4})} + (0.4)\overset{0.4019}{(P/F_{20,5})}](0.6)$$

$$= +\$0.49 < NPV_{Sell} = +\$1.0 \quad \textit{Therefore, select sell.}$$

6-10 Solution: *All Values in Millions of Dollars*

A)

C=20 C=10	R=6	R=12	R=12	R=12		R=12

```
0      1      2      3      4 . . . . . . . . . . 10
```

B)

-	-	C=15	C=30 R= 9	R=18	R=18	R=18	R=18

```
0      1      2      3      4 ..... 10     11     12
```

Incremental Time Diagram A-B

C=10	C=14	R=27	R=33	C=6	C=6	C=18	C=18

```
0      1      2      3      4 ..... 10     11     12
```

Case A   100% Probability of Success Solutions

$$\text{NPV}_A @ 20\% = -10 - 14(P/F_{20,1}) \overset{0.8333}{} + 12(P/A_{20,9})\overset{4.031}{}(P/F_{20,1})\overset{0.8333}{} = +\$18.64$$

$$\text{NPV}_B @ 20\% = [(18(P/A_{20,9})\overset{4.031}{}-21)(P/F_{20,1})\overset{0.8333}{}-15](P/F_{20,2})\overset{0.6944}{}= +\$19.42, Select\ B$$

For mutually exclusive alternatives, select largest NPV which is alternative B. This is verified using incremental analysis.

$$\text{NPV}_A - \text{NPV}_B = 18.64 - 19.42 = -0.78,\ Reject\ A\ and\ select\ B.$$

$$\text{PVR}_A = 18.64 / [10 + 14(P/F_{20,1})] = +0.86$$

$$\text{PVR}_B = 19.42 / [15(P/F_{20,2}) + 21(P/F_{20,3})] = +0.86$$

$$\text{PVR}_{A-B} = (18.64-19.42) / [10 + 14(P/F_{20,1})] = -0.04, Reject\ A, select\ B.$$

Case B   Expected Value Analysis Solutions

$$\text{ENPV}_A @ 20\% = -10 + [-14(P/F_{20,1})\overset{0.8333}{} + 12(P/A_{20,9})\overset{4.031}{}(P/F_{20,1})\overset{0.8333}{}](0.6)= +\$7.18$$

$$\text{ENPV}_B @ 20\% = [(18(P/A_{20,9})\overset{4.031}{}-21)(P/F_{20,1})\overset{0.8333}{}(0.8)-15](P/F_{20,2})\overset{0.6944}{} = +\$13.4$$

$$\text{EPVR}_A = 7.18 / [10 + 14(P/F_{20,1})(0.6)] = +\$0.42$$

$$\text{EPVR}_B = 13.45 / [15(P/F_{20,2}) + 21(P/F_{20,3})(0.8)] = +\$0.67$$

$$\text{EPVR}_{A-B} = (7.18-13.45) / [10 + 14(P/F_{20,1})(0.6)] = -\$0.37,\ Select\ B.$$

6-11 Solution: *Values in Thousands of Dollars*

		$R=5X$	$R=5.5X=5X(F/P_{10,1})$	$R=5.83X=5X(F/P_{10,1})(F/P_{6,1})$
$C=100$	$P=0.7$	$OC=8$	$OC=9.2=8(F/P_{15,1})$	$OC=9.94=8(F/P_{15,1})(F/P_{8,1})$

```
       0              1              2                          3

            P=0.3
                   CF=$0
```

Constant Dollar PW Equation

$$0 = -100 + [(5X-8)(P/F_{7,1})(P/F_{12,1}) + (5.5X-9.2)(P/F_{7,2})(P/F_{12,2})$$
$$+ (5.83X-9.94)(P/F_{7,3})(P/F_{12,3})](0.70)$$

To work in escalated dollars, calculate i that is equivalent to i*'
of 12.0% as follows:*

$$(1+i) = (1+f)(1+i') \text{ so } i^* = 19.84\%$$

19.84% is equivalent to $i^{*'} = 12\%$ for inflation of 7% per year.

Escalated Dollar PW Equation

$$\overset{0.83445}{}\qquad\qquad\qquad\overset{0.69630}{}$$
$$0 = -100 + [(5X-8)(P/F_{19.84,1}) + (5.5X-9.2)(P/F_{19.84,2})$$
$$\overset{0.58102}{}$$
$$+ (5.83X-9.94)(P/F_{19.84,3})](0.70)$$

*For either approach, the constant dollar or escalated dollar present
worth equation simplifies to the following:*

$$0 = -100 + [11.389X - 18.8569](0.70)$$

$$113.19 = 7.9723X$$

Escalated Dollar Selling Price X = $14.20 per unit in year 1.

$X(1.1) = \$15.62$ per unit in year 2

$X(1.1)(1.06) = \$16.56$ per unit in year 3

6-12 Solution: All Values in Millions

```
                    Rev=$200              Rev=$200
       C=$400       OC=$100               OC=$100
    _____
       0              1                  5, 10 or 15 yr(s)
```

Present Worth Equation

$0 = -400 + (200-100)(P/A_{i,n})$ where n = 5, 10, or 15 years

Project Life Yrs		Cost=$400	Cost=$600	Cost=$800
5	ROR =	7.9%	-5.8%	-13.9%
10	ROR =	21.4%	10.5%	4.3%
15	ROR =	24.0%	14.5%	9.1%

CHAPTER 7 PROBLEM SOLUTIONS

7-1 Solution: *All Dollar Values in Thousands*

Modified ACRS & Straight Line Depreciation With Half-Year Convention

Period	200% DB Switching to St Line		Straight Line Depreciation	
Yr 1	(2,000)(2/7)(.5) =	285.7	2,000(1/7)(.5) =	142.9
Yr 2	(2,000-285.7)(2/7) =	489.8	2,000(1/7) =	285.7
Yr 3	(1,714.3-489.8)(2/7)=	349.9	2,000(1/7) =	285.7
Yr 4	(1,224.5-349.9)(2/7)=	249.9	2,000(1/7) =	285.7
Yr 5	(874.6-249.9)(1/3.5)=	178.5*	2,000(1/7) =	285.7
Yr 6	(624.7)(1/3.5) =	178.5	2,000(1/7) =	285.7
Yr 7	(624.7)(1/3.5) =	178.5	2,000(1/7) =	285.7
Yr 8	(624.7)(1/3.5)(.5) =	89.2	2,000(1/7)(.5) =	142.9
Total Cumulative Depreciation		$2,000.0		$2,000.0

* *Switch in the year you get equal or more depreciation with straight line than you would get by continuing with 200% double declining balance.*

Alternatively, you could also calculate the depreciation using modified ACRS rates from Table 7-3 of the text. Some round-off error does exist due to the number of decimals carried in the table.

Period	Using Table 7-3 Modified ACRS Depreciation		
Yr 1	2,000(0.1429)	=	285.8
Yr 2	2,000(0.2449)	=	489.8
Yr 3	2,000(0.1749)	=	349.8
Yr 4	2,000(0.1249)	=	249.8
Yr 5	2,000(0.0893)	=	178.6
Yr 6	2,000(0.0892)	=	178.4
Yr 7	2,000(0.0893)	=	178.6
Yr 8	2,000(0.0446)	=	89.2
Total Cumulative Depreciation		$2,000.0	

7-2 Solution: *Values in Thousands of Dollars*

Period	Modified ACRS Depreciation		
Yr 1	(100)(30/120)	=	25.0
Yr 2	(100)(30/120)	=	25.0
Yr 3	(100)(20/120)	=	16.7
Yr 4	(100)(10/120)	=	8.3
Yr 5	(100)(10/120)	=	8.3
Yr 6	(100)(10/120)	=	8.3
Yr 7	(100)(10/120)	=	8.3
Total Cumulative Depreciation		$100.0 *Within Round-off*	

7-3 Solution: *All Dollar Amounts in Thousands*

Modified ACRS & Straight Line Depreciation With Mid-Quarter Convention

Modified ACRS Depreciation

Yr	Light Trucks, Purchased, 1st Qtr		R&D Equipment Purchased, 4th Qtr	
1	(100.0)(2/5)(10.5/12)	= 35.0	(500.0)(2/5)(1.5/12)	= 25.0
2	(100.0-35.0)(2/5)	= 26.0	(500.0-25.0)(2/5)	= 190.0
3	(65.0-26.0)(2/5)	= 15.6	(475.0-190.0)(2/5)	= 114.0
4	(39.0-15.6)(1/2.125)	= 11.0*	(285.0-114.0)(2/5)	= 68.4
5	(39.0-15.6)(1/2.125)	= 11.0	(171.0-68.4)(1/1.875)	= 54.7
6	(23.5)(1/2.125)(1.5/12)	= 1.4	(102.6)(1/1.875)(10.5/12)	= 47.9
Cumulative Depreciation		$100.0		$500.0

* *Switch in the year you get equal or more depreciation with straight line than you would by continuing with 200% double declining balance.*

Straight Line Depreciation

Yr	Light Trucks, Purchased, 1st Qtr		R&D Equipment Purchased, 4th Qtr	
1	(100.0)(1/5)(10.5/12)	= 17.5	(500.0)(1/5)(1.5/12)	= 12.5
2	(100.0)(1/5)	= 20.0	(500.0)(1/5)	= 100.0
3	(100.0)(1/5)	= 20.0	(500.0)(1/5)	= 100.0
4	(100.0)(1/5)	= 20.0	(500.0)(1/5)	= 100.0
5	(100.0)(1/5)	= 20.0	(500.0)(1/5)	= 100.0
6	(100.0)(1/5)(1.5/12)	= 2.5	(500.0)(1/5)(10.5/12)	= 87.5
Cumulative Depreciation		$100.0		$500.0

7-4 Solution:

Depreciable Residential Rental Real Property

Straight Line Depreciation		
Year 1	$800,000(1/27.5)(9.5/12) =	23,030.3
Year 2-27	$800,000(1/27.5) =	29,090.9
Year 28*	$800,000(1/27.5)(8.5/12) =	20,606.1
Cumulative Depreciation		$800,000.0 *Within Round-off*

* *The ratio of 8.5:12 in year 28 occurs because in the first year we generated 9.5 out of 12 months depreciation leaving 2.5 months to be depreciated, plus half-a-year at the 27.5 year rate remaining, therefore, 2.5 months + 6 months = 8.5 months.*

7-5 Solution: Petroleum Property Evaluation - Project Cash Flows

Year	0	1
Min. Rts. Acq. Cost	500,000	
Intangible (IDC)	2,000,000	
Tangible Equipment	1,000,000	
Production (Bbls)		200,000
Selling Price ($/Bbl)		18.00
Operating Cost		200,000

Case A, Independent, i.e.
Non-Integrated Producer (< 1,000 Bbl's/day)

Case B
Integrated Producer

Year	Time 0	1	Time 0	1
Production		200,000		200,000
Gross Revenue		3,600,000		3,600,000
-Royalties (16%)		-576,000		-576,000
Net Revenue		3,024,000		3,024,000
-Operating Costs		-200,000		-200,000
-IDC	-2,000,000		-1,400,000	
-Depreciation		-142,900		-142,900
-Amortization			-60,000	-120,000
Taxable Before Depl.	-2,000,000	2,681,100	-1,460,000	2,561,100
-100% Limit		2,681,100		n/a
-Percentage Depletion		-453,600		n/a
-Cost Depletion		100,000		-100,000
-Loss Forward		-2,000,000		-1,460,000
Taxable Income	-2,000,000	227,500	-1,460,000	1,001,100
-Tax Due @ 40%	0	-91,000	0	-400,440
Net Income	-2,000,000	136,500	-1,460,000	600,660
+Depreciation		142,900		142,900
+Amortization			60,000	120,000
+Depletion Taken		453,600		100,000
+Loss Forward		2,000,000		1,460,000
-Tang. Equip.(Depr)	-1,000,000		-1,000,000	
-30% IDC (Amort)			-600,000	
-Min. Rts.(Cost Depl)	-500,000		-500,000	
Cash Flow	-3,500,000	2,733,000	-3,500,000	2,423,560

Depreciation ($1,000,000)(0.1429) = $142,900

Cost Depletion = ($500,000)(200,000 bbls / 1,000,000 bbls) = $100,000

Independent Only

Petroleum 100% Percent Depletion Limit = $2,681,100(1.0) = $2,681,100
Percentage Depletion = 0.15($3,024,000) = $453,600

7-6 Solution: Corporate Mining Cash Flows

Year	0	1
Min Rts Acq Cost	500,000	
Mine Development	2,000,000	
Mining Equipment	1,000,000	
Production (Tons Ore)		200,000
Selling Price ($/Ton)		18.00
Operating Cost		200,000

Year	Time 0	1
Production		200,000
Gross Revenue		3,600,000
-Royalties (16%)		-576,000
Net Revenue		3,024,000
-Operating Costs		-200,000
-Mine Development	-1,400,000	
-Depreciation		-142,900
-Amortization	-60,000	-120,000
Taxable Before Depl.	-1,460,000	2,561,100
-50% Limit		1,280,550
-Percentage Depletion		-453,600
-Cost Depletion		100,000
-Loss Forward		-1,460,000
Taxable Income	-1,460,000	647,500
-Tax Due @ 40%	0	-259,000
Net Income	-1,460,000	388,500
+Depreciation		142,900
+Amortization	60,000	120,000
+Depletion Taken		453,600
+Loss Forward		1,460,000
-Mining Equip (Deprec)	-1,000,000	
-30% Mine Dev (Amort)	-600,000	
-Min Rts (Cost Depl)	-500,000	
Cash Flow	-3,500,000	2,565,000

Depreciation ($1,000,000)(0.1429) = $142,900

Mining 50% Percentage Depletion Limit = 2,561,100(0.5) = $1,280,550
Percentage Depletion = (0.15)($3,024,000) = $453,600
Cost Depletion = ($500,000)(200,000 tons/1,000,000 tons) = $100,000

If no other income exists, losses (negative taxable income) must be carried forward and used against project income in later years. This loss forward deduction is a non-cash deduction similar to depreciation, depletion and amortization so it is added back to net income in determining project cash flow.

7-7 Solution: Gold Property, Corporate Investor, Values in (000's)

Development Cost	900
Min. Rights Acq. Cost	800
Mining Equipment Cost	1,000
Working Capital Cost	1,000

Assume year 5 working capital return → from inventory liquidation is $1,000. (Not given in the problem statement.)

Year	0	1	2	3	4	5	Salv
Gross Revenue		2,400	2,700	3,000	3,300	3,600	1,000
-Royalties @ 5.0%		-120	-135	-150	-165	-180	-
Net Revenue		2,280	2,565	2,850	2,135	3,420	1,000
-Operating Cots		-900	-1,000	-1,100	-1,200	-1,300	
-Depreciation		-143	-245	-175	-125	-89	
-Deprec. Write-off							-223
-Work.Cap.Write-off							-1,000
-Development	-630						
-Amortization	-27	-54	-54	-54	-54	-27	
Taxable Before Depl.	-657	1,183	1,266	1,521	1,756	2,004	-223
-50% Limit		591	633	760	878	1,002	0
-Percentage Depl.(15%)		-342	-385	-427	-469	-513	0
-Cost Depletion		160	114	23			
-Loss Forward		-657					
Taxable Income	-657	184	881	1,094	1,287	1,491	-223
-Tax @ 40%		-74	-352	-438	-515	-596	89*
Net Income	-657	110	529	656	772	895	-134
+Depreciation		143	245	175	125	89	
+Deprec. Write-off							223
+Work.Cap.Write-off							1,000
+Depletion Taken		342	385	427	469	513	
+Amortization	27	54	54	54	54	27	
+Loss Forward		657					
-Equip Cost (Deprec)	-1,000						
-Min.Rts (Cost Depl)	-800						
-30% Develop (Amort)	270						
-Work.Cap.Investment	-1,000						
Cash Flow	-3,700	1,306	1,213	1,312	1,420	1,524	1,089

$$\underbrace{\qquad\qquad}_{2,613}$$

Depreciation based on the $1,000 equipment cost
using Table 7-3 and rounding the decimal places:
Yr 1 = 1,000(0.1429) = 143,   Yr 2 = 1,000(0.2449) = 245 etc...

Amort. Time 0 and Year 5 = 270(6/60) = 27, Years 1-4 = 270(12/60) = 54

Cost Depletion calculations follow:
Yr 1   (800)(20/100)   = 160
Yr 2   (800-342)(20/80) = 114
Yr 3   (458-385)(20/60) = 23 No cost depletion in yr 4, basis = 0.

DCFROR = 27.7%

7-8 Solution: *Values in Thousands of Dollars & Gallons*

Processing Facility Project

Year	0	1	2	3
Patent Cost	2,000			
Equipment Cost	3,000			
R & D Cost	1,500			
Revenues		5,000	5,500	6,000
Operating Costs		3,000	3,300	3,600
Production (gallons)		500	500	500

Cash Flow Calculations

Year	0	1	2	3
Gross Revenue		5,000	5,500	6,000
-Royalties		-500	-550	-600
-Operating Cost		-3,000	-3,300	-3,600
-R & D Cost	-1,500			
-Depreciation*		-429	-735	-525
-Amortization**	-200	-400	-400	-400
-Loss Forward		↗-1,700	↗-1,029	↗-513
Taxable Income	-1,700 ↗	-1,029 ↗	-513 ↗	362
-Tax Due @ 40%	0	0	0	-145
Net Income	-1,700	-1,029	-513	217
+Depreciation		429	735	525
+Amortization	200	400	400	400
+Loss Forward		1,700	1,029	513
-Equipment (Deprec)	-3,000			
-Patent Costs (Amort)	-2,000			
Cash Flow	-6,500	1,500	1,650	1,655

* Depreciation calculations using Table 7-3:

    Yr 1: 3,000(0.1429) = $429
    Yr 2: 3,000(0.2449) = $735
    Yr 3: 3,000(0.1749) = $525

Because write-off was not asked for in the problem statement, it is neglected in the year 3 cash flow.

** *Amortization calculations:*

    Yr 0:   2,000(6/60) = 200
    Yrs 1-4: 2,000(12/60) = 400
    Yr 5:   2,000(6/60) = 200

7-9 Solution: Case A, Corporate Mining, Values in (000's)

Acquisition Cost	2,000
Equipment Cost	3,000
Development Cost	1,500
Total Reserves(tons)	5,000

	1	2	3
Production (tons)	500	500	500

Cash Flow Calculations

Year	0	1	2	3
Gross Revenue		5,000	5,500	6,000
-Royalties (10%)		-500	-550	-600
Net Revenue		4,500	4,950	5,400
-Operating Cost		-3,000	-3,300	-3,600
-Development (70%)	-1,050			
-Depreciation*		-429	-735	-525
-Amortization**	-45	-90	-90	-90
Before Depletion	-1,095	981	825	1,185
-50% Limit		-491	-413	-593
-Percent Depletion (15%)		675	742	810
-Cost Depletion***		200	168	137
-Loss Forward		-1,095	-605	-193
Taxable Income	-1,095	-605	-193	399
-Tax Due @ 40%	0	0	0	-160
Net Income	-1,095	-605	-193	239
+Depreciation		429	735	525
+Depletion Taken		491	413	593
+Amortization	45	90	90	90
+Loss Forward		1,095	605	193
-Equipment (Deprec)	-3,000			
-30% Dev. (Amort)	-450			
-Min Rts (Cost Depl)	-2,000			
Cash Flow	-6,500	1,500	1,650	1,640

*Depreciation Calculated Using Table 7-3 in Text:
  Yr 1   3,000(0.1429) = 429
  Yr 2   3,000(0.2449) = 735   No writeoff was asked for in statement
  Yr 3   3,000(0.1749) = 525   so it is neglected in year 3 cash flow

**Amortization Calculations on   ***Cost Depletion Calculations:
  30% of Mine Develop=0.3(1,500):
  Yr 1   450(6/60) = 45   Yr 1   (2,000)(500/5,000)   = 200
  Yr 2   450(12/60) = 90   Yr 2   (2,000-491)(500/4,500) = 168
  Yr 3   450(12/60) = 90   Yr 3   (1,509-413)(500/4,000) = 137

7-9 Solution: Case B, Individual Mining, Values (000's)

Acquisition Cost	2,000			
Equipment Cost	3,000			
Development Cost	1,500			
Total Reserves(tons)	5,000			
Production (tons)		500	500	500

Cash Flow Calculations

Year	0	1	2	3
Gross Revenue		5,000	5,500	6,000
-Royalties		-500	-550	-600
Net Revenue		4,500	4,950	5,400
-Operating Cost		-3,000	-3,300	-3,600
-Development (100%)	-1,500			
-Depreciation*		-429	-735	-525
Before Depletion	-1,500	1,071	915	1,275
-50% Limit		-536	-458	-638
-Percent Depletion (15%)		675	742	810
-Cost Depletion**		200	163	126
-Loss Forward		↗ -1,500	↗ -964	↗ -507
Taxable Income	-1,500	-964	-507	131
-Tax Due @ 40%	0	0	0	-52
Net Income	-1,500	-964	-507	79
+Depreciation		429	735	525
+Depletion Taken		536	458	638
+Loss Forward		1,500	964	507
-Equipment (Deprec)	-3,000			
-Min Acq (Cost Depl)	-2,000			
Cash Flow	-6,500	1,500	1,650	1,749

*Depreciation Calculated Using Table 7-3:

    Yr 1   3,000(0.1429) = 429
    Yr 2   3,000(0.2449) = 735   No writeoff was asked for so it is
    Yr 3   3,000(0.1749) = 525   neglected in year 3 cash flow.

**Cost Depletion Calculations Follow:

    Yr 1   (2,000)(500/5,000)   = 200
    Yr 2   (2,000-536)(500/4,500) = 163
    Yr 3   (1,454-458)(500/4,000) = 126

7-10 Solution: Case A, Integrated Producer, All Values in (000's)

Acquisition Cost	2,000			
Equipment Cost	3,000			
IDC	1,500			
Total Reserves (Bbl)	5,000			
Production (Bbl)		500	500	500

Cash Flow Calculations:

Year	0	1	2	3
Gross Revenue		5,000	5,500	6,000
-Royalties		-500	-550	-600
-Operating Cost		-3,000	-3,300	-3,600
-IDC (70%)	-1,050			
-Depreciation*		-429	-735	-525
-Amortization**	-45	-90	-90	-90
-Cost Depletion***		-200	-200	-200
-Loss Forward		-1,095	-314	
Taxable Income	-1,095	-314	312	985
-Tax Due @ 40%	0	0	-125	-394
Net Income	-1,095	-314	187	591
+Depreciation		429	735	525
+Cost Depletion		200	200	200
+Amortization	45	90	90	90
+Loss Forward		1,095	314	
-Tang Equip (Deprec)	-3,000			
-30% IDC (Amort)	-450			
-Min Acq (Cost Depl)	-2,000			
Cash Flow	-6,500	1,500	1,525	1,406

*Depreciation Calculated Using Table 7-3 in Text:

    Yr 1   3,000(0.1429) = 429
    Yr 2   3,000(0.2449) = 735   No writeoff was asked for so it
    Yr 3   3,000(0.1749) = 525   is neglected in year 3 cash flows.

**Amortization Calculations on   ***Cost Depletion Calculations:
   30% of IDC = 0.3(1500):
   Yr 1   450(6/60) = 45   Yr 1 (2,000)(500/5,000)   = 200
   Yr 2   450(12/60) = 90   Yr 2 (2,000-200)(500/4,500) = 200
   Yr 3   450(12/60) = 90   Yr 3 (1,800-200)(500/4,000) = 200

7-10 Solution: Case B, Independent Producer < 1,000 Bbl/day
All Values in (000's)

Acquisition Cost	2,000			
Equipment Cost	3,000			
IDC	1,500			
Total Reserves(Bbl)	5,000			
Production (Bbl)		500	500	500

Cash Flow Calculations:

Year	0	1	2	3
Gross Revenue		5,000	5,500	6,000
−Royalties		−500	−550	−600
Net Revenue		4,500	4,950	5,400
−Operating Cost		−3,000	−3,300	−3,600
−IDC (100%)	−1,500			
−Depreciation*		−429	−735	−525
Before Depletion	−1,500	1,071	915	1,275
100% Limit		1,071	915	1,275
Percent Depletion (15%)		−675	−743	−810
Cost Depletion**		200	147	73
−Loss Forward		↗−1,500	↗−1,104	↗−931
Taxable Income	−1,500	−1,104	−931	−466
−Tax Due @ 40%	0	0	0	186***
Net Income	−1,500	−1,104	−931	−280
+Depreciation		429	735	525
+Depletion Taken		675	743	810
+Loss Forward		1,500	1,104	931
−Equip (Deprec)	−5,000			
−Min Acq (Cost Depl)	−2,000			
Cash Flow	−6,500	1,500	1,650	1,986

* Depreciation Calculated Using Table 7-3 in Text:

    Yr 1   3,000(0.1429) = 429
    Yr 2   3,000(0.2449) = 735   No writeoff was asked for so it
    Yr 3   3,000(0.1749) = 525   neglected in year 3 cash flow.

** Cost Depletion Calculations:

    Yr 1   (2,000)(500/5,000)   = 200
    Yr 2   (2,000−675)(500/4,500) = 147
    Yr 3   (1,325−743)(500/4,000) = 73

*** Crediting the project with tax savings of 186 in year 3 assumes other taxable income will exist against which to use the year 3 negative taxable income.

7-10 Solution: Case C, Independent Producer > 1,000 Bbl/day
All Values in (000's)

Acquisition Cost	2,000			
Equipment Cost	3,000			
IDC	1,500			
Total Reserves (Bbl)	5,000			
Production (Bbl)		500	500	500

Cash Flow Calculations:

Year	0	1	2	3
Gross Revenue		5,000	5,500	6,000
-Royalties		-500	-550	-600
Net Revenue		4,500	4,950	5,400
-Operating Cost		-3,000	-3,300	-3,600
-IDC (100%)	-1,500			
-Depreciation*		-429	-735	-525
-Cost Depletion**		-200	-200	-200
-Loss Forward		-1,500	-629	
Taxable Income	-1,500	-629	87	1,075
-Tax Due @ 40%	0	0	-35	-430
Net Income	-1,500	-629	52	645
+Depreciation		429	735	525
+Cost Depletion		200	200	200
+Loss Forward		1,500	629	
-Tang Equip (Deprec)	-3,000			
-Min Rts (Cost Depl)	-2,000			
Cash Flow	-6,500	1,500	1,615	1,370

*Depreciation Calculated Using Table 7-3 in Text:

```
    Yr 1    3,000(0.1429) = 429
    Yr 2    3,000(0.2449) = 735    No writeoff was asked for so it is
    Yr 3    3,000(0.1749) = 525    neglected in year 3 cash flow.
```

**Cost Depletion Calculations:

```
    Yr 1    (2,000)(500/5,000)    = 200
    Yr 2    (2,000-200)(500/4,500) = 200
    Yr 3    (1,800-200)(500/4,000) = 200
```

7-11 Solution: Case A, Integrated, Values in (000's)

Acquisition Cost	200						
Intangible Drilling	500						
Tangible Completion	400						
Initial Reserves(bbl)	200						
Production/Year(bbl)		30	27	24	21	18	

Year	0	1	2	3	4	5	Sale
Gross Revenue		700	600	500	400	300	250
-Royalties		-105	-90	-75	-60	-45	-
Net Revenue		595	510	425	340	255	250
-Operating Costs		-50	-50	-50	-50	-50	
-Intangible	-350						
-Depreciation		-57	-98	-70	-50	-36	
-Deprec Write-off							-89
-Amortization	-15	-30	-30	-30	-30	-15	
-Cost Depletion		-30	-27	-24	-21	-18	
-Cost Depl Write-off							-80
-Loss Forward		-365					
Taxable Income	-365	63	305	251	189	136	81
-Tax @ 40%		-25	-122	-100	-76	-54	-32
Net Income	-365	38	183	151	113	82	49
+Depreciation		57	98	70	50	36	
+Cost Depletion		30	27	24	21	18	
+Write-offs							169
+Amortization	15	30	30	30	30	15	
+Loss Forward		365					
-Tang Equip (Deprec)	-400						
-30% IDC	-150						
-Min Rts (Cost Depl)	-200						
Cash Flow	-1,100	520	338	275	214	151	218

369

Depreciation Calculations:	Cost Depletion Calculations:
Yr 1: 400(0.1429) = 57	Yr 1: (200)(30/200) = 30
Yr 2: 400(0.2449) = 98	Yr 2: (200-30)(27/170) = 27
Yr 3: 400(0.1749) = 70	Yr 3: (170-27)(24/143) = 24
Yr 4: 400(0.1249) = 50	Yr 4: (143-24)(21/119) = 21
Yr 5: 400(0.0893) = 36	Yr 5: (119-21)(18/98) = 18
Writeoff: 400-311 = 89	Writeoff: 200-120 = 80

Amortization (30% of IDC):
Yr 0&5: 500(0.3)(6/60) = 15, Yr 1-4: 500(0.3)(12/60) = 30

PW Eq: $0 = -1,100 + 520(P/F_{i,1}) + 338(P/F_{i,2}) + 275(P/F_{i,3})$

$$+ 214(P/F_{i,4}) + 369(P/F_{i,5})$$

i = DCFROR = 19.0%   (by financial calculator)

7-11 Solution: Case B, Independent < 1,000 Bbl/day, Values in (000's)

Acquisition Cost	200						
Intangible Drilling	500						
Tangible Completion	400						
Initial Reserves (bbl)	200						
Production/Year (bbl)		30	27	24	21	18	

Year	0	1	2	3	4	5	Sale
Gross Revenue		700	600	500	400	300	250
-Royalties		-105	-90	-75	-60	-45	-
Net Revenue		595	510	425	340	255	250
-Operating Costs		-50	-50	-50	-50	-50	
-Intangible	-500						
-Depreciation		-57	-98	-70	-50	-36	
-Deprec Write-off							-89
Taxable Before Depl	-500	488	362	305	240	169	161
-100% Limit		488	362	305	240	169	-
-Percentage Depl.		-89	-77	-64	-51	-38	-
-Cost Depletion		30	18	6			
-Loss Forward		-500	-101				
Taxable Income	-500	-101	184	241	189	131	161
-Tax @ 40%			-74	-96	-76	-52	-64
Net Income	-500	-101	110	145	113	79	97
+Depreciation		57	98	70	50	36	
+Depletion Taken		89	77	64	51	38	
+Deprec Write-off							89
+Loss Forward		500	101				
-Equipment (Deprec)	-400						
-Min Rts (Cost Depl)	-200						
Cash Flow	-1,100	545	386	278	214	153	186

339

Depreciation Calculations:
Yr 1: 400(0.1429) = 57
Yr 2: 400(0.2449) = 98
Yr 3: 400(0.1749) = 70
Yr 4: 400(0.1249) = 50
Yr 5: 400(0.0893) = 36
Writeoff: 400-311 = 89

Cost Depletion Calculations:
Yr 1: (200)(30/200)   = 30
Yr 2: (200-89)(27/170) = 18
Yr 3: (111-77)(24/143) = 6
Yr 4: (34-64)(21/119) < 0, stop

PW Eq: $0 = -1,100 + 545(P/F_{i,1}) + 386(P/F_{i,2}) + 278(P/F_{i,3})$

$+ 214(P/F_{i,4}) + 339(P/F_{i,5})$

i = DCFROR = 21.1%   (by financial calculator)

7-11 Solution: Case C, Independent > 1,000 Bbl/day, Values in (000's)

Acquisition Cost	200						
Intangible Drilling	500						
Tangible Completion	400						
Initial Reserves(bbl)	200						
Production/Year(bbl)		30	27	24	21	18	

Year	0	1	2	3	4	5	Sale
Gross Revenue		700	600	500	400	300	250
−Royalties		105	90	75	60	45	−
Net Revenue		595	510	425	340	255	250
−Operating Costs		−50	−50	−50	−50	−50	
−IDC (100%)	−500						
−Depreciation		−57	−98	−70	−50	−36	
−Deprec Write-off							−89
−Cost Depletion		−30	−27	−24	−21	−18	
−Cost Depl. Write-off							−80
−Loss Forward		↗−500	↗−42				
Taxable Income	−500	−42	293	281	219	151	81
−Tax Due @ 40%			−100	−96	−74	−60	−32
Net Income	−500	−42	193	185	145	91	49
+Depreciation		57	98	70	50	36	
+Cost Depletion		30	27	24	21	18	
+Write-offs							169
+Loss Forward		500	42				
−Tang.Equip (Deprc)	−400						
−Min Acq(Cost Depl)	−200						
Cash Flow	−1,100	545	360	279	216	145	218

363

Depreciation Calculations:
Yr 1: 400(0.1429) = 57
Yr 2: 400(0.2449) = 98
Yr 3: 400(0.1749) = 70
Yr 4: 400(0.1249) = 50
Yr 5: 400(0.0893) = 36
Writeoff: 400-311 = 89

Cost Depletion Calculations:
Yr 1: (200)(30/200)   = 30
Yr 2: (200-30)(27/170) = 27
Yr 3: (170-27)(24/143) = 24
Yr 4: (143-24)(21/119) = 21
Yr 5: (119-21)(18/98) = 18
Writeoff: 200-120 = 80

PW Eq: $0 = -1{,}100 + 545(P/F_{i,1}) + 360(P/F_{i,2}) + 279(P/F_{i,3})$

$$+ 216(P/F_{i,4}) + 363(P/F_{i,5})$$

i = DCFROR = 20.7%   (by financial calculator)

7-12 Solution: General Process Evaluation, All Values (000's) $.

Patent Acquisition	600	
Research & Exper.	500	
Equipment	1,000	
Revenues		2,000 escalating 10% per yr ...
Operating Costs		1,000 escalating 10% per yr ...

Year	0	1	2	3	4	5
Revenue		2,000	2,200	2,420	2,662	2,928
-Operating Costs		-1,000	-1,100	-1,210	-1,331	-1,464
-Research & Exper.	-500					
-Depreciation		-200	-320	-192	-115	-115
-Deprec. Write-off						-58
-Amortization	-60	-120	-120	-120	-120	-60
-Loss Forward		-560				
Taxable Income	-560	120	660	898	1,096	1,231
-Tax Due @ 40%		-48	-264	-359	-438	-493
Net Income	-560	72	396	539	657	738
+Depreciation		200	320	192	115	115
+Deprec. Write-off						58
+Amortization	60	120	120	120	120	60
+Loss Forward		560				
-Equipment (Deprec)	-1,000					
-Patent (Amort)	-600					
Cash Flow	-2,100	952	836	851	893	972

Revenue Calculations:
Yr 2 = 2,000(1.1) = 2,200
Yr 3 = 2,200(1.1) = 2,420 etc.

Operating Costs:
Yr 2 = 1,000(1.1) = 1,100
Yr 3 = 1,100(1.1) = 1,210 etc.

The patent is assumed to have a remaining life of 5 years upon which amortization has been based. Assuming the patent cost was incurred in the middle of tax year zero gives the following amortization:

Year   0 = (600)(6 months / 60 months) = 60
Year 1-4 = (600)(12 months / 60 months) = 120
Year   5 = (600)(6 months / 60 months) = 60

Depreciation of Equipment (Using MACRS Table 7-3):

Year 1 = 1,000(0.2000) = 200
Year 2 = 1,000(0.3200) = 320
Year 3 = 1,000(0.1920) = 192 etc...

PW Eq: $0 = -2,100 + 952(P/F_{i,1}) + 836(P/F_{i,2}) + 851(P/F_{i,3})$

$$+ 893(P/F_{i,4}) + 972(P/F_{i,5})$$

i = DCFROR = 32.2% by trial and error.

7-13 Five Megawatt Hydroelectric Plant Economics

Before-tax Economic Analysis:

Annual Revenue = 5,000,000 watts * 6,000 hrs/yr * 1 kwh/1,000 watts

$\quad\quad\quad\quad\quad$ = 30,000,000 kwh per year

30,000,000 kwh * \$0.35 profit / kwh = \$1,050,000 profit per year.

NPV Eq: $-6,000,000 + 1,050,000(P/A_{i,n})$

Sensitivity Analysis Summary:

Life (Years)	ROR	NPV @ i* = 10.0%	NPV @ i* = 15.0%
10	11.72%	451,795	-730,293
20	16.70%	2,939,242	572,298
30	17.35%	3,898,260	894,278
40	17.47%	4,268,003	973,867

After-tax Economic Analysis:

Assume straight line 10 year depreciation life, starting in year one with a full year deduction. Assume an effective income tax rate of 30%. All values in (000's).

Year	0	1-10	11-n
Revenue @ \$0.04/kwh	–	1,200	1,200
- O.C. @ \$0.005/kwh	–	-150	-150
- Depreciation*	–	-600	–
Taxable Income	–	450	1,050
- Tax @ 30%	–	-135	-315
Net Income	–	315	735
+ Depreciation	–	600	–
- Capital Cost	-6,000	–	–
Cash Flow	-6,000	915	735

NPV = $-6,000 + 915(P/A_{i},10) + 735(P/A_{i},n-10)(P/F_{i},10)$

Life (Years)	ROR	NPV @ i* = 10.0%
10	8.51%	-377,700
20	13.41%	1,363,491
30	14.23%	2,034,804
40	14.41%	2,293,624

CHAPTER 8 PROBLEM SOLUTIONS

8-1 Solution: *All Values in Dollars*

Case A) Straight Line ACRS Depreciation, Half-Year Convention

Equipment Cost	20,000			
Working Capital	2,000			
Salvage (Including WC Return)				14,000
Revenue		35,000	35,000	35,000
Operating Costs		25,000	25,000	25,000
Year	0	1	2	3

Depreciation Calculations:
Straight Line 5 Year With Half-Year Convention

Yr 1:   20,000(1/5)(0.5) = 2,000,   Remaining Book Value = 18,000
Yr 2:   20,000(1/5)   = 4,000,   Remaining Book Value = 14,000
Yr 3:   20,000(1/5)   = 4,000,   Remaining Book Value = 10,000

Yr 3: Working Capital Book Value Equals Initial Cost of 2,000

Cash Flow Calculations:

Year	0	1	2	3
Revenue		35,000	35,000	49,000*
-Operating Costs		-25,000	-25,000	-25,000
-Depreciation		-2,000	-4,000	-4,000
-Depreciation Write-off				-10,000
-Work Capital Write-off				-2,000
Taxable Income		8,000	6,000	8,000
Tax @ 40%		-3,200	-2,400	-3,200
Net Income		4,800	3,600	4,800
+Depreciation		2,000	4,000	4,000
+Depreciation Write-off				10,000
+Work Capital Write-off				2,000
-Capital Costs	-22,000**			
Cash Flow	-22,000	6,800	7,600	20,800

*   *Year 3 revenue includes sale value of $14,000.*

** *Capital Costs include $20,000 for business equipment*
    plus $2,000 for working capital.

PW Eq: $-22,000 + 6,800(P/F_{i,1}) + 7,600(P/F_{i,2}) + 20,800(P/F_{i,3})$

i = DCFROR = 22.3% *by trial and error*

8-1 Solution: *Continued - All Values in Dollars*

Case B) *Modified ACRS Depreciation 5 Year Life, Half-Year Convention*

	0	1	2	3
Equipment Cost	20,000			
Working Capital	2,000			
Salvage (Including WC Return)				14,000
Revenue		35,000	35,000	35,000
Operating Costs		25,000	25,000	25,000
Year	0	1	2	3

MACRS Depreciation, 5 Year Life With Half-Year Convention:

Yr 1: 20,000(0.200) = 4,000,   Remaining Book Value = 16,000
Yr 2: 20,000(0.320) = 6,400,   Remaining Book Value = 9,600
Yr 3: 20,000(0.192) = 3,840,   Remaining Book Value = 5,760

Yr 3: Working Capital Book Value Equals Initial Cost, or $2,000.

Cash Flow Calculations:

Year	0	1	2	3
Revenue		35,000	35,000	49,000*
-Operating Costs		-25,000	-25,000	-25,000
-Depreciation		-4,000	-6,400	-3,840
-Depreciation Write-off				-5,760
-Work Capital Write-off				-2,000
Taxable Income		6,000	3,600	12,400
Tax @ 40%		-2,400	-1,440	-4,960
Net Income		3,600	2,160	7,440
+Depreciation		4,000	6,400	3,840
+Depreciation Write-off				5,760
+Work Capital Write-off				2,000
-Capital Costs	-22,000**			
Cash Flow	-22,000	7,600	8,560	19,040

*   Year 3 revenue includes sale value of $14,000.

** Capital Costs include $20,000 for business equipment
   plus $2,000 for working capital.

PW Eq: $-22,000 + 7,600(P/F_{i,1}) + 8,560(P/F_{i,2}) + 19,040(P/F_{i,3})$

i = **DCFROR** = 23.2% *by trial and error*

8-2 Solution: *All Values in Dollars*

Case A) *Expense R&D as an Operating Cost Against Other Income*

	0	1-4	5
Working Capital	50,000		
Research & Experimentation	100,000 *(Expense at year 0)*		
Working Capital Return Revenue			50,000
Sales Revenue		500,000	500,000
Operating Costs		400,000	400,000
Year	0	1-4	5

Cash Flow Calculations:

Year	0	1-4	5
Sales/Year		500,000	550,000*
-Operating Costs		-400,000	-400,000
-R&D as O.C.	-100,000		
-Working Capital Write-off			-50,000
Taxable Income	-100,000	100,000	100,000
Tax @ 40%	40,000	-40,000	-40,000
Net Income	-60,000	60,000	60,000
+Working Capital Write-off			50,000
-Capital Costs	-50,000		
Cash Flow	-110,000	60,000	110,000

* *Year 5 revenue includes working capital return.*

PW Eq: $0 = -110{,}000 + 60{,}000(P/A_{i,4}) + 110{,}000(P/F_{i,5})$

   $i = DCFROR = 50.4\%$

8-2 Solution: *Continued - All Values in Dollars*

Case B)   *Expense R&D as an Operating Cost and Carry Forward to Use Against Project Income (Stand Alone Economics)*

Working Capital	50,000		
Research & Experimentation	100,000		
Working Capital Return Revenue			50,000
Sales Revenue		500,000	500,000
Operating Costs		400,000	400,000
Year	0	1-4	5

Cash Flow Calculations:

Year	0	1	2-4	5
Sales/Year		500,000	500,000	550,000*
-Operating Costs		-400,000	-400,000	-400,000
-R&D as O.C.	-100,000			
-Working Capital Write-off				-50,000
-Loss Forward		-100,000		
Taxable Income	-100,000	0	100,000	100,000
Tax @ 40%	0	0	-40,000	-40,000
Net Income	-100,000	0	60,000	60,000
+Working Capital Write-off				50,000
+Loss Forward		100,000		
-Capital Costs	-50,000			
Cash Flow	-150,000	100,000	60,000	110,000

* Year 5 revenue includes working capital return.

PW Eq: $0 = -150,000 + 100,000(P/F_{i,1}) + 60,000(P/A_{i,3})(P/F_{i,1})$

$+ 110,000(P/F_{i,5})$

i = DCFROR = 44.1%

8-2 Solution: *Continued*

Case C) *Capitalize R&D and Deduct by Amortization*

Working Capital	50,000	
Research & Experimentation	100,000	
Working Capital Return Revenue		50,000
Sales Revenue	500,000	500,000
Operating Costs	400,000	400,000

Cash Flow Calculations:

Year	0	1-4	5
Sales/Year		500,000	550,000*
-Operating Costs		-400,000	-400,000
-Amortization		-20,000	-20,000
-Working Capital Write-off			-50,000
Taxable Income		80,000	80,000
Tax @ 40%		-32,000	-32,000
Net Income		48,000	48,000
+Amortization		20,000	20,000
+Working Capital Write-off			50,000
-Capital Costs	-150,000		
Cash Flow	-150,000	68,000	118,000

* Year 5 revenue includes working capital return.

PW Eq: $0 = -150{,}000 + 68{,}000(P/A_{i,4}) + 118{,}000(P/F_{i,5})$

$i = \text{DCFROR} = 39.1\%$

Case D) *Expense R&D, Deutschemark (DM) Analysis*

Case D1): ($0.70 US/DM)(833,330 DM) = $583,333 US revenue per year
Case D2): ($0.50 US/DM)(833,330 DM) = $416,667 US revenue per year

Case D1) Cash Flows: Case D2) Cash Flows:

Year	0	1-4	5	0	1-4	5
Sales/yr		583,333	633,333		416,667	466,667
-Oper. Costs		-400,000	-400,000		-400,000	-400,000
-R&D	-100,000			-100,000		
-WC Write-off			-50,000			-50,000
Taxable Income	-100,000	-183,333	-183,333	-100,000	16,667	16,667
-Tax @ 40%	+40,000	-73,333	-73,333	+40,000	-6,667	-6,667
Net Income	-60,000	+110,000	+110,000	-60,000	+10,000	+10,000
+WC Write-off			+50,000			+50,000
-Capital Costs	-50,000			-50,000		
Cash Flow	-110,000	+110,000	+160,000	-110,000	+10,000	+60,000

Case D1 DCFROR = 98.2%   **Case D2 DCFROR = -2.3%**

Foreign sales projects are very sensitive to exchange rate variations. Weakened domestic currency always enhances export project economics.

8-3 Solution: *All Values in Thousands of Dollars*

Case A) *Stand Alone Economics*

Acquisition Cost= 10,000						
Working Capital = 2,000						
Equipment Cost = 15,000	I=30,000	I=33,000	I=36,300	I=39,930	I=43,923	
Mine Develop = 10,000	OC=12,000	OC=13,200	OC=14,520	OC=15,972	OC=17,569	
	0	1	2	3	4	5

Cash Flow Calculations:

Year	Time 0	1	2	3	4	5	Salv
Production		1,000	1,000	1,000	1,000	1,000	
Gross Revenue		30,000	33,000	36,300	39,930	43,923	5,000
-Royalties		-2,400	-2,640	-2,904	-3,194	-3,514	
Net Revenue		27,600	30,360	33,396	36,736	40,409	
-Operating Costs		-12,000	-13,200	-14,520	-15,972	-17,569	
-Development	-7,000						
-Depreciation	-2,143	-3,673	-2,624	-1,874	-1,339	-1,339	-2,008
-Amortization	-600	-600	-600	-600	-600		
-WC Write-off							-2,000
Before Depletion	-9,743	11,327	13,936	16,402	18,825	21,501	992
50% Limit		5,663	6,968	8,201	9,412	10,751	
Percent Depletion		-2,760	-3,036	-3,340	-3,112*	-3,233	
Cost Depletion		2,000	1,810	1,401	432		
-Loss Forward		-9,743	-1,176				
Taxable Income	-9,743	-1,176	9,724	13,062	15,713	18,268	992
-Tax Due @ 40%	0	0	-3,890	-5,225	-6,285	-7,307	-397
Net Income	-9,743	-1,176	5,834	7,837	9,428	10,961	595
+Depreciation	2,143	3,673	2,624	1,874	1,339	1,339	2,008
+Depletion Taken		2,760	3,036	3,340	3,112	3,233	
+Amortization	600	600	600	600	600		
+Loss Forward		9,743	1,176				
+WC Write-off							2,000
-Capital Costs	-30,000**						
Cash Flow	-37,000	15,600	13,270	13,651	14,478	15,533	4,603

** Time 0 capital cost includes $15,000 for equipment, $2,000 for working capital, $3,000 for 30% of the $10,000 development cost and $10,000 for mineral rights acquisition.

* Cumulative percentage depletion in years 1, 2 and 3 is $9,136, so $864 more depletion equals $10,000 mineral rights acquisition cost. $864/.10 = $8,640 net revenue after royalty is needed for 10% depletion, balance is 8% depletion. 8% depletion revenue = ($36,736-$8,640)(0.08) = $28,096(0.08) = $2,248. Cumulative year 4 percentage depletion = $2,248 + $864 = $3,112.

8-3 Solution: *Case A Continued*

Depreciation Calculations:

```
Yr 0   15,000(.1429) = 2,143
Yr 1   15,000(.2449) = 3,673
Yr 2   15,000(.1749) = 2,624
Yr 3   15,000.(.1249) = 1,874
Yr 4   15,000(.0893) = 1,339
Yr 5   15,000(.0892) = 1,339

Yr 5 Remaining Book Write-off
       15,000(.1339) = 2,008
```

Cost Depletion Calculations:

```
Yr 1   10,000(1,000/5,000)          = 2,000
Yr 2   (10,000-2,760)(1,000/4,000) = 1,810
Yr 3   (7,240-3,036)(1,000/3,000)  = 1,401
Yr 4   (4,204-3,340)(1,000/2,000)  =   432
Yr 5   (864-3,112) < 0, stop cost depletion
```

Amortization of 30% of Development:

Yrs 0-4 $10,000(.30)(12/60) = 600$

PW Eq: $0 = -37,000 + 15,600(P/F_{i,1}) + 13,270(P/F_{i,2}) + 13,651(P/F_{i,3})$
$+ 14,478(P/F_{i,4}) + 20,047(P/F_{i,5});$ **i = DCFROR = 29.4%**

NPV $= -37,000 + 15,600(P/F_{20,1}) + 13,270(P/F_{20,2}) + 13,651(P/F_{20,3})$
$+ 14,478(P/F_{20,4}) + 20,047(P/F_{20,5}) = +\$8,154$

Case B) Expense Economics

Year	0	1	2	3	4	5	Salv
Production		1,000	1,000	1,000	1,000	1,000	
Gross Revenue		30,000	33,000	36,300	39,930	43,923	5,000
-Royalties		-2,400	-2,640	-2,904	-3,194	-3,514	
Net Revenue		27,600	30,360	33,396	36,736	40,409	
-Operating Costs		-12,000	-13,200	-14,520	-15,972	-17,569	
-Development	-7,000						
-Depreciation	-2,143	-3,673	-2,624	-1,874	-1,339	-1,339	-2,008
-Amortization	-600	-600	-600	-600	-600		
-Write-off							-2,000
Before Depletion	-9,743	11,327	13,936	16,402	18,825	21,501	992
Percent Depletion		2,760	3,036	3,340	3,112*	3,233	
50% Limit		5,663	6,968	8,201	9,412	10,751	
Cost Depletion		2,000	1,810	1,401	432		
-Depletion Taken		-2,760	-3,036	-3,340	-3,112	-3,233	
Taxable Income	-9,743	8,567	10,900	13,062	15,713	18,268	992
-Tax Due @ 40%	3,897	-3,427	-4,360	-5,225	-6,285	-7,307	-397
Net Income	-5,846	5,140	6,540	7,837	9,428	10,961	595
+Depreciation	2,143	3,673	2,624	1,874	1,339	1,339	2,008
+Depletion		2,760	3,036	3,340	3,112	3,233	
+Amortization	600	600	600	600	600		
+Write-off							2,000
-Capital Costs	-30,000**						
Cash Flow	-33,103	12,173	12,800	13,651	14,478	15,533	4,603

8-3 Solution: *Case B Continued*

** Capital cost includes $15,000 for equipment, $2,000 for working capital, $3,000 which is 30% of the $10,000 development cost and $10,000 for mineral rights acquisition.

* Cumulative percentage depletion in years 1, 2 and 3 = $9,136 so $864 more depletion equals $10,000 mineral rights acquisition cost. $864/0.10 = $8,640 which is the net revenue after royalty needed for 10% depletion, the balance of revenue is 8% depletion. 8% depletion revenue = ($36,736-$8,640)(0.08) = $28,096(0.08) = $2,248. Cumulative year 4 percentage depletion = $2,248 + $864 = $3,112.

$$NPV = -33,103 + 12,173(P/F_{20,1}) + 12,800(P/F_{20,2}) + 13,651(P/F_{20,3})$$
$$+ 14,478(P/F_{20,4}) + 20,136(P/F_{20,5}) = +\$8,904$$

DCFROR = 30.8% *is the interest rate that makes NPV = 0.*

8-4 Solution: *Values in Dollars*

Growth Rate of Return

Cash Flows	-150,000	60,000	70,000	80,000	90,000
Year	0	1	2	3	4

Project DCFROR PW Eq: $150,000 = [60,000 + 10,000(A/G_{i,4})](P/A_{i,4})$

$$i = DCFROR = 32\%$$

To calculate the project Growth DCFROR, you must account for 40% tax to be paid on 12% treasury bond interest each year, therefore money grows at 7.2% per year after taxes.

$$\qquad\qquad 1.2319 \qquad\qquad 1.1492 \qquad\qquad 1.072$$
PW Eq: $150,000 = [60,000(F/P_{7.2,3}) + 70,000(F/P_{7.2,2}) + 80,000(F/P_{7.2,1})$
$$+ 90,000](P/F_{i,4})$$

$$150,000 = 330,118(P/F_{i,4})$$

$$i = Growth\ DCFROR = 21.8\%$$

8-5 Solution: *All Values in Thousands of Dollars*

Manufacturing Plant Evaluation

Working Capital	= 20	I =100		I =100	
Depreciable Equipment	= 180	OC=40		OC=40	WC Return = 20
					Salvage = 150

0	1 15	

Project Cash Flow Calculations:

Year	0	1	2-7	8	9-15	Salvage 15
Revenue		100.00	100.00	100.00	100.00	170.00
-Operating Costs		-40.00	-40.00	-40.00	-40.00	
-Depreciation		-12.86	-25.71	-12.86		
-WC Write-off						-20.00
Taxable Income		47.14	34.29	47.14	60.00	150.00
-Tax @ 40%		-18.86	-13.71	-18.86	-24.00	-60.00
Net Income		28.29	20.57	28.29	36.00	90.00
+Depreciation		12.86	25.71	12.86		
+WC Return						20.00
Capital Costs	-200.00					
Cash Flow	-200.00	41.14	46.29	41.14	36.00	110.00

$$\text{NPV @ 15\%} = -200.00 + 41.14(P/F_{15,1}) + 46.29(P/A_{15,6})(P/F_{15,1})$$
$$+ 41.14(P/F_{15,8}) + 36.00(P/A_{15,7})(P/F_{15,8}) + 110.00(P/F_{15,15})$$
$$= +\$64.0$$

DCFROR = 21.1% *is the interest rate that makes NPV equal to zero.*

8-6 Solution: *Values in Thousands*

Corporate Mining, Stand Alone Economics

Acquisition Cost	$1,000					
Development Cost		$500 (Assume incurred 1st month of tax year)				
Equipment Cost	−	$1,000				
Units Produced	−	−	100	100	150	150

Year	Time 0	1	2	3	4	5 Salvage
Production			100	100	150	150
Net Revenue			2,000	2,000	3,000	3,000
−Operating Costs			−800	−800	−1,200	−1,200
−Development		−350				
−Depreciation			−143	−245	−175	−125 −312
−Amortization		−30	−30	−30	−30	−30
Before Depletion		−380	1,027	925	1,595	1,645 −312
50% Limit			514	463	798	823
Percent Depletion			−440	−440	−660	−660
Cost Depletion			200	140	60	
−Loss Forward			−380			
Taxable Income		−380	207	485	935	985 −312
−Tax Due @ 40%		0	−83	−194	−374	−394 125
Net Income		−380	124	291	561	591 −187
+Depreciation			143	245	175	125 312
+Depletion Taken			440	440	660	660
+Amortization		30	30	30	30	30
+Loss Forward			380			
−Capital Costs	−1,000	−1,150				
Cash Flow	−1,000	−1,500	1,117	1,006	1,426	1,406 125

$$\underbrace{\qquad\qquad}$$
1,531

Depreciation Calculations:

Yr 2	1,000(0.1429)	= 143
Yr 3	1,000(0.2449)	= 245
Yr 4	1,000(0.1749)	= 175
Yr 5	1,000(0.1249)	= 125

Depreciable Write-off = 312

Cost Depletion Calculations:

Yr 2	1,000(100/500)	= 200
Yr 3	560(100/400)	= 140
Yr 4	120(150/300)	= 60
Yr 5	*Basis < 0, no cost depletion*	

PW Eq: $0 = -1,000 - 1,500(P/F_{i,1}) + 1,117(P/F_{i,2}) + 1,006(P/F_{i,3})$
$+ 1,426(P/F_{i,4}) + 1,531(P/F_{i,5})$

DCFROR = 27.3%

NPV @ i* = 15% = +$778

PVR = $778 / [1,000 + 1,500(P/F_{15,1})]$ = +0.34

Pay-back from start of project = $3 + (377/1,426)$ = 3.26 years

8-7 Solution: *All Values in Thousands*

Petroleum Property Evaluation, Independent Producer

Acquisition Cost:	$100							
IDC :	$750	$250						
Depreciable Cost:		$1,000						
Production :				70	56	42	28	14
Year	0	1		2	3	4	5	6

Case A and B Cash Flows for Expense Against Other Income:

			Success						Fail
Year	0	1	2	3	4	5	6	6	1
Gross Revenue			1,540	1,331	1,078	776	419		
-Royalties			-216	-186	-151	-109	-59		
Net Revenue			1,324	1,145	927	667	360		
-Oper Costs			-175	-193	-212	-233	-256		-50
-Intangible	-750	-250							
-Depreciation			-143	-245	-175	-125	-89		
-Write-off								-223	
Before Depln	-750	-250	1,006	707	540	309	15	-223	-50
-100% Limit			1,006	707	540	309	-15		
-% Depln(15%)			-199	-172	-139	-100	54		
-Cost Depln			33	0	0	0	0		-100
Taxable Inc	-750	-250	807	535	401	209	0	-223	-150
-Tax @ 38%	285	95	-307	-203	-152	-80	0	85	57
Net Income	-465	-155	500	332	249	130	0	-138	-93
+Depreciation			143	245	175	125	89		
+Write-off								223	
+Depletion			199	172	139	100	15		100
-Cap. Costs	-100	-1,000							
Cash Flow	-565	-1,155	842	749	563	355	104	85	7

PW Eq: $0 = -565 - 1,155(P/F_{i,1}) + 842(P/F_{i,2}) + 749(P/F_{i,3}) + 563(P/F_{i,4})$
$+ 355(P/F_{i,5}) + 189(P/F_{i,6})$ **DCFROR = 19.0%**

NPV @ 15% = +$140

*Risk adjust Case A for a 40% probability of success after the year 0
expenditures. A $50,000 abandonment cost is incurred in year 1 if the
project fails along with a write-off of the $100,000 acquisition cost.*

Risk Adjusted PW Eq:

$0 = -565 + [-1,155(P/F_{i,1}) + 842(P/F_{i,2}) + 749(P/F_{i,3}) + 563(P/F_{i,4})$
$+ 355(P/F_{i,5}) + 189(P/F_{i,6})](.4) + 7(P/F_{i,1})(.6)$

Expected DCFROR = 1.8%, **Expected NPV @ 15%** = -$279

8-7 Solution: *Continued*

Case C)   Integrated Producer Viewpoint
         Drilling Costs Incurred at Month 7 of Years 0 and 1

Year	0	1	2	3	4	5	6	1
			Success					Fail
Gross Revenue			1,540	1,331	1,078	776	419	
-Royalties			-216	-186	-151	-109	-59	
Net Revenue			1,324	1,145	927	667	360	
-Oper Costs			-175	-193	-212	-233	-256	-50
-IDC's	-525	-175						
-Depreciation			-143	-245	-175	-125	-89	
-Write-off							-223	
-Amortization	-23	-53	-60	-60	-60	-38	-8	-202
-Cost Depln			-33	-27	-20	-13	-7	-100
Taxable Inc	-548	-227	913	620	460	258	-223	-352
-Tax @ 38%	208	86	-347	-236	-175	-98	89	134
Net Income	-339	-141	566	384	285	160	-134	-218
+Depreciation			143	245	175	125	89	
+Write-off							223	
+Amortization	23	53	60	60	60	38	8	202
+Depletion			33	27	20	13	7	100
-Cap. Costs	-325	-1,075						
Cash Flow	-642	-1,164	802	716	540	336	193	84

PW Eq: $0 = -642 - 1,164(P/F_{i,1}) + 802(P/F_{i,2}) + 716(P/F_{i,3}) + 540(P/F_{i,4})$

$\qquad + 336(P/F_{i,5}) + 193(P/F_{i,6})$

DCFROR = 14.5%
NPV @ 15% = -$18

*Risk adjust Case A for a 40% probability of success after the year 0
expenditures. A $50,000 abandonment cost is incurred in year 1 if the
project fails along with a write-off of the $100,000 acquisition cost.*

Risk Adjusted PW Eq:

$0 = -642 + [-1,164(P/F_{i,1}) + 802(P/F_{i,2}) + 716(P/F_{i,3}) + 540(P/F_{i,4})$

$\quad + 336(P/F_{i,5}) + 193(P/F_{i,6})](0.4) + 84(P/F_{i,1})(0.6)$

Applying the probabilities to the cash flow streams and combining gives:

$0 = -642 + -415.2(P/F_{i,1}) + 320.8(P/F_{i,2}) + 286.4(P/F_{i,3}) + 216.0(P/F_{i,4})$

$\quad + 134.4(P/F_{i,5}) + 77.2(P/F_{i,6})$

Expected DCFROR = -0.7%,   **Expected NPV @ 15%** = -$348

8-7 Solution: *Continued*

Case D) *Independent Producer, Stand Alone Economic Analyses*

			Success					Fail	
Year	0	1	2	3	4	5	6	6	1
Gross Revenue			1,540	1,331	1,078	776	419		
−Royalties			−216	−186	−151	−109	−59		
Net Revenue			1,324	1,145	927	667	360		
−Oper Costs			−175	−193	−212	−233	−256		−50
−Intangible	−750	−250							
−Depreciation			−143	−245	−175	−125	−89		
−Write-off								−223	
Before Depln	−750	−250	1,006	707	540	309	15	−223	−50
−100% Limit			1,006	707	540	309	−15		
−% Depl (15%)			−199	−172	−139	−100	54		
−Cost Depln			33	0	0	0	0		−100
−Loss Forward		−750	−1,000	−193					
Taxable Inc	−750	−1,000	−193	342	401	209	0	−223	−150
−Tax @ 38%	0	0	0	−130	−152	−79	0	85	57
Net Income	−750	−1,000	−193	212	249	130	0	−138	−93
+Depreciation			143	245	175	125	89		
+Write-off								223	
+Depletion			199	172	139	100	15		100
+Loss Forward		750	1,000	193					
−Cap. Costs	−100	−1,000							
Cash Flow	−850	−1,250	1,149	822	563	355	104	85	7

PW Eq: $0 = -850 - 1{,}250(P/F_{i,1}) + 1{,}149(P/F_{i,2}) + 822(P/F_{i,3}) + 563(P/F_{i,4})$

$$+ 355(P/F_{i,5}) + 189(P/F_{i,6}) \qquad \text{DCFROR} = 16.3\%$$

NPV @ 15% = +$52.4

*Risk adjust Case A for a 40% probability of success after the year 0
expenditures. A $50,000 abandonment cost is incurred in year 1 if the
project fails along with a write-off of the $100,000 acquisition cost.*

Risk Adjusted PW Eq:

$0 = -850 + [-1{,}250(P/F_{i,1}) + 1{,}149(P/F_{i,2}) + 822(P/F_{i,3}) + 563(P/F_{i,4})$

$$+ 355(P/F_{i,5}) + 189(P/F_{i,6})](.4) + 7(P/F_{i,1})(.6)$$

Applying the probabilities to the cash flow streams and combining gives:

$0 = -850 - 495.8(P/F_{i,1}) + 459.6(P/F_{i,2}) + 328.8(P/F_{i,3}) + 225.2(P/F_{i,4})$

$$+ 142.0(P/F_{i,5}) + 75.6(P/F_{i,6})$$

Expected DCFROR = -3.0%,   **Expected NPV @ 15%** = -$485

8-8 Solution: *Values in Thousands of Dollars*

Case A) *9 Year Evaluation Life*

Year	0	1	2-7	8	9
Revenue		400	400	400	500*
-Operating Costs		-200	-200	-200	-200
-Depreciation		-30	-60	-30	
-Write-offs					-100
Taxable Income		170	140	170	200
-Tax @ 35%		-59	-49	-59	-70
Net Income		111	91	111	130
+Depreciation		30	60	30	
+Write-offs					100
-Capital Costs	-520				
Cash Flow	-520	141	151	141	230

* *Revenue includes Working Capital Return.*

PW Eq: $0 = -520 + 141(P/F_{i,1}) + 151(P/A_{i,6})(P/F_{i,1}) + 141(P/F_{i,8})$
$$+ 230(P/F_{i,9})$$

DCFROR = 25.2%

NPV @ 15% = +$210

Case B) *18 Year Evaluation Life*

Year	0	1	2-7	8	9-17	18
Revenue		400	400	400	400	500*
-Operating Costs		-200	-200	-200	-200	-200
-Depreciation		-30	-60	-30		
-Write-offs						-100
Taxable Income		170	140	170	200	200
-Tax @ 35%		-59	-49	-59	-70	-70
Net Income		111	91	111	130	130
+Depreciation		30	60	30		
+Write-offs						100
-Capital Costs	-520					
Cash Flow	-520	141	151	141	130	230

* *Revenue includes Working Capital Return.*

PW Eq: $0 = -520 + 141(P/F_{i,1}) + 151(P/A_{i,6})(P/F_{i,1}) + 141(P/F_{i,8})$
$$+ 130(P/A_{i,9})(P/F_{i,8}) + 230(P/F_{i,18})$$

DCFROR = 27.7%

NPV @ 15% = +$366

8-9 Solution: *Costs ($) and Production (Gal) in Thousands*

Processing Facility

Production, (Gal)		62	53	35	24	17
Research & Exper.	750	250				
Equipment		670				
Patent Rights	100					
Operating Costs		175	193	212	233	256
Price, ($/Gal)		26.0	26.0	26.0	27.3	28.7

Case 1A, Expense Cash Flows

Year	Time 0	1	2	3	4	5	Salv
Production		62	53	35	24	17	
Gross Revenue		1,612	1,378	910	655	488	
-Royalties		-226	-193	-127	-92	-68	
Net Revenue		1,386	1,185	783	563	420	
-Operating Costs		-175	-193	-212	-233	-256	
-Research	-750	-250					
-Depreciation		-96	-164	-117	-84	-60	-149
-Amortization	-20	-20	-20	-20	-20		
Taxable Income	-770	846	808	433	227	104	-149
-Tax Due @ 40%	308	-338	-323	-173	-91	-42	60
Net Income	-462	507	485	260	136	62	-89
+Depreciation		96	164	117	84	60	149
+Amortization	20	20	20	20	20		
-Capital Costs	-100*	-670**					
Cash Flow	-542	-47	669	397	240	122	60

$$\underbrace{\qquad\qquad}_{182}$$

* The year 0 capital cost is the $100 patent rights acquisition cost.
** The year 1 capital cost is the $670 equipment cost.

PW Eq: $0 = -542 - 47(P/F_{i,1}) + 669(P/F_{i,2}) + 397(P/F_{i,3}) + 240(P/F_{i,4})$
$$+ 182(P/F_{i,5}) \quad i = \text{DCFROR} = 40.6\% > i^* \text{ of } 15\%, \textit{ accept}$$

NPV @ 15% $= -542 - 47(P/F_{15,1}) + 669(P/F_{15,2}) + 397(P/F_{15,3}) + 240(P/F_{15,4})$
$$+ 182(P/F_{15,5}) = +\$412 > 0, \textit{ accept}$$

PVR $= 412 / [542 + 47(P/F_{15,1})] = +0.71 > 0, \textit{ accept}$

8-9 Solution: *Continued*

Case 1B, Stand Alone Cash Flows

Year	Time 0	1	2	3	4	5	Salv
Production		62	53	35	24	17	
Gross Revenue		1,612	1,378	910	655	488	
−Royalties		−226	−193	−127	−92	−68	
Net Revenue		1,386	1,185	783	563	420	
−Operating Costs		−175	−193	−212	−233	−256	
−Research	−750	−250					
−Depreciation		−96	−164	−117	−84	−60	−149
−Amortization	−20	−20	−20	−20	−20		
−Loss Forward		−770					
Taxable Income	−770	76	808	433	227	104	−149
−Tax Due @ 40%		−30	−323	−173	−91	−42	60
Net Income	−770	45	485	260	136	62	−89
+Depreciation		96	164	117	84	60	149
+Amortization	20	20	20	20	20		
+Loss Forward		770					
−Capital Costs	−100*	−670**					
Cash Flow	−850	261	669	397	240	122	60

$$\underbrace{\qquad\qquad}_{182}$$

* The year 0 Capital Cost is the $100 patent rights acquisition cost.

** The year 1 capital cost is the $670 equipment cost.

PW Eq: $O = -850 + 261(P/F_{i,1}) + 669(P/F_{i,2}) + 397(P/F_{i,3}) + 240(P/F_{i,4})$

$\qquad + 182(P/F_{i,5})$ **i = DCFROR** = 33.9% > i* of 15%, *accept*

NPV @ 15% = $-850 + 261(P/F_{15,1}) + 669(P/F_{15,2}) + 397(P/F_{15,3})$

$\qquad + 240(P/F_{15,4}) + 182(P/F_{15,5}) = +\$371 > 0$, *accept*

PVR = 371 / 850 = +0.44 > 0, *accept*

8-9 Solution: *Continued*

Case 2, Risk Analysis for Part 1A
Non-Risk Adjusted Cash Flows

Cash Flow	-542 p=0.40	-47	669	397	240	182
Year	0	1	2	3	4	5

p=0.60

-Abandonment Cost	-70
-Patent Bk Value Write-off	-80
Taxable Income	-150
-Tax @ 40%	60
Net Income	-90
+ Write-off	80
Failure Cash Flow	-10

Risk Adjusted Cash Flows

Expected
Value

Cash Flows	-542	-25*	268	159	96	73
Year	0	1	2	3	4	5

* *Yr 1 cash flow is determined by combining the two expected cash flows as follows: (-10)(.6) + (-47)(.4) = -25.*

Expected Discounted Cash Flow Rate of Return:

PW Eq: $0 = -542 - 25(P/F_{i,1}) + 268(P/F_{i,2}) + 159(P/F_{i,3}) + 96(P/F_{i,4})$

$\qquad + 73(P/F_{i,5})$, **i = Expected DCFROR** = 1.7% < i* of 15%, *reject*

Expected Net Present Value:

ENPV @ 15% = $-542 - 25(P/F_{15,1}) + 268(P/F_{15,2}) + 159(P/F_{15,3})$

$\qquad + 96(P/F_{15,4}) + 73(P/F_{15,5}) = -\$166 < 0$, reject

Expected Present Value Ratio:

$$\qquad\qquad\qquad 0.8696$$
EPVR = $-166 / [542+25(P/F_{15,1})] = -0.29 < 0$, *reject*

8-9 Solution: *Continued*

Case 3, Break-even Analysis of Case 1A Cash Flows

Year	Time 0	1	2	3	4	5	Salvage
Total Production		62	53	35	24	17	
Net Production (86%)		53	46	30	21	15	
Net Revenue		53X	46X	30X	21X	15X	
-Operating Costs		-175	-193	-212	-233	-256	
-Research	-750	-250					
-Depreciation		-96	-164	-117	-84	-60	-149
-Amortization	-20	-20	-20	-20	-20		
Taxable Income	-770	53X-541	46X-377	30X-349	21X-337	15X-316	-149
-Tax Due @ 40%	308	-21X+216	-18X+151	-12X+140	-8X+135	-6X+126	60
Net Income	-462	32X-325	28X-226	18X-209	13X-202	9X-190	-89
+Depreciation		96	164	117	84	60	149
+Amortization	20	20	20	20	20		
-Capital Costs	-100	-670					
Cash Flow	-542	32X-879	28X-42	18X-72	13X-98	9X-130	60

Present Worth Equation:

$$0 = -542 + (32X-879)(P/F_{15,1}) + (28X-42)(P/F_{15,2}) + (18X-72)(P/F_{15,3})$$

with values 0.8696, 0.7561, 0.6575

$$+ (13X-98)(P/F_{15,4}) + (9X-70)(P/F_{15,5})$$

with values 0.5718, 0.4972

$$0 = 72.74X - 1,476.32, \text{ therefore, } X = \$20.30$$

Break-even Selling Price X = $20.30 per gallon

8-9 Solution: *Continued*

Case 4, *Before-tax Acquisition Cost Analysis*

A break-even cost analysis assuming the acquisition cost will be treated like a patent cost for tax purposes and amortized over 5 years.

Cash Flows From Part 1A

Cash Flow	-542	-47	669	397	240	182
Year	0	1	2	3	4	5

NPV from Part 1A = $412

This NPV represents additional after-tax acquisition cost that can be incurred and still give the investor a 15% DCFROR. Let the before-tax acquisition cost equal "X" and be subject to 5 year amortization. The tax savings generated from the additional amortization deductions above those associated with the $100,000 patent rights fee are calculated as follows:

Before-Tax Value		Tax Savings	
Yr 0:	X(1/5) = .20X	.20X(.4) = .08X
Yr 1:	X(1/5) = .20X	.20X(.4) = .08X
Yr 2:	X(1/5) = .20X	.20X(.4) = .08X
Yr 3:	X(1/5) = .20X	.20X(.4) = .08X
Yr 4:	X(1/5) = .20X	.20X(.4) = .08X

$$X = 412 + 0.08X + 0.08X\overset{2.855}{(P/A_{15,4})}$$

Break-even Acquisition Cost = $596

Therefore, X = $596 is the before-tax break-even acquisition cost that could be incurred and still have the project earn the desired 15% after-tax minimum rate of return.

8-10 Solution: *Costs ($) and Production (Bbl) in Thousands*

Petroleum Project

Production (Bbls)		62	53	35	24	17
Intangibles (IDC's)	750	250				
Tangible (Completion)		670				
Mineral Rights Acq.	100					
Operating Costs		175	193	212	233	256
Price, ($/Bbl)		26.0	26.0	26.0	27.3	28.7

Case 1A) Integrated Producer, Expense Cash Flows

Year	0	1	2	3	4	5
Gross Revenue		1,612	1,378	910	655	488
-Royalties		-226	-193	-127	-92	-68
Net Revenue		1,386	1,185	783	563	420
-Oper Costs		-175	-193	-212	-233	-256
-Intangible	-525	-175				
-Depreciation		-96	-164	-117	-84	-60
-Deprec Write-off						-149
-Amortization	-45	-60	-60	-60	-60	-15
-Cost Depln		-32	-28	-18	-13	-9
Taxable Income	-570	848	740	376	173	-69
-Tax @ 40%	228	-339	-296	-150	-70	27
Net Income	-342	509	444	226	103	-42
+Deprec/Write-off		96	164	117	84	209
+Depletion		32	28	18	13	9
+Amortization	45	60	60	60	60	15
-Capital Costs	-325*	-745**				
Cash Flow	-622	-48	696	421	260	191

* *Capital cost includes $100 mineral rights acquisition and 30% of $750
IDC's that must be amortized over 60 months.*

** *Capital cost includes $670 tangible cost and 30% of $250 IDC's.*

PW Eq: $0 = -622 - 48(P/F_{i,1}) + 696(P/F_{i,2}) + 421(P/F_{i,3}) + 260(P/F_{i,4})$

$$+ 191(P/F_{i,5}), \quad \textbf{i = DCFROR} = 36.3\% > i^* \text{ of } 15\%, \text{ } accept$$

$$ 0.8696 0.7561 0.6575 0.5718$$
NPV @ 15% $= -622 - 48(P/F_{15,1}) + 696(P/F_{15,2}) + 421(P/F_{15,3}) + 260(P/F_{15,4})$

$$ 0.4972$$
$$+ 191(P/F_{15,5}) = +383 > 0, \text{ } accept$$

PVR $= 383 / \{622 + 48(P/F_{15,1})\} = 0.58 > 0, \text{ } accept$

8-10 Solution: *Continued*

Case 1B) Integrated Producer, Stand Alone Cash Flows

Year	0	1	2	3	4	5
Gross Revenue		1,612	1,378	910	655	488
-Royalties		-226	-193	-127	-92	-68
Net Revenue		1,386	1,185	783	563	420
-Oper Costs		-175	-193	-212	-233	-256
-Intangible	-525	-175				
-Depreciation		-96	-164	-117	-84	-60
-Deprec Write-off					-149	
-Amortization	-45	-60	-60	-60	-60	-15
-Cost Depletion		-32	-28	-18	-13	-9
-Loss Forward		-570				
Taxable Income	-570	278	740	376	173	-69
-Tax @ 40%		-111	-296	-150	-70	27
Net Income	-570	167	444	226	103	-42
+Deprec/Write-off		96	164	117	84	209
+Cost Depletion		32	28	18	13	9
+Amortization	45	60	60	60	60	15
+Loss Forward		570				
-Capital Costs	-325*	-745**				
Cash Flow	-850	180	696	421	260	191

* Capital cost includes $100 mineral rights acquisition and 30% of $750 IDC's that must be amortized over 60 months.

** Capital cost includes $670 tangible cost and 30% of $250 IDC's.

PW Eq: $0 = -850 + 180(P/F_{i,1}) + 696(P/F_{i,2}) + 421(P/F_{i,3}) + 260(P/F_{i,4}) + 191(P/F_{i,5})$, i = **DCFROR** = 32.1% > i^* of 15%, *accept*

NPV @ 15% = $-850 + 180(P/F_{15,1}) + 696(P/F_{15,2}) + 421(P/F_{15,3}) + 260(P/F_{15,4}) + 191(P/F_{15,5})$ = +353 > 0, *accept*

PVR = 353 / 850 = 0.42 > 0, *accept*

8-10 Solution: *Continued*

Case 2) *Integrated Producer, Risk Adjusted Case 1A Cash Flows*

Non-Risk Adjusted Cash Flows

Cash Flow	-622 p=0.40	-48	696	421	260	191
Year	0	1	2	3	4	5

p=0.60

-Abandonment Cost	-70
-30% Unamortized IDC	-180
-Cost Depl Write-off	-100
Taxable Income	-350
-Tax @ 40%	140
Net Income	-210
+ Write-offs	280
Failure Cash Flow	+70

Risk Adjusted Cash Flows (40% Probability of Success)

Expected
Value

Cash Flows	-622	23*	278	168	104	76
Year	0	1	2	3	4	5

* *Cash Flow = -48(0.4) + 70(0.6) = +23*

Expected Discounted Cash Flow Rate of Return:

PW Eq: $0 = -622 + 23(P/F_{i,1}) + 278(P/F_{i,2}) + 168(P/F_{i,3}) + 104(P/F_{i,4})$

$+ 76(P/F_{i,5})$, **i = Expected DCFROR** = 1.5% < i* of 15%, *reject*

Expected Net Present Value:

ENPV @ 15% = $-622 + 23(P/F_{15,1}) + 278(P/F_{15,2}) + 168(P/F_{15,3})$

$+ 104(P/F_{15,4}) + 76(P/F_{15,5}) = -184.1 < 0$, *reject*

Expected Present Value Ratio:

EPVR = -184.1 / 622 = -0.296 < 0, *reject*

8-10 Solution: *Continued*

Case 3) Independent Producer > 1,000 Bbls/Day, Expense Cash Flows

Year	Time 0	1	2	3	4	5	Salv
Production		62	53	35	24	17	
Gross Revenue		1,612	1,378	910	655	488	
-Royalties		-226	-193	-127	-92	-68	
Net Revenue		1,386	1,185	783	563	420	
-Operating Costs		-175	-193	-212	-233	-256	
-Intangible Drilling	-750	-250					
-Depreciation		-96	-164	-117	-84	-60	-149
-Cost Depletion		-32	-28	-18	-13	-9	
Taxable Income	-750	833	800	435	234	95	-149
-Tax Due @ 40%	300	-333	-320	-174	-94	-38	60
Net Income	-450	500	480	261	141	57	-89
+Depreciation		96	164	117	84	60	149
+Cost Depletion		32	28	18	13	9	
-Capital Costs*	-100*	-670**					
Cash Flow	-550	-42	672	397	237	126	60

* The year 0 capital cost equals the $100 mineral rights acquisition.
** Year 1 capital cost is the $670 tangible cost.

PW Eq: $0 = -550 - 42(P/F_{i,1}) + 672(P/F_{i,2}) + 397(P/F_{i,3}) + 237(P/F_{i,4})$
$+ 186(P/F_{i,5})$,   **i = DCFROR** = 40.3% > i* of 15%, *accept*

$$\qquad\qquad 0.8696 \qquad\quad 0.7561 \qquad\quad 0.6575 \qquad\qquad 0.5718$$
NPV @ 15% = $-550 - 42(P/F_{15,1}) + 672(P/F_{15,2}) + 397(P/F_{15,3}) + 237(P/F_{15,4})$
$$0.4972$$
$+ 186(P/F_{15,5}) = +\$410 > 0$, *accept*

$$0.8696$$
PVR = $410 / \{550 + 42(P/F_{15,1})\} = +0.70 > 0$, *accept*

8-10 Solution: *Continued*

Case 3) Independent Producer > 1,000 Bbls/Day, Stand Alone Cash Flows

Year	Time 0	1	2	3	4	5	Salv.
Production		62	53	35	24	17	
Gross Revenue		1,612	1,378	910	655	488	
-Royalties		-226	-193	-127	-92	-68	
Net Revenue		1,386	1,185	783	563	420	
-Operating Costs		-175	-193	-212	-233	-256	
-Intangible Drilling	-750	-250					
-Depreciation		-96	-164	-117	-84	-60	-149
-Cost Depletion		-32	-28	-18	-13	-9	
-Loss Forward		-750					
Taxable	-750	83	800	435	234	95	-149
-Tax Due		-33	-320	-174	-94	-38	60
Net Income	-750	50	480	261	141	57	-89
+Depreciation		96	164	117	84	60	149
+Cost Depletion		32	28	18	13	9	
+Loss Forward		750					
-Capital Costs	-100*	-670**					
Cash Flow	-850	258	672	397	237	126	60

*   *The year 0 capital cost equals the $100 mineral rights acquisition.*
** *Year 1 capital cost is the $670 tangible cost.*

PW Eq: $0 = -850 + 258(P/F_{i,1}) + 672(P/F_{i,2}) + 397(P/F_{i,3}) + 237(P/F_{i,4})$

$+ 186(P/F_{i,5})$,   **i = DCFROR** = 33.9% > i^* of 15%, *accept*

$$\overset{0.8696}{} \qquad \overset{0.7561}{} \qquad \overset{0.6575}{}$$

NPV @ 15% $= -850 + 258(P/F_{15,1}) + 672(P/F_{15,2}) + 397(P/F_{15,3})$

$$\overset{0.5718}{} \qquad \overset{0.4972}{}$$

$+ 237(P/F_{15,4}) + 186(P/F_{15,5}) = +\$371 > 0$, *accept*

PVR $= 371 / 850 = +0.44 > 0$, *accept*

8-10 Solution: *Continued*

Case 3) *Independent Producer > 1,000 Bbls/Day, Risk Analysis*
Non-Risk Adjusted Cash Flows

Cash Flow	-550 p=0.40	-42	672	397	237	186
Year	0	1	2	3	4	5

p=0.60

-Abandonment Cost	-70
-Cost Depl Write-off	-100
Taxable Income	-170
-Tax @ 40%	68
Net Income	-102
+ Write-offs	100
Failure Cash Flow	-2

Risk Adjusted Cash Flows for 40% Probability of Success

Expected
Value

Cash Flows	-550	-18*	269	159	95	74
Year	0	1	2	3	4	5

* Cash Flow = -42(.4) - 2(.6) = -18

Expected Discounted Cash Flow Rate of Return:

PW Eq: $0 = -550 - 18(P/F_{i,1}) + 269(P/F_{i,2}) + 159(P/F_{i,3}) + 95(P/F_{i,4})$

$+ 74(P/F_{i,5})$, **i = Expected DCFROR** = 1.7% < i* of 15%, *reject*

Expected Net Present Value:

ENPV @ 15% = $-550 - 18(P/F_{15,1}) + 269(P/F_{15,2}) + 159(P/F_{15,3})$

$+ 95(P/F_{15,4}) + 74(P/F_{15,5}) = -167 < 0$, *reject*

Expected Present Value Ratio:

0.8696

EPVR = $-167 / [550 + 18(P/F_{15,1})] = -0.30 < 0$, *reject*

8-10 Solution: *Continued*

Case 4) *Independent Producer < 1,000 Bbls/Day, Expense Cash Flows*

Year	0	1	2	3	4	5	5 Salv
Gross Revenue		1,612	1,378	910	655	488	
-Royalties		-226	-193	-127	-92	-68	
Net Revenue		1,386	1,185	783	563	420	
-Operating Costs		-175	-193	-212	-233	-256	
-Intangible	-750	-250					
-Depreciation		-96	-164	-117	-84	-60	
-Deprec Write-off							-149
Before Depletion	-750	866	828	453	247	104	-149
-100% Limit		866	828	453	247	104	
-Percent Deplet		-208	-178	-117	-85	-63	
-Cost Depletion		32					
Taxable Income	-750	658	650	336	162	41	-149
-Tax @ 40%	300	-263	-260	-134	-65	-16	60
Net Income	-450	395	390	202	97	25	-89
+Depreciation		96	164	117	84	60	149
+Depletion		208	178	117	85	63	
-Capital Costs	-100*	-670**					
Cash Flow	-550	28	732	436	266	148	60

$$\underbrace{}_{208}$$

* *Capital Cost is the $100 mineral rights acquisition cost.*
** *Capital Cost is the $670 tangible equipment cost.*

PW Eq: $0 = -550 + 28(P/F_{i,1}) + 732(P/F_{i,2}) + 436(P/F_{i,3}) + 266(P/F_{i,4})$
$+ 208(P/F_{i,5})$, **i = DCFROR** $= 50.3\% > i^*$ *of* 15%, *accept*

NPV @ 15% $= -550 + 28(P/F_{15,1}) + 732(P/F_{15,2}) + 436(P/F_{15,3}) + 266(P/F_{15,4})$
$+ 208(P/F_{15,5}) = 570.0 > 0$, *accept*

PVR $= 570 / 550 = 1.04 > 0$, *accept*

8-10 Solution: *Continued*

Case 4) Independent Producer < 1,000 Bbls/Day, Stand Alone Cash Flows

Year	0	1	2	3	4	5	5 Salv
Gross Revenue		1,612	1,378	910	655	488	
-Royalties		-226	-193	-127	-92	-68	
Net Revenue		1,386	1,185	783	563	420	
-Oper Costs		-175	-193	-212	-233	-256	
-Intangible	-750	-250					
-Depreciation		-96	-164	-117	-84	-60	
-Deprec Write-off							-149
Before Deplet	-750	866	828	453	247	104	-149
-100% Limit		866	828	453	247	104	
-Percent Depl		-208	-178	-117	-85	-63	
-Cost Depltn		32					
-Loss Forward		-750	-92				
Taxable Income	-750	-92	558	336	162	41	-149
-Tax @ 40%			-223	-134	-65	-16	60
Net Income	-750	-92	335	202	97	25	-89
+Depreciation		96	164	117	84	60	149
+Depletion		208	178	117	85	63	
+Loss Forward		750	92				
-Capital Costs	-100*	-670**					
Cash Flow	-850	291	769	436	266	148	60

$$\underbrace{}_{208}$$

* *Capital Cost is the $100 mineral rights acquisition cost.*

** *Capital Cost is the $670 tangible equipment cost.*

PW Eq: $0 = -850 + 291(P/F_{i,1}) + 769(P/F_{i,2}) + 436(P/F_{i,3}) + 266(P/F_{i,4})$

$+ 208(P/F_{i,5}),$ **i = DCFROR** $= 41.25\% > i^{*}$ of 15%, *accept*

NPV @ 15% $= -850 + 291(P/F_{15,1}) + 769(P/F_{15,2}) + 436(P/F_{15,3})$

$+ 266(P/F_{15,4}) + 208(P/F_{15,5}) = +526.7 > 0,$ *accept*

PVR $= 526.7 \ / \ 850 = 0.62 > 0$ *accept*

8-10 Solution: *Continued*

Case 4)   Independent Producer < 1,000 Bbls/Day,   Risk Analysis
Non-Risk Adjusted Cash Flows

Cash Flow	-550	p=0.40	28	732	436	266	208

Year	0	1	2	3	4	5

p=0.60

-Abandonment Cost	-70
-Cost Depl Write-off	-100
Taxable Income	-170
-Tax @ 40%	68
Net Income	-102
+ Write-offs	100
Failure Cash Flow	-2

Risk Adjusted Cash Flows

Expected
Value

Cash Flows	-550	10*	293	174	106	83

Year	0	1	2	3	4	5

*   Cash Flow is 28(0.4) - 2(0.6) = +10

Expected Discounted Cash Flow Rate of Return:

PW Eq: $0 = -550 + 10(P/F_{i,1}) + 293(P/F_{i,2}) + 174(P/F_{i,3}) + 106(P/F_{i,4})$
$+ 83(P/F_{i,5})$,   **i = Expected DCFROR = 6.8% < i* of 15%**, *reject*

Expected Net Present Value:

ENPV @ 15% $= -550 + 10(P/F_{15,1}) + 293(P/F_{15,2}) + 174(P/F_{15,3})$
$+ 106(P/F_{15,4}) + 83(P/F_{15,5}) = -103 < 0$, *reject*

Expected Present Value Ratio:

EPVR $= -103 / 550 = -0.19 < 0$, *reject*

8-10 Solution: *Continued*

Case 5) *Integrated Producer, Break-even Price/Unit Analysis* *Case 1A, Expense Economics*

Year	0	1	2	3	4	5
Net Revenue		.86X(62)	.86X(53)	.86X(35)	.86X(24)	.86X(17)
-Oper Costs		-175	-193	-212	-233	-256
-Intangible	-525	-175				
-Depreciation		-96	-164	-117	-84	-60
-Deprec Write-off						-149
-Amortization	-45	-60	-60	-60	-60	-15
-Cost Depletion		-32	-28	-18	-13	-9
Taxable Income	-570	53X-538	46X-445	30X-408	21X-389	15X-489
-Tax @ 40%	228	-21X+215	-18X+178	-12X+163	-8X+156	-6X+196
Net Income	-342	32X-323	28X-267	18X-245	13X-234	9X-294
+Depreciation		96	164	117	84	209
+Cost Depletion		32	28	18	13	9
+Amortization	45	60	60	60	60	15
-Capital Costs	-325	-745				
Cash Flow	-622	32X-880	28X-15	18X-49	13X-77	9X-60

$$0 = -622 + (32X-880)\underset{0.8696}{(P/F_{15,1})} + (28X-15)\underset{0.7561}{(P/F_{15,2})} + (18X-49)\underset{0.6575}{(P/F_{15,3})}$$

$$+ (13X-77)\underset{0.5718}{(P/F_{15,4})} + (9X-60)\underset{0.4972}{(P/F_{15,5})}$$

$0 = 72.74X - 1,504.63$, *therefore,* $X = \$20.69$

Break-even Selling Price Per Unit = $20.69 per barrel

8-10 Solution: *Continued*

Case 6)   Integrated Producer, Acquisition Break-even Cost
Cash Flows from Part 1A:

Year	0	1	2	3	4	5
Cash Flow	-622	-48	696	421	261	191

Part 1A Net Present Value = $383.54

This NPV represents additional after-tax acquisition cost that can be incurred and still give the investor a 15% DCFROR. Let the before-tax acquisition cost equal "X" and be subject to cost depletion. The tax savings generated from the additional cost depletion deductions above those associated with the $100,000 acquisition fee are calculated as follows:

	Before-Tax Value		Tax Savings	
Yr 1:	X(62/191)	= .32X	.32X(.4) =	.13X
Yr 2:	.68X(53/129)	= .28X	.28X(.4) =	.11X
Yr 3:	.40X(35/76)	= .18X	.18X(.4) =	.07X
Yr 4:	.22X(24/41)	= .13X	.13X(.4) =	.05X
Yr 5:	.09X(17/17)	= .09X	.09X(.4) =	.04X

$$\begin{array}{ccc} 0.8696 & 0.7561 & 0.6575 \end{array}$$
$$0 = .13X(P/F_{15,1}) + .11X(P/F_{15,2}) + .07X(P/F_{15,3})$$

$$\begin{array}{cc} 0.5718 & 0.4972 \end{array}$$
$$+ .05X(P/F_{15,4}) + .04X(P/F_{15,5}) = .2907X$$

$X - .2907X = \$383.54$ NPV, *therefore*, $X = 540.73$

Break-even Acquisition Cost = $540,730

An integrated producer who can expense deductions against other income could invest $540,730 to acquire the mineral rights to this project and still have the project earn a 15% DCFROR.

8-11 Solution: *Costs and Production in Thousands*

Mining Project

Production in Tons		62	53	35	24	17
Mineral Develop	750	250				
Mining Equipment		670				
Mineral Rights Acq.	100					
Operating Costs		175	193	212	233	256
Price, $ Per Ton		26.0	26.0	26.0	27.3	28.7

Case 1A) *Corporate Mining, Expense Cash Flows*

Year	0	1	2	3	4	5	Salv
Gross Revenue		1,612	1,378	910	655	488	
-Royalties		-226	-193	-127	-92	-68	
Net Revenue		1,386	1,185	783	563	420	
-Oper Costs		-175	-193	-212	-233	-256	
-Development	-525	-175					
-Depreciation		-96	-164	-117	-84	-60	
-Deprec Write-off							-149
-Amortization	-45	-60	-60	-60	-60	-15	
Before Depletion	-570	881	768	393	187	89	-149
-50% Limit		440	384	197	93	-45	
-Percent Depletion		-208	-178	-117	-85	63	
-Cost Depletion		32					
Taxable Income	-570	673	590	276	102	44	-149
-Tax @ 40%	228	-269	-236	-110	-41	-18	60
Net Income	-342	404	354	166	61	26	-89
+Depreciation		96	164	117	84	60	149
+Depletion Taken		208	178	117	85	45	
+Amortization	45	60	60	60	60	15	
-Capital Costs	-325*	-745**					
Cash Flow	-622	22	756	460	290	146	60

$$\underbrace{}_{206}$$

* Capital cost includes $100 mineral rights acquisition and 30% of $750 development that must be amortized over 60 months.

** Capital cost includes $670 equipment cost and 30% of $250 development cost.

PW Eq: $0 = -622 + 22(P/F_{i,1}) + 756(P/F_{i,2}) + 460(P/F_{i,3}) + 290(P/F_{i,4})$

$+ 206(P/F_{i,5})$ **i = DCFROR** = 45.1%

NPV @ 15% = $-622 + 22(P/F_{15,1}) + 756(P/F_{15,2}) + 460(P/F_{15,3}) + 290(P/F_{15,4})$

$+ 206(P/F_{15,5}) = +\$539$

PVR = 539 / 622 = 0.87

8-11 Solution: *Continued*

Case 1B) *Corporate Mining, Stand Alone Cash Flows*

Year	0	1	2	3	4	5	Salv
Gross Revenue		1,612	1,378	910	655	488	
-Royalties		-226	-193	-127	-92	-68	
Net Revenue		1,386	1,185	783	563	420	
-Oper Costs		-175	-193	-212	-233	-256	
-Development	-525	-175					
-Depreciation		-96	-164	-117	-84	-60	
-Deprec Write-offs							-149
-Amortization	-45	-60	-60	-60	-60	-15	
Before Depletion	-570	881	768	393	187	89	-149
-50% Limit		440	384	197	93	-45	
-Percent Depl.		-208	-178	-117	-85	63	
-Cost Depletion		32					
-Loss Forward		-570					
Taxable Income	-570	103	590	276	102	44	-149
-Tax @ 40%		-41	-236	-110	-41	-18	60
Net Income	-570	62	354	166	61	26	-89
+Deprec/Write-offs		96	164	117	84	60	149
+Depletion Taken		208	178	117	85	45	
+Amortization	45	60	60	60	60	15	
+Loss Forward		570					
-Capital Costs	-325*	-745**					
Cash Flow	-850	250	756	460	290	146	60

$$\underbrace{\qquad\qquad}_{206}$$

* *Capital cost includes $100 mineral rights acquisition and 30% of $750 development that must be amortized over 60 months.*

** *Capital cost includes $670 equipment cost and 30% of $250 development cost.*

PW Eq: $0 = -850 + 250(P/F_{i,1}) + 756(P/F_{i,2}) + 460(P/F_{i,3}) + 290(P/F_{i,4})$

$+ 206(P/F_{i,5})$ **i = DCFROR = 39.7%**

NPV @ 15% $= -850 + 250(P/F_{15,1}) + 756(P/F_{15,2}) + 460(P/F_{15,3})$

$+ 290(P/F_{15,4}) + 206(P/F_{15,5}) = +\$510$

PVR $= 510 / 850 = .60$

8-11 Solution: Continued

Case 2) *Corporate Mining, Risk Adjustment Based on Case 1A*
Non-Risk Adjusted Cash Flows

Cash Flow	-622	p=0.40	22	756	460	290	206
Year	0		1	2	3	4	5

p=0.60

-Abandonment Cost	-70
-30% Unamortized Develop.	-180
-Cost Depl Write-off	-100
Taxable Income	-350
-Tax @ 40%	140
Net Income	-210
+ Write-offs	280
Failure Cash Flow	+70

Risk Adjusted Cash Flows

Cash Flows	-622		51*	302	184	116	82
Year	0		1	2	3	4	5

* Cash Flow is 22(.4) + 70(.6) = +51

Expected Discounted Cash Flow Rate of Return:

PW Eq: $0 = -622 + 51(P/F_{i,1}) + 302(P/F_{i,2}) + 184(P/F_{i,3}) + 116(P/F_{i,4})$

$+ 82(P/F_{i,5})$ **i = Expected DCFROR** = 6.1% < i* of 15%, *reject*

Expected Net Present Value:

ENPV @ 15% $= -622 + 51(P/F_{15,1}) + 302(P/F_{15,2}) + 184(P/F_{15,3})$

$+ 116(P/F_{15,4}) + 75(P/F_{15,5}) = -121 < 0$, *reject*

Expected Present Value Ratio:

EPVR = -121 / 622 = -0.195 < 0, *reject*

8-11 Solution: *Continued*

Case 3)   *Individual Mineral Producer, Expense Cash Flows*

Year	0	1	2	3	4	5	Salv
Gross Revenue		1,612	1,378	910	655	488	
−Royalties		−226	−193	−127	−92	−68	
Net Revenue		1,386	1,185	783	563	420	
−Oper Costs		−175	−193	−212	−233	−256	
−Development	−750	−250					
−Depreciation		−96	−164	−117	−84	−60	
−Deprec Write-off							−149
Before Depln	−750	866	828	453	247	104	−149
−50% Limit		433	414	227	123	−52	
−Percent Depln		−208	−178	−117	−85	63	
−Cost Depletion		32					
Taxable Income	−750	658	650	336	162	52	−149
−Tax @ 40%	300	−263	−260	−134	−65	−21	60
Net Income	−450	395	390	202	97	31	−89
+Depreciation		96	164	117	84	60	
+Write-off							149
+Depletion Taken		208	178	117	85	52	
−Capital Costs	−100*	−670**					
Cash Flow	−550	28	732	436	266	143	60

$$\underbrace{\qquad\qquad}_{203}$$

*   *Capital cost is the $100 mineral rights acquisition cost.*

** *Capital cost is the $670 equipment cost.*

PW Eq: $0 = -550 + 28(P/F_{i,1}) + 732(P/F_{i,2}) + 436(P/F_{i,3}) + 266(P/F_{i,4})$

$+ 203(P/F_{i,5})$ $i = DCFROR = 50.3\% > 15\%$, *accept*

NPV @ 15% $= -550 + 28(P/F_{15,1}) + 732(P/F_{15,2}) + 436(P/F_{15,3}) + 266(P/F_{15,4})$

$+ 203(P/F_{15,5}) = 567.5 > 0$, *accept*

PVR $= 567.5 / 550 = 1.03 > 0$, *accept*

8-11 Solution: *Continued*

Case 3) *Individual Mineral Producer, Stand Alone Cash Flows*

Year	0	1	2	3	4	5	Salv
Gross Revenue		1,612	1,378	910	655	488	
-Royalties		-226	-193	-127	-92	-68	
Net Revenue		1,386	1,185	783	563	420	
-Oper Costs		-175	-193	-212	-233	-256	
-Development	-750	-250					
-Depreciation		-96	-164	-117	-84	-60	
-Deprec Write-off							-149
Before Depletion	-750	866	828	453	247	104	
-50% Limit		433	414	227	123	-52	
-Percent Depl.		-208	-178	-117	-85	63	
-Cost Depletion		32					
-Loss Forward		-750	-92				
Taxable Income	-750	-92	558	336	162	52	-149
-Tax @ 40%			-223	-134	-65	-21	60
Net Income	-750	-92	335	202	97	31	-89
+Depreciation		96	164	117	84	60	149
+Depletion Taken		208	178	117	85	52	
+Loss Forward		750	92				
-Capital Costs	-100*	-670**					
Cash Flow	-850	291	769	436	266	143	60

203

* Capital cost is the $100 mineral rights acquisition cost.

** Capital cost is the $670 equipment cost.

PW Eq: $0 = -850 + 291(P/F_{i,1}) + 769(P/F_{i,2}) + 436(P/F_{i,3}) + 266(P/F_{i,4})$
$+ 203(P/F_{i,5})$, **i = DCFROR = 41.2% > 15%,** *accept*

NPV @ 15% $= -850 + 291(P/F_{15,1}) + 769(P/F_{15,2}) + 436(P/F_{15,3})$
$+ 266(P/F_{15,4}) + 203(P/F_{15,5}) = +524.2 > 0,$ *accept*

PVR $= 524.2 / 850 = 0.62 > 0,$ *accept*

8-11 Solution: *Continued*

Case 3)   *Individual Mineral Producer,*
Risk Adjustment Based on "Expense" Cash Flows

Non-Risk Adjusted Cash Flows

Cash Flow	-550	p=0.40	28	732	436	266	203
Year		0	1	2	3	4	5

p=0.60

-Abandonment Cost	-70
-Cost Depl Write-off	-100
Taxable Income	-170
-Tax @ 40%	68
Net Income	-102
+ Write-offs	100
Failure Cash Flow	-2

Risk Adjusted Cash Flows

Expected
Value

Cash Flows	-550	10*	293	174	106	80
Year	0	1	2	3	4	5

*   Cash Flow is $28(.4) - 2(.6) = +10$

Expected DCFROR:

PW Eq: $0 = -550 + 10(P/F_{i,1}) + 293(P/F_{i,2}) + 174(P/F_{i,3}) + 106(P/F_{i,4})$

$+ 80(P/F_{i,5})$ **i = Expected DCFROR = 6.67% < i*** of 15%, *reject*

Expected Net Present Value:

ENPV @ 15% $= -550 + 10(P/F_{15,1}) + 293(P/F_{15,2}) + 174(P/F_{15,3})$

$+ 106(P/F_{15,4}) + 80(P/F_{15,5}) = -105 < 0,$ *reject*

Expected Present Value Ratio:

PVR $= -105 / 550 = -0.19 < 0,$ *reject*

8-11 Solution: *Continued*

Case 4) *Corporate Mineral Producer, Break-even Selling Price Analysis*

Year	Time 0	1	2	3	4	5	Salv
Total Production		62	53	35	24	17	
Net Production (86%)		53	46	30	21	15	
Net Revenue		53X	46X	30X	21X	15X	
-Operating Costs		-175	-193	-212	-233	-256	
-Development	-525	-175					
-Depreciation		-96	-164	-117	-84	-60	
-Deprec Write-off							-149
-Amortization	-45	-60	-60	-60	-60	-15	
Before Depletion	-570	53X-506	46X-417	30X-389	21X-377	15X-331	-149
-50% Limit		27X-253	23X-208	15X-195	0*	0	
-Percent Depl. (15%)		-8X	-7X	-5X			
-Cost Depletion		32					
Taxable Income	-570	45X-506	39X-417	25X-389	21X-377	15X-331	-149
-Tax @ 40%		228-18X	+202-16X	+167-10X	+156 -8X	+151 -6X	+132 60
Net Income	-342	27X-304	23X-250	15X-233	13X-226	9X-199	-89
+Depreciation		96	164	117	84	60	149
+Depletion Taken		8X	7X	5X			
+Amortization	45	60	60	60	60	15	
-Capital Costs	-325	-745					
Cash Flow	-622	35X-893	30X-26	20X-56	13X-82	9X-124	60

$$9X-64$$

By iterative calculations, percentage depletion is the largest depletion deduction in years 1, 2 & 3 and the 50% limit is zero or near zero in years 4 and 5. Since the cost depletion basis is recovered by the year 1 percentage depletion, no depletion exists in years 4 and 5.

$$
\begin{aligned}
&\qquad\quad 0.8696 \qquad\qquad\qquad 0.7561 \qquad\qquad\qquad 0.6575 \\
0 = {}&-622 + (35X-893)(P/F_{15,1}) + (30X-26)(P/F_{15,2}) + (20X-56)(P/F_{15,3}) \\
&\qquad\quad 0.5718 \qquad\qquad 0.4972 \\
&+ (13X-82)(P/F_{15,4}) + (9X-64)(P/F_{15,5})
\end{aligned}
$$

$$0 = 78.18X - 1{,}533.71, \text{ therefore, } X = \$19.62$$

Break-even Selling Price Per Unit = $19.62 per ton

8-11 Solution: *Continued*

Case 5) *Corporate Mineral Producer, Acquisition Break-even Cost Analysis*

Year	0	1	2	3	4	5	Salv
Revenue		1,612	1,378	910	655	488	
-Royalties		-226	-193	-127	-92	-68	
Net Revenue		1,386	1,185	783	563	420	
-Oper Costs		-175	-193	-212	-233	-256	
-Development	-525	-175					
-Depreciation		-96	-164	-117	-84	-60	
-Deprec Write-off							-149
-Amortization	-45	-60	-60	-60	-60	-15	
Before Depletion	-570	881	768	393	187	89	-149
-50% Limit		440	384	197	93	-45	
-Percent Depl.		-208	-178	-117	-85	63	
-Cost Depletion		32					
Taxable	-570	673	590	276	102	44	-149
-Tax @ 40%	228	-269	-236	-110	-41	-18	60
Net Income	-342	404	354	166	61	26	-89
+Deprec/Write-off		96	164	117	84	60	149
+Depletion		208	178	117	85	45	
+Amortization	45	60	60	60	60	15	
-Capital Costs	-325	-745					
Cash Flow	-622	22	756	460	290	146	60

$$\underbrace{}_{206}$$

Net Present Value = $539

Since percentage depletion is allowed for all mineral producers, if we assume percentage depletion deductions will continue to be larger than the new cost depletion deductions, the before-tax value we could afford to pay for the property is the same as the after-tax net present value of $539,000. Checking this assumption, additional mineral rights cost of $539,000 added to the $100,000 in the analysis statement gives $639,000 total acquisition cost. The first year cost depletion would be $639,000(62/191) = $207,420 which is less than year 1 percentage depletion of $208,000 so percent depletion would still be taken. The additional mineral rights acquisition cost would not affect the depletion deduction so $539,000 is the incremental break-even acquisition cost.

CHAPTER 9 PROBLEM SOLUTIONS

9-1 Solution: *All Values in Dollars*

```
                    525,000(.259)   470,000(.259)   460,000(.259)
               OC =135,980           =121,730          =119,140
OLD:
     _____
     0              1               2                 3

                    C=8,000
                    525,000(.183)   470,000(.183)   460,000(.183)
     C=39,000       OC=96,080        = 86,010         = 84,180
New:
     _____
     0              1               2                 3

                    C=8,000
                    525,000(.076)   470,000(.076)   460,000(.076)
NEW  C=39,000       Savings = 39,900  = 35,720        = 34,960
-OLD:
     _____
     0              1               2                 3
```

Incremental Cash Flows in Escalated Dollars:

Year	0	1	2	3
Savings		39,900	35,720	34,960
-Development		-8,000		
-Depreciation		-3,900	-7,800	-7,800
-Deprec Write-off				-19,500
Taxable Income		28,000	27,920	7,660
-Tax @ 40%		-11,200	-11,168	-3,064
Net Income		16,800	16,752	4,596
+Depreciation		3,900	7,800	27,300
-Capital Costs	-39,000			
Cash Flow	-39,000	20,700	24,552	31,896

Case A) PW Eq: $0 = -39,000+20,700(P/F_{i,1})+24,552(P/F_{i,2})+31,896(P/F_{i,3})$

i = **DCFROR** = 39.9%

Case B) Non-Discounted Pay-back = $1 + (39,000-20,700)/24,552 = 1.75$

Case C) *From Equation 5-1:* $1 + i = (1 + f)(1 + i')$

Constant Dollar DCFROR = $i' = \{(1.399)/(1.1)\} - 1 = .2716$ or 27.2%

Alternatively, Constant Dollar Cash Flows:

```
               20,700(P/F_{10,1})   24,552(P/F_{10,2})   31,896(P/F_{10,3})
-39,000             =18,818             =20,290             =23,963
     _____
     0              1               2                 3
```

PW Eq: $0 = -39,000+18,818(P/F_{i',1})+20,290(P/F_{i',2})+23,963(P/F_{i',3})$

i' = **Constant Dollar DCFROR** = 27.2%, *the same as from Eq 5-1.*

9-2 Solution: *All Values in Thousands of Dollars*

Abandon Now at Yr 0:

	Sunk Costs	
Acq Cost=400	IDC=600	*Write-off All Capital Costs Against Other Income at Yr0*
-2	0	0 *Now* 1

Develop in Month 7 of Year 0 (now):

(Assume $600 IDC was in Month 5 of Yr 0)

Yr 1 Abandon
Salvage=100

$C_{IDC}=100$ P=0.4

$C_{tang}=200$ Rev=420

        P=0.6   OC= 35

	Sunk Costs	
Acq Cost=400	IDC=600	
-2	0	0 *Now* 1

The $400 year -2 acquisition cost and the $600 year 0 IDC are sunk along with the tax deduction for 70% of the $600 year 0 IDC. These values are not relevant to our analysis; the remaining tax effects are.

Depreciation Calculations		Cost Depletion Calculations	
Yr 1: 200(.1429) = 29		Yr 1: 400(25% of Reserves) = 100	
Yr 1: Sale Write-off = 171		Yr 1: Sale Write-off = 300	

Amortization Calculations		
Year 0 $600 IDC	*Year 0 $100 IDC*	*Total*
Yr 0: 180(8/60) = 24		24
Yr 1: 180(12/60) = 36	Yr 0: 30(6/60) = 3	39
Yr 1: Write-off = 120	Yr 1: Write-off = 27	147

Year	*Abandon* 0 *Now*	*Develop & Succeed* 0 *Now*	1	Yr 1 *Sale*	*Fail and* Abandon Yr 1
Gross Revenue			420	350	100
-Royalties			-76		
Net Revenue			344	350	100
-Oper Costs			-60		
-Intangible		-70			
-Depreciation			-29	-171	-200
-Amortization	-180 *write-off*	-27	-36	-147	-183
-Cost Depletion	-400 *write-off*		-100	-300	-400
Taxable Income	-580	-97	119	-268	-683
-Tax @ 40%	232	39	-48	107	273
Net Income	-348	-58	71	-161	-410
+Depreciation			29	171	200
+Cost Depletion	400		100	300	400
+Amortization	180	27	36	147	183
-Capital Costs		-230			
Cash Flow	232	-261	236	457	373

Prob.Success=0.6   Prob.Fail=0.4

$NPV_{Abandon}$ = +$232

$ENPV_{Develop}$ = -261+[236(P/F_{20,1}) + 457(P/F_{20,1})](.6) + 373(P/F_{20,1})(.4)

= +$210 < $NPV_{Abandon}$, *therefore, abandon now.*

9-3 Solution: *All Values in Thousands of Dollars*

Land Acquisition Break-even Sale Price: *Let X = Sale Value*

SELL Cash Flow Calculation:		*ABANDON Cash Flow Calculation:*	
Sale Value	X	Equipment Salvage Value	30
-Book Value Write-off	-5	-Abandon Cost	-20
Taxable Income	X-5	-Book Value Write-off	-5
-Tax @ 40%	-.4X+2	Taxable Income	5
Net Income	.6X-3	-Tax @ 40%	-2
+Book Value Write-off	5	Net Income	3
Cash Flow	.6X+2	+Book Value Write-off	5
		Cash Flow	8

Set "Sale Cash Flow" equal to "Abandon Cash Flow" and solve for the unknown break-even sale value "X":

.6X + 2 = 8, *therefore,* X = $10

9-4 Solution:

C = $60,000   Esc $ Sale Value = $X
```
_____
0                                               2
```

Sale Value in Escalated Dollars	X
-Book Value Write-off	-60,000
Taxable Income	X-60,000
-Tax @ 30%	-.3X+18,000
Net Income	.7X-42,000
+Book Value Write-off	60,000
Cash Flow in Escalated Dollars	.7X+18,000

Constant Dollar Present Worth Equation:

$60,000 = (.7X+18,000)(P/F_{f=10\%,2})(P/F_{i*'=20\%,2})$

$60,000 = .4017X + 10,330$

Break-even Selling Price: X = $123,649

Alternate Solution:

$1 + i = (1 + f)(1 + i')$; so $i^* = (1 + .10)(1 + .20) - 1 = .32$ or 32%

$i^* = 32\%$ is equivalent to $i^{*'} = 20\%$ for 10%/yr inflation, f.

Escalated Dollar Present Worth Equation:

$60,000 = (.7X+18,000)(P/F_{32,2})$ *therefore,* X = $123,649

9-5 Solution: *Values in Thousands of Dollars*

Land Acquisition Break-even Sales Price Analysis:

```
         C=500 (Sunk)    CF=-1,500  P=0.6   1,000 1,800 1,200  800   400
DEVELOP: ───────────────────────────────────────────────────────────────
           -2              0                  1     2     3     4     5
                             P=0.4
                                      CF=0
```

```
         C=500 (Sunk)       CF=800    (Opportunity Cost if Developed)
SELL:    ───────────────────────────────────────────────────────────────
           -2                 0         1     2     3     4     5
```

Yr 0 Sell Cash Flow:

Sale Revenue	1,000
-Book Value Write-off	500
Taxable Income	500
-Tax @ 40%	-200
Net Income	300
+Book Value Write-off	500
Cash Flow	800

Sell NPV:

Sell CF = Sell NPV = +$800

Develop Expected NPV for $i^* = 20\%$:

$$ENPV = -1,500 + [1,000(P/F_{20,1}) + 1,800(P/F_{20,2}) + 1,200(P/F_{20,3})$$
$$+ 800(P/F_{20,4}) + 400(P/F_{20,5})](0.6) = +\$495$$

Therefore, select the maximum NPV and Sell.

Incremental ENPV generates the same economic conclusion:

$ENPV_{Develop-Sell}$ = 495 - 800 = -$305, *reject the develop alternative*

Break-even Probability of Occurrence :

Let "X" equal the break-even probability of success, which is the value of "X" that makes the $ENPV_{DEV} = NPV_{Sell} = +\$800$

```
                  0.8333          0.6944          0.5787
800 = -1,500 + [1,000(P/F20,1) + 1,800(P/F20,2) + 1,200(P/F20,3)
             0.4823          0.4019
      + 800(P/F20,4) + 400(P/F20,5)](X)
```

$$800 = -1,500 + X(3,324.3), \text{ therefore, } X = 0.69 \text{ or } 69\%$$

9-6 Solution: *All Values in Dollars*

Depreciable Costs	100,000	50,000
Working Capital	25,000	
Sale Value		
Revenue		200,000
Operating Costs		140,000

Sale Value: 250,000
Revenue: 200,000, 280,000, 280,000
Operating Costs: 140,000, 190,000, 190,000

Cash Flow Calculations

Year	0	1	2	3	3 Salv.
Revenue		200,000	280,000	280,000	250,000
-Operating Costs		-140,000	-190,000	-190,000	
-Depreciation		-21,429	-36,735	-26,239	
-Deprec Write-off					-65,598
-WC Write-off					-25,000
Taxable Income		38,571	53,265	63,761	159,402
-Tax @ 40%		-15,429	-21,306	-25,504	-63,761
Net Income		23,143	31,959	38,257	95,641
+Depreciation		21,429	36,735	26,239	65,598
+WC Write-off					25,000
-Capital Costs	-125,000	-50,000			
Cash Flow	-125,000	-5,429	68,694	64,496	186,239

250,735

PW Eq: $0 = -125{,}000 - 5{,}429(P/F_{i,1}) + 68{,}694(P/F_{i,2}) + 250{,}735(P/F_{i,3})$

i = DCFROR = 39%

NPV @ i* = 15% = +$87,084

NPV represents additional after-tax cost (negative cash flow) that may be incurred at time zero in addition to $125,000 for the project to yield a DCFROR of 15%. If the equivalent before-tax value is deductible as a development cost at time zero, convert after-tax NPV to the equivalent before tax value by dividing NPV by the sum of one minus the tax rate as follows:

$$87{,}084 / (1-0.4) = \$145{,}140$$

This is the before-tax research or development cost that could be incurred in year 0 and still have the project earn a 15% discounted cash flow rate of return.

9-7 Solution: *All Values in Dollars*

Land Acquisition:

			Rev=250,000
C_{Land}=100,000	OC=2,500	OC=2,500	OC=2,500

0	1	2	3

Cash Flow Calculations:

Year	0	1-3	Yr 3 Sale
Revenue			250,000
-Property Taxes		-2,500	
-Write-off Bk Value			-100,000
Taxable Income		-2,500	150,000
-Tax @ 30%		750	-45,000
Net Income		-1,750	105,000
+Write-off Bk Value			100,000
-Capital Cost	-100,000		
Cash Flow	-100,000	-1,750	205,000

PW Eq: $0 = -100,000 - 1,750(P/A_{i,3}) + 205,000(P/F_{i,3})$

Escalated Dollar DCFROR, i, = 25.6%

Use Equation 5-1 to convert the escalated dollar DCFROR to the equivalent constant dollar DCFROR as follows:

$$1+i = (1+f)(1+i')$$

Constant Dollar DCFROR for 8% inflation:

$i' = (1.256 / 1.08) - 1 = 0.163$ or 16.3%.

9-8 Solution: *All Values in Thousands of Dollars*

Common Stock versus Bonds:

Investment Alternative #1, Purchase Common Stock

```
C=100
_____        F = 100(F/P_10,10) = 259.4
0                                          10
```

Taxable Gain = 259.4 - 100 = $159.4
Tax on Gain = 159.4(0.30) = -$47.8

Yr 10 After-Tax Cash Flow (Future Value) = 259.4 - 47.8 = $211.6

Investment Alternative #2, Purchase Bond

```
C=100     I=10      I=10 . . . . . . . . .  I=10
_____      L=100
0          1         2 . . . . . . . . . . 10
```

Interest Income of $10,000 per year is before-tax and needs to be converted to an after-tax value that represents the actual dollars available to be reinvested at the after-tax money market interest rate of 7.0% (10% - 3%) as follows:

Net Cash Flow From Bond Dividends Each Year: 10 - 10(0.3) = $7.0

Year 10 after-tax cash flow (future value):

$$\text{Year 10 FW} = 7.0\overset{13.816}{(F/A_{7,10})} + 100 \text{ maturity value} = \$196.7$$

Purchase common stock to maximize future value of $211.6 versus $196.7

The required before-tax growth rate for common stock that would make the alternatives economically equivalent is shown below:

Let X = before-tax common stock sale value at year 10 to give after-tax cash flow of $196.7 which equals the bank investment projected future value.

196.7 = Required after-tax year 10 value
196.7 = X - (X-100)(0.3)
196.7 = X - 0.3X + 30
196.7 = 0.7X + 30

Therefore, 0.7X = 196.7 - 30, so X = $238.1

PW Eq: 100 = 238.1(P/F$_{i,10}$),   **Growth Rate, i** = 9.06%

9-9 Solution: *Values in Thousands of Dollars*

Break-even Sales Analysis

Let X = the break-even sales revenue required to give a 25% DCFROR.

Year	0	1	2	3	4	5
Revenue		X	X+10	X+20	X+30	X+40
-Operating Costs		-50.0	-60.0	-70.0	-80.0	-90.0
-Depreciation	-71.5	-122.5	-87.5	-62.5	-45.0	-45.0
-Depr Write-off						-67.0
Taxable Income	-71.5	X-172.5	X-137.5	X-112.5	X-95.0	X-162.0
-Tax @ 40%	28.6	-.4X+69.0	-.4X+55.0	-.4X+45.0	-.4X+38.0	-.4X+64.8
Net Income	-42.9	.6X-103.5	.6X-82.5	.6X-67.5	.6X-57.0	.6X-97.2
+Depreciation	71.5	122.5	87.5	62.5	45.0	45.0
-Depr Write-off						67.0
-Capital Cost	-500.0					
Cash Flow	-471.4	.6X+19.0	.6X+5.0	.6X-5.0	.6X-12.0	.6X+14.8

PW Eq:

$$0 = -471.4 + (.6X + 19)\overset{0.8000}{(P/F_{25,1})} + (.6X + 5)\overset{0.6400}{(P/F_{25,2})}$$

$$+ (.6X - 5.0)\overset{0.512}{(P/F_{25,3})} + (.6X - 12.0)\overset{0.4096}{(P/F_{25,4})}$$

$$+ (.6X + 14.8)\overset{0.3277}{(P/F_{25,5})}$$

$$0 = 1.6136X - 455.63, \textit{ therefore, } X = \$282.37$$

Year 1 Break-even Revenue: $282.37.

This amount will increase by $10 in each succeeding year.

9-10 Solution: *All Values in Thousands of Dollars*

Cash Flows

Year	0	1	2	3	4	5	6
Revenue			900	900	900	900	1,300*
-Operating Costs			-200	-200	-200	-200	-200
-Research/Develop	-100	-300					
-Depreciation		-50	-100	-100	-100	-100	-50
-Work Cap Book Value							-200
Taxable Income	-100	-350	600	600	600	600	850
-Tax @ 40%	40	140	-240	-240	-240	-240	-340
Net Income	-60	-210	360	360	360	360	510
+Depreciation		50	100	100	100	100	50
+Work Cap Book Value							200
-Equipment (Deprec)	-500						
-Working Capital	-200						
Cash Flow	-60	-860	460	460	460	460	760

* Revenue includes working capital return and salvage.

Case A) Net Present Value Analysis

$$NPV = -60-860(P/F_{15,1})+460(P/A_{15,4})(P/F_{15,1})+760(P/F_{15,6}) = +\$663$$

Case B) Additional Before-Tax Research and Development Cost at Year 0

An additional development cost of $X at year 0 that is expensed against other taxable income saves 0.4X in income tax, increasing the negative year 0 cash flow by -0.6X. Setting 0.6X equal to NPV of +663 and solving for X gives the year 0 break-even research or development cost that will exactly make NPV = 0 for i* = 15%.

NPV / (1-tax rate) = 663 / (1-0.4) = $1,105

Case C) Consider $900,000 Sale Offer at Year 1.

Sale CF = 900-(900-0)(0.4 tax rate)=540 after taxes at year 1 = NPV_{Sell}

Yr 1 NPV_{Dev} = -860 + 460$(P/A_{15,4})$ + 760$(P/F_{15,5})$ = 831

NPV_{Dev} > NPV_{Sell} so select Develop.

Case D) What sale value at year 1 makes selling a break-even with developing?

Let X = break-even before-tax sale price at year 1.

X - (X-0)(0.4 tax rate) = 0.6X = CF_{Sell} = NPV_{Sell} = NPV_{Dev} = 831

X = $1,385 = Break-even Project Sale Price

9-10 Solution: *Continued*

Case E) *Additional Cost to Allow a 15% Minimum ROR*

Let X = the unknown additional year zero depreciable cost

Year	0	1	2	3	4	5	6 Salv
Total Rev			900	900	900	900	900	400
-Oper Costs			-200	-200	-200	-200	-200
-Res/Dev	-100	-300					
-Yr 1 Depr		-50	-100	-100	-100	-100	-50
-Acq Depr		-.1X	-.2X	-.2X	-.2X	-.2X	-.1X
-Work Cap								-200

| Taxable | -100 | -350-.1X | 600-.2X | 600-.2X | 600-.2X | 600-.2X | 650-.1X | 200 |
| -Tax Due | 40 | 140+.04X | -240+.08X | -240+.08X | -240+.08X | -240+.08X | -260+.04X | -80 |

Net Income	-60	-210-.06X	360-.12X	360-.12X	360-.12X	360-.12X	390-.06X	120
+Depr		50+.1X	100+.2X	100+.2X	100+.2X	100+.2X	50+.1X	
+Work Cap								200
-Cap Costs	-X	-700						

| Cash Flow | X-60 | -860+.04X | 460+.08X | 460+.08X | 460+.08X | 460+.08X | 440+.04X | 320 |

PW Equation:

$$0 = -X - 60 + (-860 + .04X)\underset{0.8696}{(P/F15,1)} + (460 + .08X)\underset{2.855}{(P/A15,4)}\underset{0.8696}{(P/F15,1)}$$

$$+ (760 + .04X)\underset{0.4323}{(P/F15,6)}$$

$$0 = -X - 60 - 739.16 + .0348X + 1,117.22 + 0.1986X + 328.55 + 0.0173X$$

Calculating the value of X to make NPV = 0.

$$0 = -X + 663 + 0.2507X$$

Re-arranging the above equation gives text Equation 9-1:

X = 663 + .2507X *or,* X = NPV + Present Worth of Tax Savings on X (Eq 9-1)

Solving for X gives the following:

0.7493X = 663, *therefore,* X = $885

Verification of Problem 9-10, Case B

Additional before-tax research/development cost = NPV/(1-tax rate) = $663/(1-0.4) = $1,105. This research/development cost, in addition to the $100 research cost already built into the analysis at year 0, makes NPV equal to 0 as the following cash flow and NPV calculations show.

Problem 9-10 *Case B, Verification of Results*

Year	0	1	2	3	4	5	6
Revenue			900	900	900	900	1,300*
-Operating Costs			-200	-200	-200	-200	-200
-Development	-1,205	-300					
-Depreciation		-50	-100	-100	-100	-100	-50
-Work Cap Book Val							-200
Taxable Income	-1,205	-350	600	600	600	600	850
-Tax @ 40%	482	140	-240	-240	-240	-240	-340
Net Income	-723	-210	360	360	360	360	510
+Depreciation		50	100	100	100	100	50
+Work Cap Book Val							200
-Capital Costs		-700					
Cash Flow	-723	-860	460	460	460	460	760

* Revenue includes working capital return and salvage.

NPV $= -723 - 860(P/F_{15,1}) + 460(P/A_{15,4})(P/F_{15,1}) + 760(P/F_{15,6}) = 0$

9-11 Solution: *Constant Dollar Analysis of Problem 9-10*

Case A) *NPV Analysis*

$i^{*'} = (1+i)/(1+f) - 1$, therefore $i^{*'} = (1.15/1.10) - 1 = 4.55\%$

Constant Dollar NPV:

$$NPV = -60 - 860\underset{0.9091}{(P/F_{10,1})}\underset{0.9565}{(P/F_{4.55,1})} + 460\underset{0.8264}{(P/F_{10,2})}\underset{0.9149}{(P/F_{4.55,2})}$$

$$+ 460\underset{0.7513}{(P/F_{10,3})}\underset{0.8750}{(P/F_{4.55,3})} + 460\underset{0.6830}{(P/F_{10,4})}\underset{0.8370}{(P/F_{4.55,4})}$$

$$+ 460\underset{0.6209}{(P/F_{10,5})}\underset{0.8005}{(P/F_{4.55,5})} + 760\underset{0.5654}{(P/F_{10,6})}\underset{0.7657}{(P/F_{4.55,6})} = +\$663$$

If handled properly, constant dollar and escalated dollar NPV results will always be equivalent within round-off error of the factors used.

Case B) *Additional Before-Tax Research and Development Cost*

NPV / (1 - tax rate) = 663 / (1-.4) = $1,105

Case C) *Consider $900,000 Sale Offer at Year 1*

Sale Cash Flow = Sale Value - Tax on Gain

Sale CF = 900-(900-0)(0.4 tax rate)=$540 after taxes at year 1 = NPV_{Sell}

Yr 1 NPV$_{Dev}$ $= -860 + 460(P/A_{15,4}) + 760(P/F_{15,5}) = \$831$

$NPV_{Dev} > NPV_{Sell}$ *so select develop*

9-11 Solution: *Continued*

Case D) *What value at yr 1 makes selling break-even with developing?*

Let X = break-even before-tax sale price at year 1
Sale Cash Flow = Sale Value - Tax on Gain

$$= X - (X-0)(0.4 \text{ tax rate}) = 0.6X = CF_{Sell} = NPV_{Sell} = NPV_{Dev} = \$831$$

Break-even Selling Price: $X = 831/0.6 = \$1,385$

9-12 Solution: *All Values in Thousands of Dollars*

Accounting for Risk in Problem 9-10

Success Cash Flows: -60   P=0.4   -860   P=0.7   460   460   460   460   760

                       0   1   2   3   4   5   6

                  P=0.6   P=0.3

Failure Cash Flows: 0   200+500(.4) = 400

Case A)

                0.8696   2.855   0.8696

ENPV @ 15% $= -60 + [-860(P/F_{15,1}) + \{460(P/A_{15,4})(P/F_{15,1})$

              0.4323   0.7561

        $+ 760(P/F_{15,6})\}(0.7)](0.4) + 400(P/F_{15,2})(.3)(.4) = +\$88.92$

Case B) *Additional Before-Tax Research and Development Cost That Could be Incurred on a Risk-Adjusted Analysis Basis:*

$$NPV / (1\text{-tax rate}) = 88.92 / (1 - .4) = \$148.19$$

9-13 Solution: *All Values in Thousands of Dollars*

Break-even Before-Tax Revenue Analysis for Problem 9-10A

Year	0	1	2	3	4	5	6
Revenue			X	X	X	X	X+400*
-Operating Costs			-200	-200	-200	-200	-200
-Development	-100	-300					
-Depreciation		-50	-100	-100	-100	-100	-50
-Work Cap Bk Val							-200
Taxable Income	-100	-350	X-300	X-300	X-300	X-300	X-50
-Tax @ 40%	40	140	-.4X+120	-.4X+120	-.4X+120	-.4X+120	-.4X+ 20
Net Income	-60	-210	.6X-180	.6X-180	.6X-180	.6X-180	.6X- 30
+Depreciation		50	100	100	100	100	50
+Work Cap Bk Val							200
-Capital Costs		-700					
Cash Flow	-60	-860	.6X-80	.6X-80	.6X-80	.6X-80	.6X+220

* Revenue includes working capital return and salvage.

9-13 Solution: *Continued*

Break-even Before-Tax Revenue Analysis for Problem 9-10A Continued

$$\text{PW Eq: } 0 = -60 - 860\underset{0.8696}{(P/F_{15,1})} + (.6X-80)\underset{2.855}{(P/A_{15,4})}\underset{0.8696}{(P/F_{15,1})}$$

$$+ (.6X+220)\underset{0.4323}{(P/F_{15,6})}$$

$$0 = 1.749X - 911.37, \quad \textit{therefore, } X = \$521.07$$

Break-even Revenue Per Year: $521,070

$$\textbf{Break-even Selling Price: } = \frac{521{,}070 \text{ break - even revenue per year}}{10{,}000 \text{ units produced per year}}$$

$$= \$52.11/\text{unit break-even selling price}$$

9-14 Solution: *All Values in Dollars*

R = Revenue, OC = Operating Costs, P =Probability of Occurrence

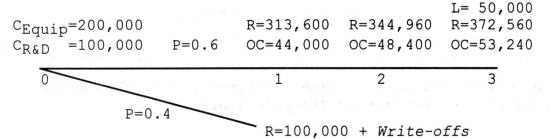

$$L= 50{,}000$$

C_{Equip}=200,000		R=313,600	R=344,960	R=372,560
$C_{R\&D}$ =100,000	P=0.6	OC=44,000	OC=48,400	OC=53,240

0   1   2   3

P=0.4

R=100,000 + *Write-offs*

Escalated Dollar Cash Flow Calculations

		60% Probability of Success				Fail 40%
Year	0	1	2	3	Salv	1
Revenue		313,600	344,960	372,560	50,000	100,000
-Oper Costs		-44,000	-48,400	-53,240		
-Develop	-100,000					
-Deprec	-28,571	-48,980	-34,985	-24,990		
-Write-off					62,474	-171,429
-Loss Forward		-128,571				-128,571
Taxable	-128,571	92,049	261,575	294,330	-12,474	-200,000
-Tax @ 40%		-36,819	-104,630	-117,732	4,990	80,000
Net Income	-128,571	55,228	156,945	176,598	-7,484	-120,000
+Deprec	28,571	48,980	34,985	24,990	62,474	171,429
+Loss Forward		128,571				128,571
-Cap Costs	-200,000					
Cash Flow	-300,000	232,779	191,930	201,588	54,990	180,000

256,578

9-14 Solution: *Continued*

Constant Dollar ENPV @ 10%:

$$
\begin{aligned}
&\qquad\qquad\qquad\qquad\; \overset{0.9434}{}\;\; \overset{0.9091}{} \qquad\qquad\quad \overset{0.9434}{}\;\; \overset{0.9259}{}\;\; \overset{0.8264}{}\\
&= -300{,}000 + [232{,}779(P/F_{6,1})(P/F_{10,1}) + 191{,}930(P/F_{6,1})(P/F_{8,1})(P/F_{10,2})\\
&\qquad\qquad\quad \overset{0.9434}{}\;\; \overset{0.9259}{}\;\; \overset{0.9091}{}\;\; \overset{0.7513}{}\\
&\quad + 256{,}578(P/F_{6,1})(P/F_{8,1})(P/F_{10,1})(P/F_{10,3})](.6)\\
&\qquad\qquad\quad \overset{0.9434}{}\;\;\; \overset{0.9091}{}\\
&\quad + 180{,}000(P/F_{6,1})(P/F_{10,1})(.4) = +\$56{,}508
\end{aligned}
$$

Using Equation 5-1, it is necessary to calculate the equivalent escalated dollar minimum rate of return accounting for the various inflation rates each year as follows:

$$i^* = (1+i^{*\prime})(1+f) - 1$$

Yr 1: Escalated \$ Minimum DCFROR = (1.1)(1.06) − 1 = .1660 or 16.6%
Yr 2: Escalated \$ Minimum DCFROR = (1.1)(1.08) − 1 = .1880 or 18.8%
Yr 3: Escalated \$ Minimum DCFROR = (1.1)(1.10) − 1 = .2110 or 21.1%

Escalated Dollar ENPV:

$$
\begin{aligned}
&\qquad\qquad\qquad\qquad \overset{0.8576}{} \qquad\qquad\qquad \overset{0.8576}{} \qquad \overset{0.8418}{}\\
&ENPV = -300{,}000 + [232{,}779(P/F_{16.6,1}) + 191{,}930(P/F_{16.6,1})(P/F_{18.8,1})\\
&\qquad\qquad\quad \overset{0.8576}{}\;\; \overset{0.8418}{}\;\; \overset{0.8258}{} \qquad\qquad\qquad\qquad \overset{0.8576}{}\\
&+ 256{,}578(P/F_{16.6,1})(P/F_{18.8,1})(P/F_{21.1,1})](.6) + 180{,}000(P/F_{16.6,1})(.4)\\
&\quad = +\$56{,}440
\end{aligned}
$$

Factor round-off error causes a slight difference between this result and the constant dollar result.

9-15 Solution: *All Values in Thousands of Dollars*

Natural Gas Pipeline Break-even Analysis With Mid-Period Compounding
Let X = Break-even Transportation Price

Year	0	0.5	1.5	2.5	3.5	4.5	5.5
Revenue		1900X	1440X	1030X	730X	440X	150X
-Oper Costs		-5	-5	-5	-5	-5	-5
-Depreciation		-31	-54	-38	-27	-20	-20
-Depr Write-off							-30
Taxable Income		1900X-36	1440X-59	1030X-43	730X-32	440X-25	150X-55
-Tax @ 40%		- 760X+14	-576X+23	-412X+17	-292X+12	-176X+10	-60X+22
Net Income		1140X-22	864X-36	618X-26	438X-20	264X-15	90X-33
+Depreciation		31	54	38	27	20	50
-Cap Costs	-220						
Cash Flow	-220	1140X+9	864X+18	618X+12	438X+7	264X+5	90X+17

PW Eq:
$$0 = -220 + (1{,}140X + 9)\overset{0.9449}{(P/F_{12,0.5})} + (864X + 18)\overset{0.8437}{(P/F_{12,1.5})}$$
$$+ (618X + 12)\overset{0.7533}{(P/F_{12,2.5})} + (438X + 7)\overset{0.6726}{(P/F_{12,3.5})}$$
$$+ (264X + 5)\overset{0.6005}{(P/F_{12,4.5})} + (90X + 17)\overset{0.5362}{(P/F_{12,5.5})}$$

$$0 = 2{,}773X - 170.4, \textit{ rearranging gives: } 170.4 = 2{,}773X$$

Break-even Price Per MCF: X = \$0.06145 per Mcf < \$0.10 / Mcf offer, so reject the offer and build the gathering line.

The break-even transport charge for a 12% escalated dollar DCFROR on the $220,000 pipeline investment is $0.0614 per Mcf based on mid-year values and compounding which treats year 1 values at period n = 0.5, year 2 values as occurring at period n = 1.5, and so forth.

$$P/F_{12,0.5} = (1/1.12)^{0.5} = \$0.9449$$

$$P/F_{12,1.5} = (1/1.12)^{1.5} = \$0.8437$$

and so forth for n = 2.5, 3.5, etc. . . .

9-16 Solution: *All Values in Thousands of Dollars*

```
Development       = 10,000   Rev = 30,000  33,000  36,300  39,930  43,923
Deprec Equipment  = 15,000   OC  = 12,000  13,200  14,520  15,972  17,569
Working Capital   =  2,000
Salvage (Including Working Capital Return)                           5,000
```

	0	1	2	3	4	5

The $10,000 mineral rights acquisition cost incurred at year -2 is sunk, but remaining tax effects and sale value are not.

Development Cash Flow Calculations

Year	0	1	2	3	4	5	Salv
Gross Revenue		30,000	33,000	36,300	39,930	43,923	5,000
-Royalties		-2,400	-2,640	-2,904	-3,194	-3,514	
Net Revenue		27,600	30,360	33,396	36,736	40,409	5,000
-Oper Costs		-12,000	-13,200	-14,520	-15,972	-17,569	
-Development	-7,000						
-Depreciation	-2,143	-3,673	-2,624	-1,874	-1,340	-1,338	-2,008
-Amortization	-600	-600	-600	-600	-600		
-WC Write-off							-2,000
Before Depltn	-9,743	11,327	13,936	16,402	18,824	21,502	992
-50% Limit		5,663	6,968	8,201	9,412	10,751	
-Percent Depl		-2,760	-3,036	-3,340	-3,112*	-3,233	
-Cost Depltn		2,000	1,810	1,401	432		
Taxable Income	-9,743	8,567	10,900	13,062	15,712	18,269	992
-Tax @ 40%	3,897	-3,427	-4,360	-5,225	-6,285	-7,308	-397
Net Income	-5,846	5,140	6,540	7,837	9,427	10,961	595
+Depreciation	2,143	3,673	2,624	1,874	1,340	1,338	2,008
+Depletion		2,760	3,036	3,340	3,112	3,233	
+Amortization	600	600	600	600	600		
+WC Write-off							2,000
-Capital Costs	-20,000**						
Cash Flow	-23,103	12,173	12,800	13,651	14,479	15,532	4,603

$$\underbrace{}_{20,135}$$

* Cumulative percentage depletion in years 1, 2 and 3 = $9,136 so $864 more depletion equals $10,000 mineral rights acquisition cost. $864/0.10 = $8,640 net revenue after royalty is needed for 10% depletion, balance is 8% depletion. 8% depletion revenue = ($36,736-$8,640)(0.08) = $28,096(0.08) = $2,248. Cumulative year 4 percentage depletion = $2,248 + $864 = $3,112.

** Capital cost includes $15,000 for equipment, $2,000 for working capital, $3,000 for 30% of the $10,000 development cost.

9-16 Solution: *Continued*

Case 1) *Calculating DCFROR and NPV ($10,000 acquisition cost is sunk)*

PW Eq: $0 = -23{,}103 + 12{,}173(P/F_{i,1}) + 12{,}800(P/F_{i,2}) + 13{,}651(P/F_{i,3})$

$+ 14{,}479(P/F_{i,4}) + 20{,}135(P/F_{i,5})$ **i = DCFROR = 50.7%**

NPV $= -23{,}103 + 12{,}173(P/F_{20,1}) + 12{,}800(P/F_{20,2}) + 13{,}651(P/F_{20,3})$

$+ 14{,}479(P/F_{20,4}) + 20{,}135(P/F_{20,5}) = +\$18{,}904$

After-tax Cash Flow of Yr 0 Sale Offer:

Before-tax sale value minus the tax due from the sale equals the sale cash flow and net present value. At the point of the sale, (time zero) the only cost incurred was 2 years ago. That cost is sunk and not relevant except for remaining tax effects. If we sell the property the remaining book value is deducted from the sale revenue to determine the taxable gain as follows:

$20{,}000 - (20{,}000 - 10{,}000)(0.4) = \$16{,}000 < \$18{,}904$ Develop NPV, *so develop*

Case 2) Break-even Selling Price with Developing

In this analysis you are determining the break-even sale price the makes the sale NPV equal to the develop NPV. This calculation is very similar to the analysis just made, except the selling price becomes an unknown variable. Let "X" equal the break-even selling price.

$X - (X - 10{,}000)(0.4) = \$18{,}904$

$0.6X + 4{,}000 = \$18{,}904$, *therefore*, $X = \$14{,}904/0.6 = \$24{,}840$

Case 3) Additional Development Cost that Could be Incurred

Neglecting sale value opportunity cost considerations, this question asks you to determine the additional development cost (above the current $10,000) that can be incurred and still have the project earn a 20% DCFROR on invested dollars. As in the previous solutions to this problem, if we let "X" be the unknown break-even development cost, then "X" less the tax savings from deductions on "X" will be equal to the after-tax NPV of development ($18,904). 70% of "X" can be expensed at time zero by a corporate mineral producer with the remaining 30% amortized over 5 years (year 0 to 4) as follows:

$X - (0.7)X(0.4 \text{ tax rate}) - (0.06)X(0.4) - (0.06)X(0.4)(P/A_{20,4}) = \$18{,}904$

$X - 0.28X - 0.024X - 0.024X(2.589) = \$18{,}904$

$0.634X = 18{,}904$ *therefore*, $X = \$29{,}823$

$29,823 is the additional year 0 before-tax development cost that could be incurred and still have the project earn a 20% DCFROR. Opportunity cost is neglected.

9-17 Solution:

Alternative A)   100% Working Interest, 87.5% Net Revenue Interest

Production, Bbls/yr		17,500	9,000	6,500	3,000
Selling Price, $/Bbl		$20.00	$20.00	$21.00	$22.05
Royalty, $/Bbl		$2.50	$2.50	$2.62	$2.75
Operating Cost, $/Bbl		$4.00	$4.00	$4.00	$4.00
Intangible Drilling	$250,000				
Tangible Completion	$100,000				
Lease Cost	$0				

Cash Flows:

Year	0	1	2	3	4
Gross Revenue		350,000	180,000	136,500	66,150
-Royalties		-43,750	-22,500	-17,063	-8,269
Net Interest		306,250	157,500	119,438	57,881
-Operating Expenses		-70,000	-36,000	-26,000	-12,000
-Intangibles 70	-175,000	-	-	-	-
-Depreciation		-14,290	-24,490	-17,490	-43,730
-Amortization	-7,500	-15,000	-15,000	-15,000	-22,500
Taxable Income	-167,500	206,960	82,010	60,948	-20,349
-Tax @ 38%	63,650	-78,645	-31,164	-23,160	7,733
Net Income	-103,850	128,315	50,846	37,787	-12,616
+Depreciation		14,290	24,490	17,490	43,730
+Amortization	7,500	15,000	15,000	15,000	22,500
-Capital Costs:					
-Tangible Equipment	-100,000				
-30% of IDC	-75,000				
After-tax Cash Flow	-271,350	157,605	90,336	70,277	53,614

$$\text{NPV @ 12\%} = -271,350 + \underset{0.8929}{157,605(P/F_{12,1})} + \underset{0.7972}{90,336(P/F_{12,2})}$$

$$+ \underset{0.7118}{70,277(P/F_{12,3})} + \underset{0.6355}{53,614(P/F_{12,4})} = \$25,486$$

PVR = 25,486/271,350 = 0.094

PW Eq: $0 = -271,350 + 157,605(P/F_{i,1}) + 90,336(P/F_{i,2})$

$+ 70,277(P/F_{i,3}) + 53,614(P/F_{i,4})$

ROR = 17.4% *by financial calculator*

9-17 Solution: *Continued*

Case B) 5% Carried Interest, Back-in for 25% Working Interest and
21.875% Net Revenue Interest

Pay-out Calculation Using Production:

When the cumulative value of net revenue (defined here as production times the selling price less royalties and cash operating costs) gives revenue equal to the total dollars invested, the project is at pay-out. In this case, we know we've spent $350,000, and the price in years 1 and 2 is constant at $20.00 per barrel. Due to the two royalties, the producer only gets 82.5% of each barrel to pay off the investment. Hence, pay-out in production is calculated as follows:

```
Yr 1 Pay-out Basis $350,000 - [17,500x($20.00(0.825)-$4.00)] = $131,250
Yr 2 Pay-out Basis $131,250 - [ 9,000x($20.00(0.825)-$4.00)] = $ 18,750
Yr 3 Pay-out: $18,750 = (X bbl)($21.00(0.825)-$4.00)   X = 1,407 bbl
```

Therefore, in year 3, 1,407 barrels would be subject to the over-riding royalty interest of 5.0%, after which (the reversion point), 5,093 barrels are applicable to the 25.0% working interest, and a 21.875% net revenue interest (25.0% adjusted for 12.5% royalties).

Cash Flow Calculations:

Year	0	1	2	3	4
Carried Interest Rev.(5%)		17,500	9,000	1,477	0
Net Revenue Interest(21.875%)		0	0	23,396	14,470
Total Net Revenues		17,500	9,000	24,873	14,470
-Operating Expense (25%)		0	0	-5,093	-3,000
Taxable Income		17,500	9,000	19,780	11,470
-Tax @ 38%		-6,650	-3,420	-7,517	-4,359
Net Income		10,850	5,580	12,264	7,112
-Capital Costs					
Cash Flow		10,850	5,580	12,264	7,112

$$\text{NPV @ 12\%} = 10{,}850 \overset{0.8929}{(P/F_{12,1})} + 5{,}580 \overset{0.7972}{(P/F_{12,2})}$$

$$+ 12{,}264 \overset{0.7118}{(P/F_{12,3})} + 7{,}112 \overset{0.6355}{(P/F_{12,4})} = \$27{,}386 \; select \; carried \; interest$$

From a purely economic viewpoint, selecting the largest NPV leads to the conclusion to farm out the property. However, from a practical viewpoint the NPV results are very close and effectively a break-even. This is verified by an appropriate incremental analysis (see next page).

9-17 Solution: *Continued*

Incremental Analysis:

Incremental Cash Flow Alternative A - Alternative B:

-271,350	146,755	84,756	58,013	46,502
0	1	2	3	4

ROR_{A-B} = 11.58% < i*=12%,   *reject A, accept B by very slight margin*

NPV_{A-B} = 25,486 - 27,386 = -$1,900 < 0,   *reject A, accept B*

PVR_{A-B} = -1,900/271,350 = -0.0007 < 0,   *reject A, accept B*

The "carried interest farm out" (Case B) has a slight economic advantage with all methods. Since Cases A and B are mutually exclusive alternatives, Case B with maximum total investment NPV of $27,386 is the economic choice. Incremental PVR and ROR lead to the same conclusion.

9-18 Solution:

The following incremental cash flow calculations are based on the before-tax data provided in the problem statement. The in-fill drilling alternative reflects combined adjusted production from both the new and existing wells, versus the current production forecast for the current or existing well. Notice that beginning in year 3 and beyond, the incremental production is negative which translates into reduced revenues, implying the company would pay less in royalties and operating costs (the later in year 6 only).

Incremental Cash Flow Calculations:

Year	0	1	2	3	4	5	6
Production	90,000	140,000	45,000	-10,000	-25,000	-30,000	-25,000
Price ($/MCF)	1.25	1.25	1.50	1.75	2.00	2.25	2.50
Revenue	112,500	175,000	67,500	-17,500	-50,000	-67,500	-62,500
-Royalties	-14,063	-21,875	-8,438	2,188	6,250	8,438	7,813
Net Revenue	98,438	153,125	59,063	-15,313	-43,750	-59,063	-54,688
-Op Costs	-1,000	-2,000	-2,000	-2,000	-2,000	-2,000	4,000
-IDC	-88,200						
-Deprec	-6,000	-10,286	-7,347	-5,248	-3,748	-3,748	-5,622
-Amort	-3,780	-7,560	-7,560	-7,560	-7,560	-3,780	
Taxable Inc	-542	133,279	42,156	-30,120	-57,058	-68,591	-56,310
-Tax @ 38%	206	-50,646	-16,019	11,446	21,682	26,065	21,398
Net Income	-336	82,633	26,136	-18,675	-35,376	-42,526	-34,912
+Deprec	6,000	10,286	7,347	5,248	3,748	3,748	5,662
+Amort	3,780	7,560	7,560	7,560	7,560	3,780	
-Cap. Cost	-79,800						
Cash Flow	-70,356	100,479	41,043	-5,867	-24,068	-34,998	-29,290

Depreciation, Tangible Cost = $168,000(0.25) = $42,000

Year 0:	42,000(0.1429)	= $ 6,000
Year 1:	42,000(0.2449)	= $10,286
Year 2:	42,000(0.1749)	= $ 7,347
Year 3:	42,000(0.1249)	= $ 5,248
Year 4:	42,000(0.0893)	= $ 3,748
Year 5:	42,000(0.0892)	= $ 3,748
Year 6:	42,000(0.0893)	= $ 3,748
Year 6:	Book Value	= $ 1,874 $5,622 Yr 6 Total

Amortization Deductions $168,000(0.75)(0.30) = $37,800

Year 0:	37,800(6/60)	= $3,780
Years 1-4:	37,800(12/60)	= $7,560
Year 5:	37,800(6/60)	= $3,780

9-18 Solution: *Continued*

Present Worth Equation: *(Note Cost-Income-Cost in CF's)*

$$0 = -70{,}356 + 100{,}479(P/F_{i,1}) + 41{,}043(P/F_{i,2})$$
$$- 5{,}867(P/F_{i,3}) - 24{,}068(P/F_{i,4}) - 34{,}998(P/F_{i,5}) - 29{,}290(P/F_{i,6})$$

NPV @ 12% = -\$2,093,   *reject in-fill drilling*

Note the incremental project investment pay-out period is 0.7 per year, but the incremental investment is rejected indicating pay-out is a poor economic indicator.

DCFROR analysis of this cash flow stream leads to the dual rate of return problem and requires modifying cash flow streams.

Modified Present Worth Cost ROR Analysis:

$$70{,}356 + 5{,}867\overset{0.7118}{(P/F_{12\%,3})} + 24{,}068\overset{0.6355}{(P/F_{12\%,4})}$$

$$+ 34{,}998\overset{0.5674}{(P/F_{12\%,5})} + 29{,}290\overset{0.5066}{(P/F_{12\%,6})} = \$124{,}524 = Modified\ Cost$$

$$124{,}524 = 100{,}479(P/F_{i\%,1}) + 41{,}043(P/F_{i\%,2})$$

Modified DCFROR = 10.51% < 12.0%, *reject in-fill drilling*

PVR = -2,093/70,356 = -0.0297 < 0, *reject in-fill drilling*

9-19 Solution: *All Dollar Values in Millions*

Escalated Dollar Cash Flow Calculations:

Year	Time 0	1	2	3	4	Salv.	40%fail Yr 1
Revenue		25.00	25.00	25.00	25.00		10.00
-Op. Costs		-10.00	-10.00	-10.00	-10.00		
-Develop	-12.00						
-Depreciation		-2.14	-3.67	-2.62	-1.87	-4.69	-15.00
-Amortization		-0.50	-0.50	-0.50	-0.50	-0.50	-2.50
Taxable Income	-12.00	12.36	10.83	11.88	12.63	-5.19	-7.50
-Tax @ 38%	4.56	-4.70	-4.11	-4.51	-4.80	1.97	2.85
Net Income	-7.44	7.66	6.71	7.36	7.83	-3.22	-4.65
+Depreciation		2.14	3.67	2.62	1.87	4.69	15.00
+Amortization		0.50	0.50	0.50	0.50	0.50	2.50
-Cap Cost	-15.00						
Cash Flow	-22.44	10.30	10.89	10.49	10.20	1.97	12.85

9-19 Solution: *Continued*

Depreciation Based on $15 Million Equipment Cost	Amortization Deductions on $2.5 million Patent	Year 0 Sell Cash Flow	
Yr 1 15(0.1429) = 2.14 Yr 2 15(0.2449) = 3.67 Yr 3 15(0.1749) = 2.62 Yr 4 15(0.1249) = 1.87 Yr 4 Book Value = 4.69	Years 1-4 2.5(1/5) = 0.50 Write-off 2.5(1/5) = 0.50	Revenue	4.50
		-Bk Value	-2.50
		Taxable	2.00
		-Tax @ 38%	-0.76
		Net Income	1.24
		+Bk Value	2.50
		Cash Flow$_0$	3.74

Case A) *Escalated Dollar Expected Net Present Value @ 15%:*

$$\text{ENPV} = -22.44 + (0.8)[10.30\overset{0.8696}{(P/F_{15\%,1})} + 10.89\overset{0.7561}{(P/F_{15\%,2})}$$

$$+ 10.49\overset{0.6575}{(P/F_{15\%,3})} + 12.17\overset{0.5718}{(P/F_{15\%,4})}] + (0.2)[12.85\overset{0.8696}{(P/F_{15\%,1})}]$$

$$= +\$4.63 > \$3.74 \quad \textit{choose development}$$

Case B) *Constant Dollar Expected NPV @ i*=15% With 8.7% Inflation:*

Using Equation 5-1:

Escalated Equivalent i* = (1.15)(1.087) - 1 = 0.25 or 25.0%, *therefore*

$$\text{ENPV} = -22.44 + (0.8)[10.30\overset{0.8000}{(P/F_{25\%,1})} + 10.89\overset{0.6400}{(P/F_{25\%,2})}$$

$$+ 10.49\overset{0.5120}{(P/F_{25\%,3})} + 12.17\overset{0.4096}{(P/F_{25\%,4})}] + (0.2)[12.85\overset{0.8000}{(P/F_{25\%,1})}]$$

$$= +\$0.07 < \$3.74 \quad \textit{choose selling}$$

9-20 Solution:

Purchase Compressor:

```
OC=75,000
C =1,000,000      -             -         OC=225,000      -        R=300,000
```

0	1	2	3	4	5

Lease Compressor:

```
OC= 75,000
LP=144,000   LP=288,000   LP=288,000   LP=288,000   LP=288,000   LP=144,000
```

0	1	2	3	4	5

Incremental Time Diagram Purchase - Lease:

```
 C=1,000,000
 S=144,000    S=288,000    S=288,000    S=288,000    S=288,000    S=444,000
```

0	1	2	3	4	5

Incremental Cash Flows:

Year	0	1	2	3	4	5
Savings	144,000	288,000	288,000	288,000	288,000	444,000
-Repair				-225,000		
-Depreciation	-142,857	-244,898	-174,927	-124,948	-89,249	-223,121
Taxable Income	1,143	43,102	113,073	-61,948	198,751	220,879
-Tax @40%	-457	-17,241	-45,229	24,779	-79,501	-88,351
Net Income	686	25,861	67,844	-37,169	119,251	132,527
+Depreciation	142,857	244,898	174,927	124,948	89,249	223,121
-Cap. Costs	-1,000,000					
Cash Flow	-856,457	270,759	242,771	87,779	208,499	355,649

PW Eq: $0 = -856,457 + 270,759(P/F_{i,1}) + 242,771(P/F_{i,2})$

$$+ 87,779(P/F_{i,3}) + 208,499(P/F_{i,4}) + 355,649(P/F_{i,5})$$

Annual Effective Discount Rate = $(1+0.01)^{12}-1 = 0.1268$ *or* 12.68%

ROR = i = 10.87% *by financial calculator* < $i*$=12.68%, *reject purchase*

NPV @ 12.68% = -\$38,481 < 0, *reject purchase*

PVR = -38,461 / 856,457 = -0.045 < 0, *reject purchase*

9-21 Solution: *All Values in Dollars*

Case A) 10 Year Bond Analysis

C=10,000   I=800 .... I=800

Maturity Value = 10,000

0   1 .... 10 yr

Using Eq. 3-2: **Before-Tax Yield = 8%**

After-Tax Yield = 8%(1-0.38) = 4.96%

Bond market values are based on before-tax yields (interest rates) and therefore are not affected by the investor's tax situation. Bond market value (price) is not identical to the investor's NPV from buying a bond. NPV is dependent upon an investor's tax situation.

$$\overset{7.360}{} \qquad \overset{0.5584}{}$$

At 6% interest: $P = 800(P/A_{6,10}) + 10,000(P/F_{6,10}) = \$11,472$

$$\overset{6.144}{} \qquad \overset{0.3855}{}$$

At 10% interest: $P = 800(P/A_{10,10}) + 10,000(P/F_{10,10}) = \$8,770$

Case B) 30 Year Bond Analysis

Value=?   I=$800 .... I=$800

Maturity Value = $10,000

0   1 .... 30 yr+

At 8% interest: $P = Value = \$10,000$

$$\overset{13.765}{} \qquad \overset{0.1741}{}$$

At 6% interest: $P = 800(P/A_{6,30}) + 10,000(P/F_{6,30}) = \$12,753$

$$\overset{9.427}{} \qquad \overset{0.0573}{}$$

At 10% interest: $P = 800(P/A_{10,30}) + 10,000(P/F_{10,30^*}) = \$8,115$

Case C) 30 Year Zero Coupon Bond

Value=?   −   −

Maturity Value = $10,000

0   1 .... 30 yr

$$\overset{0.099377}{}$$

At 8% interest: $P = Value = 10,000(P/F_{8,30}) = \$994$

$$\overset{0.1741}{}$$

At 6% interest: $P = Value = 10,000(P/F_{6,30}) = \$1,741$

$$\overset{0.0573}{}$$

At 10% interest: $P = Value = 10,000(P/F_{10,30}) = \$573$

CHAPTER 10 PROBLEM SOLUTIONS

10-1 Solution: *Replacement Analysis in Actual Dollars*

A, New Machine

	Cost=15,000	OC=6,000	OC=7,000	OC=8,000	
					L=2,000
	0	1	2	3	

B, Existing Machine

	Cost=21,000	OC=5,000	OC=5,000	OC=5,000	
					L=3,000
	0	1	2	3	

"A" New Machine Cash Flows

Year	0	1	2	3	Salvage
Revenue					2,000
-Operating Costs		-6,000	-7,000	-8,000	
-Depreciation	-3,000	-4,800	-2,880	-1,728	-2,592
Taxable Income	-3,000	-10,800	-9,880	-9,728	-592
-Tax @ 40%	1,200	4,320	3,952	3,891	237
Net Income	-1,800	-6,480	-5,928	-5,837	-355
+Depreciation	3,000	4,800	2,880	1,728	2,592
-Capital Costs	-15,000				
Cash Flow	-13,800	-1,680	-3,048	-4,109	2,237

PW Cost$_A$ @ 20% = $13,800+1,680(P/F_{20,1})+3,048(P/F_{20,2})+1,872(P/F_{20,3})$

$\qquad\qquad$ = \$18,400   *Select A with Minimum PW Cost*

Break-even Cost/Unit = $18,400/[(1,000)(250)(P/A_{20,3})(1-.4)]$= \$0.058/unit

"B" Existing Machine Cash Flows

Year	0	1	2	3	Salvage
Revenue					3,000
-Operating Costs		-5,000	-5,000	-5,000	
-Depreciation	-4,200	-6,720	-4,032	-2,419	-3,629
Taxable Income	-4,200	-11,720	-9,032	-7,419	-629
-Tax @ 40%	1,680	4,688	3,613	2,968	252
Net Income	-2,520	-7,032	-5,419	-4,452	-377
+Depreciation	4,200	6,720	4,032	2,419	3,629
-Capital Costs	-21,000				
Cash Flow	-19,320	-312	-1,387	-2,032	3,252

PW Cost$_B$ @ 20% = $19,320 + 312(P/F_{20,1}) + 1,387(P/F_{20,2}) - 1,220(P/F_{20,3})$

$\qquad\qquad$ =   +\$19,838   *Reject B, since A has Minimum PW Cost*

Break-even Cost/Unit = $19,838/[(1,000)(250)(P/A_{20,3})(1-.4)]$= \$0.063/unit

If the additional 500 units of Machine B productivity can be utilized,
PW Cost$_B$ of 1,000 units =19,838(2/3)=13,225 < 18,400 PW Cost$_A$. Select B.

10-2 Solution: *All Values in Actual Dollars*

```
                                   C=23,000
     C=2,000(.6)=1,200    OC=3,000 OC=4,000 OC=2,000 OC=2,500 OC=3,000
"A"  _____ L=8,000
        0                   1        2        3        4        5


     C=20,000                       OC=1,500 OC=2,000 OC=2,500 OC=3,000 OC=3,500
"B"  _____ L=3,000
        0                   1        2        3        4        5
```

Machine A Cash Flows

Year	Time 0	1	2	3	4	5	Salvage
Revenue							8,000
-Operating Costs		-3,000	-4,000	-2,000	-2,500	-3,000	
-Depreciation			-3,286	-5,633	-4,023	-2,874	-7,185
Taxable Income		-3,000	-7,286	-7,633	-6,523	-5,874	815
-Tax Due @ 40%		1,200	2,914	3,053	2,609	2,350	-326
Net Income		-1,800	-4,371	-4,580	-3,914	-3,524	489
+Depreciation			3,286	5,633	4,023	2,874	7,185
-Capital Costs	-1,200		-23,000				
Cash Flow	-1,200	-1,800	-24,086	1,053	109	-650	7,674

PW Cost$_A$ = 1,200 + 1,800(P/F$_{15,1}$) + 24,086(P/F$_{15,2}$) - 1,053(P/F$_{15,3}$)

$\qquad$ - 109(P/F$_{15,4}$) + 650(P/F$_{15,5}$) - 7,674(P/F$_{15,5}$) = \$16,731

Replacement Machine B Cash Flows

Year	Time 0	1	2	3	4	5	Salvage
Revenue							3,000
-Operating Costs		-1,500	-2,000	-2,500	-3,000	-3,500	
-Depreciation	-2,857	-4,898	-3,499	-2,499	-1,785	-1,785	-2,677
Taxable Income	-2,857	-6,398	-5,499	-4,999	-4,785	-5,285	323
-Tax Due @ 40%	1,143	2,559	2,199	2,000	1,914	2,114	-129
Net Income	-1,714	-3,839	-3,299	-2,999	-2,871	-3,171	194
+Depreciation	2,857	4,898	3,499	2,499	1,785	1,785	2,677
-Capital Costs	-20,000						
Cash Flow	-18,857	1,059	199	-500	-1,086	-1,386	2,871

PW Cost$_B$ = 18,857 - 1,059(P/F$_{15,1}$) -199(P/F$_{15,2}$) + 500(P/F$_{15,3}$)

$\qquad$ + 967(P/F$_{15,4}$) + 1,267(P/F$_{15,5}$) - 2,633(P/F$_{15,5}$) = \$17,997

Case A) Select Machine A with the lowest present worth cost of \$16,731.

Case B) If extra service can be utilized, select Machine B since 17,997/1.4 = \$12,855 is less than the Machine A present worth cost of \$16,731.

10-3 Solution: *All Values in Thousands*

Calculate the Year 0 Opportunity Cost

Salvage Tax = (30,000-21,000)(0.4) = \$3,600
Opportunity Cost = 30,000 - 3,600 = \$26,400

Year	0	1	2	3
-Repair Cost	-25,000			
-Operating Costs		-15,000	-18,000	-21,000
-Depreciation	-21,000			
Taxable Income	-46,000	-15,000	-18,000	-21,000
-Tax @ 40%	18,400	6,000	7,200	8,400
Net Income	-27,600	-9,000	-10,800	-12,600
+Depreciation	21,000			
-Opportunity Cost	-26,400			
Cash Flow	-33,000	-9,000	-10,800	-12,600

Case A) Present Worth Cost

$$33,000 + 9,000 \overset{0.8333}{(P/F_{20,1})} + 10,800 \overset{0.6944}{(P/F_{20,2})} + 12,600 \overset{0.5787}{(P/F_{20,3})} = \$55,291$$

Case B) Annual Cost

$$55,291 \overset{0.47473}{(A/P_{20,3})} = \$26,248$$

Case C) Break-even Lease Payments

Let the three uniform and equal beginning of year lease payments equal "X", 40% of "X" goes to tax, so yr 0, 1 & 2 cash flow increases by 0.6X.

PW Eq: $(.6X-33,000) + (.6X-9,000)\overset{0.8333}{(P/F_{20,1})} + (.6X-10,800)\overset{0.6944}{(P/F_{20,2})}$

$-12,600\overset{0.5787}{(P/F_{20,3})} = 0$

$1.5168X = 55,291$ *therefore*, X = 36,455

Alternative Calculation of X: *PW Cost = PW Revenue (1-tax rate)*

$55,291=[X+X(P/A_{20,2})](1-0.4 \text{ tax rate})$

$[55,291/2.528(0.6)] = 36,453 = X$ *at years 0, 1 and 2 which is the beginning of years 1, 2, and 3.*

Using annual costs would yield the following calculations:

Annual Cost = Annual Revenue (1-tax rate) $26,248 = X(1-0.4 \text{ tax rate})$

Therefore, X = \$43,748 *at years 1, 2 and 3.*

Convert to beginning of year values as follows:

$43,748\overset{0.8333}{(P/F_{20,1})} = \$36,455$

10-4 Solution: *All Values in Thousands of Dollars*

Alternative A Time Diagram

C=50	OC=12	OC=15	OC=18	OC=21	OC=24	
0	1	2	3	4	5	L=3

Alternative B Time Diagram

	C=32	C=50				
C=15	OC=20	OC=16	OC=3	OC=4	OC=5	
0	1	2	3	4	5	L=25

Alternative A Cash Flows

Year	0	1	2	3	4	5	Salvage
Revenue							3.00
-Operating Costs		-12.00	-15.00	-18.00	-21.00	-24.00	
-Depreciation	-7.14	-12.24	-8.75	-6.25	-4.46	-4.46	-6.69
Taxable Income	-7.14	-24.24	-23.75	-24.25	-25.46	-28.46	-3.69
-Tax Due @ 40%	2.86	9.70	9.50	9.70	10.18	11.38	1.48
Net Income	-4.29	-14.55	-14.25	-14.55	-15.28	-17.08	-2.22
+Depreciation	7.14	12.24	8.75	6.25	4.46	4.46	6.69
-Capital Costs	-50.00						
Cash Flow	-47.14	-2.30	-5.50	-8.30	-10.82	-12.62	4.48

$$-8.14$$

Present Worth Cost @ 15% = $69.0, *Select A with slightly lower PW Cost.*

Alternative B Cash Flows

Year	0	1	2	3	4	5	Salvage
Revenue							25.00
-Operating Costs		-20.00	-16.00	-3.00	-4.00	-5.00	
-Depreciation	-2.14	-3.67	-14.34	-20.08	-14.34	-10.25	-25.61
-Write-off			-6.56				
Taxable Income	-2.14	-23.67	-36.90	-23.08	-18.34	-15.25	-0.61
-Tax Due @ 40%	0.86	9.47	14.76	9.23	7.34	6.10	0.25
Net Income	-1.29	-14.20	-22.14	-13.85	-11.01	-9.15	-0.37
+Depreciation	2.14	3.67	14.34	20.08	14.34	10.25	25.61
+Write-Off			6.56				
-Capital Costs	-15.00	-32.00	-50.00				
Cash Flow	-14.14	-42.53	-51.24	6.23	3.34	1.10	25.25

$$26.35$$

Present Worth Cost @ 15% = $70.8

10-4 Solution: *Continued*

Incremental Analysis, Alternative A - Alternative B

The easiest way to get the incremental cash flows for incremental NPV or DCFROR analysis is to look at the differences in the individual Machine A and B cash flows. Look at the difference so that negative cash flow is followed by positive cash flow, so analyze A-B. However it is impossible to avoid the cost, income, cost dual ROR situation.

Incremental Time Diagram, A-B

-33.00	40.23	45.74	-14.53	-14.16	-34.49
0	1	2	3	4	5

Calculate NPV for a range of discount rates "i" to determine the dual "i" values.

i	NPV
0	-10.2
5	- 4.4
10	- 0.6
15	1.8
20	3.2
30	4.2
40	3.7
50	2.5
60	1.0
70	-0.6

The 1.80 incremental NPV for $i^* = 15\%$ equals the difference in the Present Worth Cost of "A" of $69.0 and the Present Worth Cost of "B" of $70.8. Remember that the sign convention is opposite for NPV and PW Cost analyses.

Dual DCFROR's are 11% and 66%, but they are not valid for decision making as ROR results. You must go to a modified ROR analysis, either Growth ROR or Present Worth Cost Modified ROR analysis discussed in Chapter Four.

Present Worth Cost Modified DCFROR Analysis

$$\overset{0.6575}{} \quad \overset{0.5717}{} \quad \overset{0.4972}{}$$

PW Mod. Cost $= 33.00 + 14.53(P/F_{15,3}) + 14.16(P/F_{15,4}) + 34.49(P/F_{15,5}) = \$67.79$

Modified DCFROR PW Eq $67.79 = 40.23(P/F_{i,1}) + 45.74(P/F_{i,2})$

i = PW Cost Modified DCFROR $= 17.0\% > i^* = 15\%$,   *accept Machine A*

Consistent with present worth cost and NPV analysis results.

If you prefer to obtain the incremental Machine A-B after-tax cash flow by taking the difference in the alternatives before-tax and converting the incremental costs and savings to after-tax cash flow, be very careful not to net incremental operating costs and capital costs against one another. Also note that the negative incremental "A-B" capital costs in years 1 and 2 are savings that result in negative depreciation in years 2, 3, 4 and 5 and a negative write-off at year 5.

10-4 Solution: *Continued*

Before-Tax Incremental Diagram, Machine A - Machine B

```
              C =-32      C =-50
  C=50-15     OC= -8      OC= -1      OC=15       OC=17       OC=19
  ─────────────────────────────────────────────────────────────────
     0           1           2           3           4           5
```

Correct handling of the depreciation calculations is the key to correct incremental cash flow analysis, but it is very easy to make mistakes.

Year	Incremental A-B Depreciation		Net Depreciation	
0	(50-15)(.1429)	= 5.0	Yr 0	5.00
1	(50-15)(.2449)	= 8.57	Yr 1	8.57
2	Write-off on (-15)	= -9.19		
2	(50)(.1749)	= 8.75		
2	(-82)(.1429)	= -11.72	Yr 2	-12.16
3	(50)(.1249)	= 6.25		
3	(-82)(.2449)	= -20.08	Yr 3	-13.83
4	(50)(.0893)	= 4.46		
4	(-82)(.1749)	= -14.34	Yr 4	-9.88
5	(50)(.0892)	= 4.46		
5	(-82)(.1249)	= -10.25	Yr 5	-5.79
5	write-off on 50	= 6.69		
5	write-off on (-82)	= -25.62	Yr 5	-18.92

Incremental Cash Flow Calculations

Year	0	1	2	3	4	5
Savings/Salvage		8.00	1.00			-22.00
-Oper Costs				-15.00	-17.00	-19.00
-Deprec/Write-off	-5.00	-8.57	12.16	13.83	9.88	24.71
Taxable Income	-5.00	-0.57	13.16	-1.17	-7.12	-16.29
-Tax @ 40%	2.00	0.23	-5.26	0.47	2.85	6.52
Net Income	-3.00	-0.34	7.90	-0.70	-4.27	-9.77
+Deprec/Write-off	5.00	8.57	-12.16	-13.83	-9.88	-24.71
-Capital Costs	-35.00	32.00	50.00			
Cash Flow	-33.00	40.23	45.74	-14.53	-14.15	-34.48

Within round-off error these incremental A-B after-tax cash flows are the same as those from analyzing the difference in the total investment cash flows.

10-5 Solution: *Values in Thousands of Dollars*

Old Machine

Case 1	*Case 2*	*Case 3 (Accounting*
C=90-36 tax if D9 sold	C=90	C=0 *Viewpoint)*
Yr 0 Book Value = 0	Yr 0 Book Value = 0	Yr 0 Book Value = 0

New Machine

Case 1	*Case 2*	*Case 3*
C=460	C=460+36 tax old sale	C=460+36 tax-90 sale
Yr 0 Bk Value = 460	Yr 0 Bk Value = 460	Yr 0 Bk Value = 460

Since the same relative differences exist between the New and Old Machines for all 3 cases (incremental cost of $406 for each), you must get the same economic conclusions using any of the 3 cases. However, do not mix the cases.

Present worth cost analysis results are presented. You can convert present worth cost results to equivalent annual cost by multiplying present worth cost times $A/P_{15,5}$, giving the same economic conclusions.

Case A) Assumes the New and Old assets give the same service

Old Machine Cash Flow Calculations

Year		0		1	2	3	4	5
Case #	1	2	3					
-Op Costs	-100.0	-100.0	-100.0	-150.0	-237.0	-184.0	-290.0	-156.0
Taxable	-100.0	-100.0	-100.0	-150.0	-237.0	-184.0	-290.0	-156.0
-Tax @ 40%	40.0	40.0	40.0	60.0	94.8	73.6	116.0	62.4
Net Income	-60.0	-60.0	-60.0	-90.0	-142.2	-110.4	-174.0	-93.6
-Cap Costs	-54.0	-90.0						
Cash Flow	-114.0	-150.0	-60.0	-90.0	-142.2	-110.4	-174.0	-93.6

Present Worth Cost for Year 0, Case 1

$$\text{PW Cost Eq: } 114.0 + 90.0\overset{0.8696}{(P/F_{15,1})} + 142.2\overset{0.0}{(P/F_{15,2})} + 110.4\overset{.6575}{(P/F_{15,3})}$$

$$+ 174.0\overset{0.5718}{(P/F_{15,4})} + 93.6\overset{0.4972}{(P/F_{15,5})}$$

Present Worth Cost, Case 1: $518.4
Present Worth Cost, Case 2: $554.4
Present Worth Cost, Case 3: $464.4

10-5 Solution: *Continued*

New Machine Cash Flow Calculations

Year		0		1	2	3	4	5
Case #	1	2	3					
Revenue								140.0
-Oper Cost				-88.0	-221.0	-108.0	-274.0	-140.0
-Deprec	-65.7	-65.7	-65.7	-112.7	-80.5	-57.5	-41.0	-41.0
-Write-off								-61.6
Taxable Inc	-65.7	-65.7	-65.7	-200.7	-301.5	-165.5	-315.0	-102.6
-Tax @ 40%	26.3	26.3	26.3	80.3	120.6	66.2	126.0	+41.0
Net Income	-39.4	-39.4	-39.4	-120.4	-180.9	-99.3	-189.0	-61.6
+Deprec	65.7	65.7	65.7	112.7	80.5	57.5	41.0	41.0
+Write-off								61.6
-Cap Costs	-460.0	-496.0	-406.0					
Cash Flow	-433.7	-469.7	-379.7	-7.7	-100.4	-41.8	-148.0	41.0

Present Worth Cost for Year 0, Case 1:

$$\text{PW Cost Eq:} \quad 433.7 + 7.7\underset{0.8696}{(P/F_{15,1})} + 100.4\underset{0.7561}{(P/F_{15,2})} + 41.8\underset{0.6575}{(P/F_{15,3})}$$

$$+ 148.0\underset{0.5718}{(P/F_{15,4})} - 41.0\underset{0.4972}{(P/F_{15,5})}$$

Present Worth Cost, Case 1: $608.0
Present Worth Cost, Case 2: $644.8
Present Worth Cost, Case 3: $554.8

Case B)

If the total productive capacity of the new D9L can be utilized, the Case 1 present worth cost of the new machine would drop to $608/1.3 = $467.7 which makes the New Machine preferable to the Old Machine, Case 1 present worth cost of $518.4.

Break-even Cost Analysis

Break-even cost per unit of service analysis is only valid for Case 1 actual after-tax year 0 costs.

Old Machine Break-even Cost Per Unit of Service Equals:

PW Cost "Old" / PW Production(1-tax rate)

$$518,400 \ / \ [2,000\underset{3.352}{(P/A_{15,5})}(1-0.4)] = \$128.88 \ / \ unit$$

New Machine Break-even Cost Per Unit of Service Equals:

$$608,000 \ / \ [2,600\underset{3.352}{(P/A_{15,5})}(1-0.4)] = \$116.27 \ / \ unit$$

Select the New Machine with the minimum cost per unit.

10-6 Solution: *Lease vs Purchase Analysis, All Values in Dollars*

Case A) Expense Economics

```
              OC=18          OC=36          OC=36          OC=18
Lease        ────────────────────────────────────────────────────  L=0
              0              1              2              3

              C=100
Purchase     ────────────────────────────────────────────────────  L=30
              0              1              2              3

              OC=-18
Purchase      C =100        OC=-36         OC=-36         OC=-18
-Lease       ────────────────────────────────────────────────────  L=30
              0              1              2              3
```

Remember that a negative incremental operating cost is equivalent to positive savings or revenue. Also, do not net incremental capital cost of 100 against the incremental operating cost of -18 in year 0. They are treated differently for tax purposes.

Incremental Analysis, Purchase - Lease Cash Flows

Year	0	1	2	3	
Savings/Salvage	18,000	36,000	36,000	48,000	*includes salvage.*
-Depreciation	-20,000	-32,000	-19,200	-11,520	
-Deprec/Write-off				-17,280	
Taxable Income	-2,000	4,000	16,800	19,200	
-Tax @ 40%	800	-1,600	-6,720	-7,680	
Net Income	-1,200	2,400	10,080	11,520	
+Deprec/Write-off	20,000	32,000	19,200	28,800	
-Capital Costs	-100,000				
Cash Flow	-81,200	34,400	29,280	40,320	

PW Eq: $0 = -81,200 + 34,400(P/F_{i,1}) + 29,280(P/F_{i,2}) + 40,320(P/F_{i,3})$

   i = DCFROR = 13.1% < 15%, *reject purchase*

NPV = $-81,200 + 34,400(P/F_{15,1}) + 29,280(P/F_{15,2}) + 40,320(P/F_{15,3})$

   = -2,636

10-6 Solution: *Case A Continued*

PW Cost of Leasing Cash Flows

Year	0	1	2	3
Revenue				
-Lease Costs	-18,000	-36,000	-36,000	-18,000
Taxable Income	-18,000	-36,000	-36,000	-18,000
-Tax @ 40%	7,200	14,400	14,400	7,200
Net Income	-10,800	-21,600	-21,600	-10,800
-Capital Costs				
Cash Flow	-10,800	-21,600	-21,600	-10,800

PW Cost = 10,800 + 21,600$(P/A_{15,2})$ + 10,800$(P/F_{15,3})$ = $53,016

PW Cost of Purchasing Cash Flows

Year	0	1	2	3
Revenue				30,000
-Depreciation	-20,000	-32,000	-19,200	-11,520
-Deprec/Write-off				-17,280
Taxable Income	-20,000	-32,000	-19,200	1,200
-Tax @ 40%	8,000	12,800	7,680	-480
Net Income	-12,000	-19,200	-11,520	720
+Deprec/Write-off	20,000	32,000	19,200	28,800
-Capital Costs	-100,000			
Cash Flow	-92,000	12,800	7,680	29,520

PW Cost = 92,000 - 12,800$(P/F_{15,1})$ - 7,680$(P/F_{15,2})$ - 29,520$(P/F_{15,3})$

$\qquad$ = $55,652 *Select leasing with the lowest present worth cost.*

Case B) Uniform Annual Equivalent Revenue Required

$\qquad$ **UAERR = Annual Cost / (1-tax rate)**

$\qquad\qquad\qquad$ 0.43798

UAERR$_{Lease}$ = $53,016$(A/P_{15,3})$ / (1-.4) = $23,220 / (1-.4) = $38,700

$\qquad\qquad\qquad$ 0.43798

UAERR$_{Purch}$ = $55,652$(A/P_{15,3})$ / (1-.4) = $24,375 / (1-.4) = $40,624

10-6 Solution: *Continued*

Case C) Stand Alone Economics
Leasing Cash Flows

Year	0	1	2	3
Revenue				
-Lease Costs	-18,000	-36,000	-36,000	-18,000
-Loss Forward		-18,000	-54,000	-90,000
Taxable Income	-18,000	-54,000	-90,000	-108,000
-Tax @ 40%	0	0	0	43,200
Net Income	-18,000	-54,000	-90,000	-64,800
+Loss Forward		18,000	54,000	90,000
-Capital Costs				
Cash Flow	-18,000	-36,000	-36,000	25,200

PW Cost $= 18,000 + 36,000(P/A_{15,2}) - 25,200(P/F_{15,3}) = \$59,956$

Purchase Cash Flows

Year	0	1	2	3
Revenue				30,000
-Depreciation	-20,000	-32,000	-19,200	-11,520
-Deprec/Write-off				-17,280
-Loss Forward		-20,000	-52,000	-71,200
Taxable Income	-20,000	-52,000	-71,200	-70,000
-Tax @ 40%	0	0	0	28,000
Net Income	-20,000	-52,000	-71,200	-42,000
+Deprec/Write-off	20,000	32,000	19,200	28,800
+Loss Forward		20,000	52,000	71,200
-Capital Costs	-100,000			
Cash Flow	-100,000	0	0	58,000

PW Cost $= 100,000 - 58,000(P/F_{15,3}) = \$61,864$

Select Leasing with the lowest present worth cost.

Carrying losses forward versus expensing against other income has little effect on lease versus purchase analysis because cumulative tax deductions are similar for both.

10-7 Solution: *All Values in Thousands of Dollars*

```
        C=240-96(tax)      OC=360           OC=390          OC=420
Old     ─────────────────────────────────────────────────────────  L=0
        0                  1                2               3


        C=1,000            OC=120           OC=160          OC=200
New     ─────────────────────────────────────────────────────────  L=240
        0                  1                2               3
```

Opportunity Cost = 240 - 96(tax) = $144 *for 3 Old Machines*

Cash Flows for Keeping the 3 Old Machine

Year	0	1	2	3
Revenue		–	–	–
-Operating Costs		-360	-390	-420
Taxable Income		-360	-390	-420
-Tax @ 40%		144	156	168
Net Income		-216	-234	-252
-Capital Costs	-144			
Cash Flow	-144	-216	-234	-252

$$\phantom{AC_{Old}}0.8696 \quad\quad 0.7561 \quad\quad 0.6575 \quad 0.43798$$

$AC_{Old} = [144+216(P/F_{15,1})+234(P/F_{15,2})+252(P/F_{15,3})](A/P_{15,3})=\$295.4$

UAERR = 295.4/(1-0.4)=$492.33 *for 3 Old Machines,* $164.1 *per Machine.*

Cash Flows for Purchasing 2 New Machines

Year	0	1	2	3
Revenue				250
-Operating Costs		-120	-160	-200
-Deprec/Write-off	-200	-320	-192	-288
Taxable Income	-200	-440	-352	-238
-Tax @ 40%	80	176	141	95
Net Income	-120	-264	-211	-143
+Depreciation	200	320	192	288
-Capital Costs	-1,000			
Cash Flow	-920	56	-19	145

$$\phantom{AC_{New}}0.8696 \quad\quad 0.7561 \quad\quad 0.6575 \quad 0.43798$$

$AC_{New} = [920 - 56(P/F_{15,1}) + 19(P/F_{15,2})-145(P/F_{15,3})](A/P_{15,3})=\$346$

UAERR$_{New}$ = 346/(1-.4)=$577 *for 2 New Machines, or* $288.5 *per Machine.*

Replacement of the Old Machines is not indicated to be economically desirable with either annual cost or UAERR analysis.

10-8 Solution: *All Values in Thousands of Dollars*

Purchase vs Leasing a Plant

Assume other income exists against which to use deductions in any year.

```
                         Rev/yr=800              800   800
            C=1,000      OC/yr =200              200   200
Purchase    ──────────────────────────────────────────────  L=400
            0              1 . . . . . . . . . . . 9    10

                         Rev/yr=800              800   800
            OC=200        OC/yr=400              400   200
Lease       ──────────────────────────────────────────────  L=0
            0              1 . . . . . . . . . . 9     10

            C=1,000
Purchase    OC=-200       OC/yr=-200            -200    0
 - Lease    ──────────────────────────────────────────────  L=400
            0              1 . . . . . . . . . 9      10
```

Purchase Plant Cash Flows

Year	0	1-9	10	Salv
Revenue		800	800	400
-Oper Costs		-200	-200	
-Deprec	-50	-100	-50	
Taxable Inc	-50	500	550	400
-Tax @ 40%	20	-200	-220	-160
Net Income	-30	300	330	240
+Deprec	50	100	50	
-Cap Cost	-1,000			
Cash Flow	-980	400	380	240

$$\underbrace{}_{620}$$

Lease Plant Cash Flows

Year	0	1-9	10
Revenue		800	800
-Oper Costs	-200	-400	-200
-Deprec			
Taxable Inc	-200	400	600
-Tax @ 40%	80	-160	-240
Net Income	-120	240	360
+Depreciation			
-Capital Costs			
Cash Flow	-120	240	360

Purchase PW EQ:

$0 = -980 + 400(P/A_{i,9}) + 620(P/F_{i,10})$

i = DCFROR = 39.7%
NPV @ 10% = +$1,563

Lease PW Eq:

$0 = -120 + 240(P/A_{i,9}) + 360(P/F_{i,10})$

i = DCFROR = 200%
NPV @ 10% = +$1,401

Mutually exclusive alternative analysis requires incremental analysis.

Incremental Analysis, Purchase - Lease Cash Flows

```
CF=-860        CF=+160 . . . . . . . . . . . . CF=+160      CF=+260
───────────────────────────────────────────────────────────────
0                1 . . . . . . . . . . . . . . 9             10
```

Incremental PW Eq: $0 = -860 + 160(P/A_{i,9}) + 260(P/F_{i,10})$,

i = Incremental DCFROR = 14% > 10%, *so purchase*

Incremental NPV = 1,563 - 1,401 = +$162 > 0, *so purchase*

10-8 Solution: *Continued*

Leave the revenues out of this analysis since they are projected to be the same whether purchase or lease is selected.

Cash Flows for Purchase of New Plant for Cost Analysis

Year	0	1-9	10	Salv
Revenue				400
-Operating Costs		-200	-200	
-Depreciation	-50	-100	-50	
Taxable Income	-50	-300	-250	400
-Tax @ 40%	20	120	100	-160
Net Income	-30	-180	-150	240
+Depreciation	50	100	50	
-Capital Costs -1,000				
Cash Flow	-980	-80	-100	240

$$\underbrace{\qquad\qquad}_{140}$$

PW Cost @ 10% = $980 + 80(P/A_{10,9}) - 140(P/F_{10,10}) = \$1,386.75$

AW Cost @ 10% = $1,386.75(A/P_{10,10}) = \$225.69$

Cash Flows for Leasing Plant for Cost Analysis

Year	0	1-9	10
Revenue			
-Oper Costs	-200	-400	-200
Taxable Income	-200	-400	-200
-Tax @ 40%	80	160	80
Net Income	-120	-240	-120
Cash Flow	-120	-240	-120

PW Cost @ 10% = $120 + 240(P/A_{10,9}) + 120(P/F_{10,10}) = \$1,548.43$

AW Cost @ 10% = $1,548.43(A/P_{10,10}) = \$252.00$

Select Purchase to minimize both present worth and annual worth cost.

The same economic conclusion to purchase has been reached with all techniques of analysis.

10-9 Solution: *All Values in Dollars*

Standard Cost of Service for a bulldozer

Let "X" equal the Before Tax Standard Cost Per Hour necessary to receive a 15% DCFROR on invested capital. Revenues are separated from costs for illustration and sensitivity analysis purposes. You may also obtain the same solutions by combining both into one cash flow calculation and solving for the standard cost of service/hr X. That solution is left to the reader.

Cash Flows for Break-even Revenues

Year	0	1	2	3	4	5
Revenue		4,000X	4,000X	3,000X	2,000X	2,000X
Taxable Income		4,000X	4,000X	3,000X	2,000X	2,000X
-Tax @ 40%		-1,600X	-1,600X	-1,200X	-800X	-800X
Cash Flow		2,400X	2,400X	1,800X	1,200X	1,800X

$$\text{PW of Revenues} = (2,400X)P/F_{15,1} + (2,400X)(P/F_{15,2}) + (1,800X)(P/F_{15,3})$$
$$+ (1,200X)(P/F_{15,4}) + (1,200X)(P/F_{15,5}) = 6,368X$$

Cash Flows for Cost of Service

Year	0	1	2	3	4	5
Salvage Revenue						136,298
-Oper Costs		-27,948	-125,364	-100,441	-150,384	-45,499
-Deprec	-69,512	-119,164	-85,117	-60,798	-43,452	-43,403
-Deprec Write-off						-65,154
Taxable Inc	-69,512	-147,112	-210,481	-161,239	-193,836	-17,758
-Tax @ 40%	27,805	58,845	84,192	64,496	77,534	7,103
Net Income	-41,707	-88,267	-126,289	-96,743	-116,302	-10,655
+Deprec	69,512	119,164	85,117	60,798	43,452	43,403
+Deprec Write-off						65,154
-Cap. Cost	-486,585					
Cash Flow	-458,780	30,897	-41,172	-35,945	-72,850	97,902

$$\text{PW Cost} = 458,780 - 30,897(P/F_{15,1}) + 41,172(P/F_{15,2}) + 35,945(P/F_{15,3})$$
$$+ 72,850(P/F_{15,4}) - 97,902(P/F_{15,5}) = \$479,657$$

By setting present worth revenues equal to present worth costs we can determine the break-even standard cost of service per hour X, as follows:

Break-even Standard Cost of Service Per Hour:

$479,657 = X(6,368 \text{ hours})$, therefore, $X = \$75.32$ per hour

10-9 Solution: *Continued*

Standard Cost of Service for a Bulldozer
For the alternate hours per year, calculate the after-tax discounted revenues and again, set equal to the present worth cost to determine X. Before-tax hours of service are 3,000 hours per year, therefore, the discounted after-tax revenues may be expressed as:

$$1,800X(P/A_{15,5}) = 6,034X$$

Break-even Standard Cost of Service *is equal to:*
$479,657 = X(6,034 \text{ hours})$ therefore, $X = \$79.46$ per hour

It becomes apparent that the faster equipment hours of operation, or production, occur over asset life, the more cost competitive equipment becomes. This happens because equipment productivity is related to product revenue generation and the faster revenues are generated, the better the economics of projects become.

10-10 Solution: *Values in Thousands of Dollars*

C=Capital Cost, OC=Operating Cost, LP=Lease Payment, L=Salvage

```
               C=200
               OC=18        OC=39         OC=45          OC=24
Purchase      ─────────────────────────────────────────────── L=50
                 0             1             2              3
               LP=36        LP=72         LP=72          LP=36
Lease          OC=18        OC=39         OC=45          OC=24
              ───────────────────────────────────────────────
                 0             1             2              3
```

Purchase Cash Flows (Cost Analysis)

Year	Time 0	1	2	3	Salvage
Revenue					50.00
-Operating Costs	-18.00	-39.00	-45.00	-24.00	
-Depreciation	-40.00	-64.00	-38.40	-23.04	-34.56
Taxable Income	-58.00	-103.00	-83.40	-47.04	15.44
-Tax Due @ 40%	23.20	41.20	33.36	18.82	-6.18
Net Income	-34.80	-61.80	-50.04	-28.22	9.26
+Depreciation	40.00	64.00	38.40	23.04	34.56
-Capital Costs	-200.00				
Cash Flow	-194.80	2.20	-11.64	-5.18	43.82

Present Worth Cost @ 15% = $176.28

10-10 Solution: *Continued*

Leasing Cash Flows (Cost Analysis)

Year	0	1	2	3
-Operating Costs	-18.00	-39.00	-45.00	-24.00
-Lease Payments	-36.00	-72.00	-72.00	-36.00
Taxable Income	-54.00	-111.00	-117.00	-60.00
-Tax Due @ 40%	21.60	44.40	46.80	24.00
Net Income	-32.40	-66.60	-70.20	-36.00
Cash Flow	-32.40	-66.60	-70.20	-36.00

Present Worth Cost @ 15% = $167.06

Selecting the alternative with the least present worth cost suggests that leasing is the economic choice.

Incremental Analysis (Purchase-Lease), Before-tax Diagram, S = Savings

```
                    C=200
                    S= 36        S=72         S=72         S=36
Purchase-Lease      ─────────────────────────────────────────────  L=50
                      0            1            2            3
```

Incremental Cash Flows

Year	0	1	2	3	Salvage
Savings	36.00	72.00	72.00	36.00	50.00
-Depreciation	-40.00	-64.00	-38.40	-23.04	-34.56
Taxable Income	-4.00	8.00	33.60	12.96	15.44
-Tax Due @ 40%	1.60	-3.20	-13.44	-5.18	-6.18
Net Income	-2.40	4.80	20.16	7.78	9.26
+Depreciation	40.00	64.00	38.40	23.04	34.56
-Capital Costs	-200.00				
Cash Flow	-162.40	68.80	58.56	30.82	43.82

Incremental NPV @ 15% = -$9.2 < 0   *reject purchase*

Incremental DCFROR   = 11.6% < 15%   *reject purchase*

10-10 Solution: *Continued*

Monthly Analysis, Lease vs Purchase

```
          C=200
          OC=3.0   OC=3.0   OC=3.0   OC=3.5   OC=3.5   OC=4.0   OC=4.0   -
Purchase ─────────────────────────────────────────────────────────────── L=50
          0        1 ..... 11        12 ..... 23        24 ..... 35    36

          LP=6.0   LP=6.0   LP=6.0   LP=6.0   LP=6.0   LP=6.0   LP=6.0
          OC=3.0   OC=3.0   OC=3.0   OC=3.5   OC=3.5   OC=4.0   OC=4.0   -
Lease    ─────────────────────────────────────────────────────────────── L=0
          0        1 ..... 11        12 ..... 23        24 ..... 35    36
```

Purchase Cash Flow Calculations, Monthly Periods

Year 0 depreciation is spread over months 0 to 5, Year 1 depreciation is spread uniformly over months 6 to 17, Year 2 depreciation spread uniformly over months 18 to 29 and year 3 depreciation is spread over months 30 to 35.

Month	0	1-5	6-11	12-17	18-23	24-29	30-35	36
Revenue								50.00
-Op Cost	-3.00	-3.00	-3.00	-3.50	-3.50	-4.00	-4.00	
-Deprec	-6.67	-6.67	-5.33	-5.33	-3.20	-3.20	-3.84	
-Write-off								-34.56
Taxable	-9.67	-9.67	-8.33	-8.83	-6.70	-7.20	-7.84	15.44
-Tax @ 40%	3.87	3.87	3.33	3.53	2.68	2.88	3.14	-6.18
Net Income	-5.80	-5.80	-5.00	-5.30	-4.02	-4.32	-4.70	9.26
+Deprec	6.67	6.67	5.33	5.33	3.20	3.20	3.84	
+Write-off								34.56
-Cap Cost	-200.00							
Cash Flow	-200.87	0.87	0.33	0.03	-0.82	-1.12	-0.86	43.82

Effective Annual Discount Rate, E = $0.15 = (1+i)^{12} - 1$

Monthly Interest Rate, i = 0.0117 or 1.17%   *by trial and error*

PW Cost Purchase:

= $200.87 - 0.87(P/A_{1.17\%,5}) - 0.33(P/A_{1.17\%,12})(P/F_{1.17\%,5})$ .... = $178.2

Note that the monthly period analysis present worth cost of $178.2 is very close to the annual period analysis present worth cost of $176.3 Use of equivalent monthly period and annual period discount rates in the two analyses together with proper timing of the costs in the annual analysis is the key to obtaining equivalent results.

10-10 Solution: *Continued*

Monthly Analysis, Lease vs Purchase

Lease Cash Flow Calculations, Monthly Periods

Month	0	1-5	6-11	12-17	18-23	24-29	30-35
-Op Cost	-3.00	-3.00	-3.00	-3.50	-3.50	-4.00	-4.00
-Lease Pmt	-6.00	-6.00	-6.00	-6.00	-6.00	-6.00	-6.00
Taxable Inc	-9.00	-9.00	-9.00	-9.50	-9.50	-10.00	-10.00
-Tax @ 40%	3.60	3.60	3.60	3.80	3.80	4.00	4.00
Net Income	-5.40	-5.40	-5.40	-5.70	-5.70	-6.00	-6.00
Cash Flow	-5.40	-5.40	-5.40	-5.70	-5.70	-6.00	-6.00

PW Cost Leasing:

$5.40 + 5.40(P/A_{1.17\%,11}) + 5.70(P/A_{1.17\%,12})(P/F_{1.17\%,11})$

$+6.00(P/A_{1.17\%,12})(P/F_{1.17\%,23}) = \$167.8$

Selecting the alternative with the least present worth cost suggests that leasing is the economic choice, consistent with the annual period evaluation.

Incremental Purchase-Lease

Cash Flows	-195.47	6.27	5.73	5.73	4.88	4.88	5.14	43.82
Month	0	1-5	6-11	12-17	18-23	24-29	30-35	36

PW Eq: $0 = -195.47 + 6.27(P/A_{i\%,5}) + 5.73(P/A_{i\%,12})(P/F_{i\%,5})$

$+ 4.88(P/A_{i\%,12})(P/F_{i\%,17}) + 5.14(P/A_{i\%,6})(P/F_{i\%,29})$

$+ 36(P/F_{i\%,36})$

Incremental NPV @ 15% Annually *(1.17% per month)*=-$10.44 < 0 reject*

Incremental DCFROR per month = 0.88% < i* = 1.17%

Nominal Rate DCFROR is calculated as follows:

    12(0.88%) = 10.56% per year, compounded monthly.

To evaluate the incremental investment using annual DCFROR, the monthly DCFROR should be converted to the equivalent effective discrete annual DCFROR rate. The effective discrete annual rate is calculated as follows:

$$E = (1+.0088)^{12}-1 = 0.1109 \text{ or } 11.09\% < i* = 15\%, \quad reject~purchase$$

10-11 Solution: *Values in Thousands of Dollars*

Service Analysis

	OC= 100	OC=200	OC=200	OC=100	
Capital	C=1,000	-	-	-	
Intensive, "A"					L=300
	0	1	2	3	

	OC=275	OC=550	OC=550	OC=275	
Less Capital					
Intensive, "B"					L=0
	0	1	2	3	

	Savings=175	S=350	S=350	S=175	
"A-B"	C=1,000	-	-	-	
Incremental					L=300
	0	1	2	3	

"A-B" Incremental Analysis

Year	0	1	2	3
Savings	175	350	350	475
-Depr/Write-off	-200	-320	-192	-288
Taxable Income	-25	30	158	187
-Tax @ 40%	10	-12	-63.2	-74.8
Net Income	-15	18	94.8	112.2
+Depr/Write-off	200	320	192	288
-Capital Cost	-1,000	-	-	-
Cash Flow	-815	338	286.8	400.2

PW Eq: $0 = -815 + 338(P/F_{i,1}) + 286.8(P/F_{i,2}) + 400.2(P/F_{i,3})$

i = Incremental DCFROR = 12% < i*=15% *so reject "A", select "B"*

Incremental NPV @ 15%:

$$\underset{0.8696}{} \quad \underset{0.7561}{} \quad \underset{0.6575}{}$$

$-815+338(P/F_{15,1})+286.8(P/F_{15,2})+400.2(P/F_{15,3})=-\$41.09 < 0$ *reject "A"*

10-11 Solution: *Continued*

Cost Analyses

Alternative "A" (Capital Intensive)

Year	0	1	2	3
Revenue	–	–	–	300
-Operating Costs	-100	-200	-200	-100
-Deprec/Write-off	-200	-320	-192	-288
Taxable Income	-300	-520	-392	-88
-Tax @ 40%	+120	+208	+156.8	+35.2
Net Income	-180	-312	-235.2	-52.8
+Deprec/Write-off	200	320	192	288
-Capital Cost	-1,000	–	–	–
Cash Flow	-980	8	-43.2	235.2

$$\text{PW Cost @ 15\%: } 980 - 8\,\overset{0.8696}{(P/F_{15,1})} + 43.2\,\overset{0.7561}{(P/F_{15,2})} - 235.2\,\overset{0.6575}{(P/F_{15,3})} = \$851.06$$

$$\text{End-of-Period Equivalent AC: } 851.06\,\overset{0.43798}{(A/P_{15,3})} = \$372.75$$

$$\text{Beginning-of-Period Equivalent AC: } 372.75\,\overset{0.8696}{(P/F_{15,1})} = \$324.14$$

Alternative "B" (Less Capital Intensive)

Year	0	1	2	3
Revenue	–	–	–	–
-Operating Costs	-275	-550	-550	-275
Taxable Income	-275	-550	-550	-275
-Tax @ 40%	+110	+220	+220	+110
Net Income	-165	-330	-330	-165
-Capital Cost	–	–	–	–
Cash Flow	-165	-330	-330	-165

10-11 Solution: *Continued*

Alternative "B"

PW Cost @ 15%:

$$165 + 330\overset{0.8696}{(P/F_{15,1})} + 330\overset{0.7561}{(P/F_{15,2})} + 165\overset{0.6575}{(P/F_{15,3})} = \$809.97$$

$809.97 < \$851.06$, *so select less capital intensive "B"*

End-of-Period Equivalent AC:

$$809.97\overset{0.43798}{(A/P_{15,3})} = \$354.75 < \$372.75, \quad \text{select "B"}$$

Beginning-of-Period Equivalent AC:

$$354.75\overset{0.8696}{(P/F_{15,1})} = \$308.49 < \$324.14 \text{ select "B"}$$

In the above analyses, the less capital-intensive alternative "B" is preferred. However, alternative "B" may be treated as an option to lease the equipment. In this case, the problem becomes a lease vs. purchase analysis. Assume, then, that a hypothetical 6% minimum discount rate, that reflects the after-tax cost of borrowing funds to finance the purchase of the asset, is used. Many companies do this. In that case, purchasing seems preferable to leasing. But is it really?

Should the appropriate minimum discount rate be affected by whether the analysis is described as lease vs purchase, or as an old asset compared to a new asset, or as labor compared to automated equipment?
It seems evident the answer is "no," unless unique borrowed money financing that does not affect other capital budgets is available for purchasing instead of leasing. In general, if you can borrow to purchase an asset instead of leasing, then you probably can borrow money to acquire automated equipment to replace labor, or to finance any investment being evaluated. However, regardless of the financing source, the economic analysis objective is to make optimum use of available investment dollars from any source. Opportunity cost of capital as a minimum discount rate enables us to achieve that objective. If unique financing exists that creates no impact on available investment dollars to invest elsewhere, then, and only then, opportunity cost of capital equals the after-tax cost of borrowed money.

CHAPTER 11 PROBLEM SOLUTIONS

11-1 Solution: **Land Acquisition Analysis, All Values in Dollars**

CASE A, Cash Investment:

Before-Tax Diagram

```
    C=60,000
    ──────────────────────────────────── L = 150,000
    0           1 ....................... 5
```

Tax on gain = $(150,000-60,000)(.4 \text{ tax rate}) = 36,000$

After-Tax Diagram

```
  CF=-60,000
    ──────────────────────────────────── CF = 114,000
    0           1 ..................... 5
```

PW Eq: $0 = 60,000 - 114,000(P/F_{i,5})$,   i=DCFROR=13.7% by trial and error.

CASE B, Leveraged Investment:

Before-Tax Diagram

```
         Int= 5,000 Int=4,000 Int=3,000 Int=2,000 Int=1,000
   C=10,000  C=10,000  C=10,000  C=10,000  C=10,000  C=10,000
    ──────────────────────────────────────────── L = 150,000
    0        1         2         3         4       5
```

Every dollar of interest saves $0.40 in tax at a 40% effective tax rate.

After-Tax Diagram

```
         Int= 3,000 Int=2,400 Int=1,800 Int=1,200   Int=600
   C=10,000  C=10,000  C=10,000  C=10,000  C=10,000  C=10,000
    ──────────────────────────────────────────── CF = 114,000
    0        1         2         3         4       5
Net CF=-10,000  -13,000  -12,400  -11,800  -11,200  -10,600
```

Costs vary by a constant gradient of $600 for years 1 to 5.

PW Eq: $0 = -10,000 - [13,000 - 600(A/G_{i,5})](P/A_{i,5}) + 114,000(P/F_{i,5})$

$\qquad i = DCFROR = 19.9\%$

The after-tax cost of borrowed money is 10%(1-.4 tax rate) or 6.0% which is less than the cash investment DCFROR of 13.7% so borrowed money leverage works for the investor and the leveraged investment DCFROR of 19.9% is greater than the cash investment DCFROR of 13.7%.

11-2 Solution: Develop vs Sell Now Leveraged Analysis

$C_{Land}=1$ (Sunk) $C_{Bldgs}=30$ Income/Yr = 65   70   75
          $C_{Equip}= 5$ OpCost/Yr = 25   30   35

| -2 | 0 (Now) | 1 | 2 | 3 |

Leveraged Develop Cash Flows:

Year	0	1	2	3	3 Salv
Revenue		65.00	70.00	75.00	40.00
-Operating Costs		-25.00	-30.00	-35.00	
-Deprec/Writeoff		-1.63	-2.18	-1.83	-30.37*
-Interest		-3.60	-3.03	-2.40	
Taxable Income		34.77	34.79	35.77	9.63
-Tax @ 35%		-12.17	-12.18	-12.52	-3.37
Net Income		22.60	22.61	23.25	6.26
+Deprec/Writeoff		1.63	2.18	1.83	30.37*
-Principal		-4.72	-5.29	-19.99	
-Cap. Costs	-35.00				
+Borrowed $	30.00				
Cash Flow	-5.00	19.51	19.50	5.09	36.53

41.72

Sale Cash Flow:

Year	0
Sale Value	7.0
-Book Writeoff	-1.0
Taxable	6.0
-Tax (35%)	-2.1
Net Income	3.9
+Book Writeoff	1.0
Cash Flow	4.9

$NPV_{Sell} = 4.9$

*Includes land and equipment.

$$NPV @ 20\% = -5.00+19.51(P/F_{20,1})+19.50(P/F_{20,2})+41.72(P/F_{20,3}) = +\$48.94$$

with 0.8333, 0.6944, 0.5787 above respective terms.

DCFROR = 401%, "i" value that makes NPV equal to zero

Since these projects are mutually exclusive we select the project with the largest NPV which is the "Develop" alternative with an NPV of +48.7.

Depreciation Calculations

Yr 1 5(0.1429)	= 0.72
Yr 1 30(1/31.5)(11.5/12)	= 0.91
Yr 2 5(0.2449)	= 1.23
Yr 2 30(1/31.5)	= 0.95
Yr 3 5(0.1749)	= 0.88
Yr 3 30(1/31.5)	= 0.95
Yr 3 Writeoff on 5	= 2.18
Yr 3 Writeoff on 30	= 27.19
Yr 3 Land Writeoff	= 1.00

Mortgage Payment: $30(A/P_{12,5}) = 8.32$

Year	1	2	3
Principal	30.00	25.28	19.99
Interest	3.60	3.03	2.40
Princ. Pd	4.72	5.29	19.99

11-3 Solution: Petroleum Property Evaluation

Develop (Before-Tax) Time Diagram

```
                              Rev=7.0
                    IDC=2.0    OC=1.2
                    Tang=1.5   IDC=2.0    Rev=11.0    Rev=9.0
Acq=3.0 (Sunk)      Borrow=4.0 Tang=1.0    OC=2.5      OC=2.1
                                                                  L=6.5
 -1                 0(Now)       1          2          3
```

Develop Cash Flows

Year	0	1	2	3	3 Salv
Revenue		7.00	11.00	9.00	6.50
-Royalties		-1.05	-1.65	-1.35	
Net Revenue		5.95	9.35	7.65	
-Oper Costs		-1.20	-2.50	-2.10	
-Intangible	-1.40	-1.40			
-Depreciation	-0.21	-0.51	-0.51	-0.36	
-Deprec Write-off					-0.91
-Amortization	-0.12	-0.24	-0.24	-0.24	-0.36
-Interest		-0.48	-0.40	-0.32	
Depletion		-0.30	-0.48	-0.42	-1.80
Taxable Inc	-1.73	1.82	5.22	4.21	3.43
-Tax @ 40%	0.69	-0.73	-2.09	-1.68	-1.37
Net Income	-1.04	1.09	3.13	2.53	2.06
+Depreciation	0.21	0.51	0.51	0.36	0.91
+Depletion		0.30	0.48	0.42	1.80
+Amortization	0.12	0.24	0.24	0.24	0.36
-Principal		-0.63	-0.71	-2.66	
-Cap. Costs	-2.10	-1.60			
+Borrowed	4.00				
Cash Flow	1.19	-0.09	3.65	0.89	5.13

Sell Cash Flow

Year	0
Sale Value	5.0
-Write-off	-3.0
Taxable Inc.	2.0
-Tax @ 40%	-0.8
Net Income	1.2
+Write-off	3.0
Cash Flow	4.2

$NPV_{Sell} = 4.2$

NPV_{Dev} @ 25% = 6.54 > 4.2, Select Develop

Since neither project has any negative cash flow upon which to properly calculate DCFROR, both alternatives offer infinite leveraged DCFROR's on total investment. Incremental DCFROR analysis is required to make a proper economic decision with DCFROR analysis. The incremental analysis is on the next page.

Loan Payment Schedule:
$4(A/P_{12,5}) = 1.11$

	Princ Bal	Interest	Principal Paid
Yr 1	4	0.48	0.63
Yr 2	3.37	0.40	0.71
Yr 3	2.67	0.32	2.66

Cost Depletion Schedule:

Yr 1	3(0.10)	= 0.30	
Yr 2	3(0.16)	= 0.48	or $[0.16X/(X-0.1X)](3-0.3) = 0.48$
Yr 3	3(0.14)	= 0.42	or $[0.14X/(0.9X-0.16X)](3-0.78) = 0.42$
Yr 3	Writeoff	= 1.80	

11-3 Solution: Continued

Incremental DCFROR Analysis:

Cash Flow "Develop"

1.19	-0.09	3.65	0.89	5.13
0	1	2	3	3+

Cash Flow "Sell Now"

4.2	-	-	-	-
0	1	2	3	3+

Incremental
"Develop-Sell Now"
Cash Flows

-3.01	-0.09	3.65	0.89	5.13
0	1	2	3	3+

6.02

Incremental PW Eq: $0 = -3.01 - 0.09(P/F_i,1) + 3.65(P/F_i,2)$
$+ 6.02(P/F_i,3)$

i = Incremental DCFROR = 56.4% > i^* of 25%, so accept development

Incremental NPV @ 25% = +2.3 > 0, so accept development

Or,

The same incremental NPV results from $NPV_{Dev} - NPV_{Sell}$:

Incremental NPV = 6.5 - 4.2 = 2.3

11-4 Solution: Silver Property, Values in Millions

Acq Cost =2.0   Rev=4.5   Rev=6.0   Rev=7.5
Equipment =3.0   OC =3.0   OC=3.37   OC=3.75
Borrowed $=4.0   Dev=1.5

$$\underset{0}{\rule{0pt}{0pt}} \qquad \underset{1}{\rule{0pt}{0pt}} \qquad \underset{2}{\rule{0pt}{0pt}} \qquad \underset{3}{\rule{0pt}{0pt}}\text{—— Salv = 6.0}$$

Loan Amortization Schedule:

$4.0(A/P_{10,10}) = 0.65$

Year	Interest	Principal
1	$4(0.1)$ $=0.4$	$0.65-0.4 = 0.25$
2	$3.75(0.1)=0.37$	$0.65-0.37=0.28$
3	$3.47(0.1)=0.35$	3.47

Cost Depletion Schedule:

Yr 1	$2(0.3/3)$	$= 0.2$
Yr 2	$(2-0.2)(0.3/2.7)$	$= 0.2$
Yr 3	$(1.8-0.71)(0.3/2.4)$	$= 0.14$

Cash Flows:

Year	0	1	2	3	3 Salv
Revenue		4.50	6.00	7.50	6.00
-Operating Costs		-3.00	-3.38	-3.75	
-Development		-1.05			
-Depreciation		-0.43	-0.73	-0.52	
-Deprec Writeoff					-1.32
-Amortization		-0.05	-0.09	-0.09	-0.22
-Interest		-0.40	-0.37	-0.35	
Before Depletion		-0.43	1.43	2.79	4.46
-50% Limit		0	-0.71	1.39	
-Percent Depl (15%)		0.68	0.90	-1.13	
-Cost Depletion		-0.20	0.20	0.14	
Taxable Income		-0.63	0.72	1.66	4.46
-Tax @ 40%		0.25	-0.29	-0.67	-1.78
Net Income		-0.38	0.43	1.00	2.68
+Depreciation		0.43	0.73	0.52	1.32
+Depletion		0.20	0.71	1.13	
+Amortization		0.05	0.09	0.09	0.22
-Principal		-0.25	-0.28	-3.47	
-Capital Costs	-5.00	-0.45*			
+Borrowed	4.00				
Cash Flow	-1.00	-0.40	1.68	-0.73	4.22

PW Eq: $0 = -1.00-0.40(P/F_{i,1})+1.68(P/F_{i,2})-0.73(P/F_{i,3})+4.22(P/F_{i,3})$

   i = Leveraged DCFROR = 73.25%

This is the "i" value that makes NPV for this leveraged investment NPV equal to zero.

11-5 Solution: Land Acquisition Analysis

	Escalated $ Sale Price = X
Borrowed $ = 160,000	Interest = 16,000
Cost of Land = 200,000	Loan Principal Payment = 160,000

```
        0                                      1 year
```

Year	0	1
Escalated $ Sale Revenue		X
-Interest		-16,000
-Book Value (Initial Cost)		-200,000
Taxable Gain		X-216,000
-Tax @ 34%		-.34X+ 73,440
Net Income		.66X-142,560
+Book Value		+200,000
-Capital Cost	-200,000	
+Borrowed $	160,000	-160,000
Cash Flow	-40,000	.66X-102,560

For a 30% constant dollar DCFROR and 10% inflation per year, the equivalent escalated dollar DCFROR is calculated as follows:

$$i = (1+0.10)(1+0.30) - 1$$

$$= 0.430 \text{ or } 43.0\%$$

$$\overset{0.6993}{\text{PW Eq: } 0 = -40,000 + (0.66X-102,560)(P/F_{43\%,1})}$$

$$40,000 = 0.46X - 71,720$$

X = $242,870 = the escalated dollar sale price to give a 30% constant dollar DCFROR on leveraged equity investment.

11-6 Solution: Rental Machinery Analysis, All Values in Thousands of Dollars

Working Capital = 10   Rev/yr =   150   180   210
Deprec Equip.   = 150   OC/yr =   50   70   90

                                                        ──────── Salv = 50
          0   1   2   3   Including WC
                                                                  Return

Escalated Dollar Cash Flow Calculations

Year	0	1	2	3	3 Salv
Revenue		150.00	180.00	210.00	50.00
-Oper Costs		-50.00	-70.00	-90.00	
-Depreciation	-21.43	-36.73	-26.24	-18.74	-46.86
-Interest		-12.00	-8.00	-4.00	
-Writeoffs					-10.00
Taxable Income	-21.43	51.27	75.76	97.26	-6.86
-Tax @ 40%	8.57	-20.51	-30.30	-38.90	2.74
Net Income	-12.86	30.76	45.46	58.35	-4.12
+Depreciation	21.43	36.73	26.24	18.74	46.86
-Principal		-40.00	-40.00	-40.00	
+Writeoffs					10.00
-Capital Costs	-160.00				
+Borrowed $	120.00				
Cash Flow	-31.43	27.49	31.70	37.10	52.74

                                           89.84

Leveraged Escalated Dollar PW Eq:

$0 = -31.43 + 27.49(P/F_{i,1}) + 31.7(P/F_{i,2}) + 89.84(P/F_{i,3})$

i = Leveraged Escalated $ DCFROR = 104.8%

NPV @ 20% = +$65.48

Constant Dollar Equivalent Cash Flows:

Year 0	Year 1	Year 2	Year 3
-31.43	$27.49(P/F_{10,1})=24.99$	$31.7(P/F_{10,2})=26.2$	$89.84(P/F_{10,3})=67.5$

Leveraged Constant Dollar PW Eq:

$0 = -31.43 + 24.99(P/F_{i',1}) + 26.2(P/F_{i',2}) + 67.5(P/F_{i',3})$

i' = Leveraged Constant $ DCFROR = 86.2%

Using Equation 5-1 we can check the results:

$(1+i) = (1+f)(1+i')$, $(1 + 1.048) = (1.1)(1.862) = 2.048$, so equivalent.

11-7 Solution: Depreciable Investment Analysis (in Thousands of Dollars)

```
Deprec Equip   = 100
Development    =  10        Revenues/yr = 150                    150
Work Capital   =  30        Op Costs/yr = 118                    118   WC Return
                                                                       = 30
              ───────────────────────────────────────────────────────
                       0                    1  . . . . . . . . . . . . . . .   5
```

Cash Investment Analysis:

Year	0	1	2	3	4	5	5 Salv
Revenue		150.0	150.0	150.0	150.0	150.0	30.0
-Oper Costs		-118.0	-118.0	-118.0	-118.0	-118.0	
-Development	-10.0						
-Depreciation	-10.0	-20.0	-20.0	-20.0	-20.0	-10.0	
-Writeoffs							-30.0
Taxable Income	-20.0	12.0	12.0	12.0	12.0	22.0	
-Tax @ 40%	8.0	-4.8	-4.8	-4.8	-4.8	-8.8	
Net Income	-12.0	7.2	7.2	7.2	7.2	13.2	
+Depreciation	10.0	20.0	20.0	20.0	20.0	10.0	
+Writeoffs							30.0
-Capital Costs	-130.0						
Cash Flow	-132.0	27.2	27.2	27.2	27.2	23.2	30.0

$$\underbrace{\qquad\qquad}_{53.2}$$

Cash PW Eq: $0 = -132 + 27.2(P/A_{i,4}) + 53.2(P/F_{i,5})$

  i = Cash Investment DCFROR = 6.5%

Leveraged Investment Cash Flows:

Year	0	1	2	3	4	5	5 Salv
Revenue		150.0	150.0	150.0	150.0	150.0	30.0
-Oper Costs		-118.0	-118.0	-118.0	-118.0	-118.0	
-Development	-10.0						
-Depreciation	-10.0	-20.0	-20.0	-20.0	-20.0	-10.0	
-Interest		-12.0	-9.6	-7.2	-4.8	-2.4	
-Writeoffs							-30.0
Taxable Income	-20.0	0.0	2.4	4.8	7.2	19.6	0.0
-Tax @ 40%	8.0	0.0	-1.0	-1.9	-2.9	-7.8	0.0
Net Income	-12.0	0.0	1.4	2.9	4.3	11.8	
+Depreciation	10.0	20.0	20.0	20.0	20.0	10.0	
-Principal		-20.0	-20.0	-20.0	-20.0	-20.0	
+Writeoffs							30.0
-Capital Costs	-130.0						
+Borrowed $	100.0						
Cash Flow	-32.0	0.0	1.4	2.9	4.3	1.8	30.0

$$\underbrace{\qquad\qquad}_{31.8}$$

11-7 Solution: Continued - Depreciable Investment Analysis,
In Thousands of Dollars

Lev. PW Eq: $0 = -32.0+1.4(P/F_{i,2})+2.9(P/F_{i,3})+4.3(P/F_{i,4})+31.8(P/F_{i,5})$

i = Leveraged Investment DCFROR = 5.2%

Results for leveraged analysis are less attractive because the after-tax cost of borrowed money (7.2%) exceeds the project cash investment DCFROR, hence leverage works against the investor.

11-8 Solution: Leveraged Evaluation of Problem 10-10

Purchase Cash Flows (Cost Analysis)

Year	Time 0	1	2	3	Salvage
Revenue					50
-Operating Costs	-18	-39	-45	-24	
-Interest Payment		-15	-10	-5	
-Depreciation	-40	-64	-38	-23	-35
Taxable Income	-58	-118	-93	-52	15
-Tax @ 40%	23	47	37	21	-6
Net Income	-35	-71	-56	-31	9
+Depreciation	40	64	38	23	35
-Princ. Paid		-50	-50	-50	
+Loan Income	150				
-Capital Costs	-200				
Cash Flow	-45	-57	-68	-58	44

Present Worth Cost @ 15% = $154.8
Present Worth Cost @ 25% = $141.3

Leasing Cash Flows (Cost Analysis)

Year	Time 0	1	2	3
-Operating Costs	-18.00	-39.00	-45.00	-24.00
-Lease Payments	-36.00	-72.00	-72.00	-36.00
Taxable Income	-54.00	-111.00	-117.00	-60.00
-Tax Due @ 40%	21.60	44.40	46.80	24.00
Net Income	-32.40	-66.60	-70.20	-36.00
Cash Flow	-32.40	-66.60	-70.20	-36.00

Present Worth Cost @ 15% = $167.1
Present Worth Cost @ 25% = $149.0

Selecting the alternative with the least present worth cost suggests that purchasing the equipment is now the economic choice. This was not the choice in evaluating the alternatives from a 100% cash equity analysis.

11-9 Solution:

Uniform mortgage payments over 3 years, at 12% annual interest:

$500,000(A/P_{12,3}) = \$208,175$

	Year 1	Year 2	Year 3
Before-Tax Interest	60,000	42,219	23,304
Principal Payment	148,175	165,955	185,870

Leveraged Cash Flows:

Year	0	1	2	3
Cash Investment CF	-800,000	400,000	500,000	550,000
-Loan Principal Pmt.	-	-148,175	-165,955	-185,870
-After-Tax Interest*	-	-36,000	-25,331	-13,382
+Borrowed Dollars	+500,000	-	-	-
Leveraged CF	-300,000	215,825	308,714	350,748

*After-Tax Interest = (1-tax rate)(interest)

A) PW Eq: $0 = -300,000+215,825(P/F_{i,1})+308,714(P/F_{i,2})+350,748(P/F_{i,3})$

NPV @ 72% = -$1,238
NPV @ 70% = $5,169

i = Leveraged DCFROR = 70%+(72%-70%)(5,169-0)/(5,169+1,238) = 71.61%

B) Calculate the NPV at i* = 25%

$NPV = -300,000+215,825(P/F_{25,1})+308,714(P/F_{25,2})+350,748(P/F_{25,3})$

= +$249,820

Let the acquisition cost in year 0 = X

X/3 is the annual amortization deduction

(X/3)(0.4) = 0.133X = tax savings per year

$$X - 0.133X \overset{1.952}{(P/A_{25,3})} = 249,820$$

X = $337,419 = acquisition cost to give a 25% DCFROR

AUXILIARY PROBLEMS

1. You have been asked to evaluate whether it is economically better to use a submersible centrifugal pump system or a rod pump system to lift crude oil 4000 feet in a well with an estimated producing life of 12 years. The submersible pump system initially will have an installed cost of $100,000 including tubing, wiring and surface gear while the installed rod pump cost, including sucker rods and surface gear will be $135,000. It is estimated that the submersible pump will need to be replaced every 3 years with a similar refurbished used pump for a cost of $35,000 at year 3, $45,000 at year 6 and $55,000 at year 9. Year 12 salvage value of the submersible pump is $50,000. The down-hole positive displacement rod pump is estimated to need replacing every 4 years for costs of $8,000 at year 4 and $12,000 at year 8. Due to corrosion, the salvage value of the rod pump system at year 12 is estimated to be 0. The minimum ROR is 15%. Use Present Worth Cost analysis to determine which pumping system is economically better. Verify your conclusion with ROR analysis.

2.

	I=100	I=250	I=375	I=500	I=500	L=100 I=400
C=100	C=500	C=100	C=125	C=150	C=150	C=200
0	1	2	3	4	5	6

A project has costs and revenues as shown on the diagram in thousands of dollars. Calculate the project rate of return. Then, assume the minimum rate of return is 15% and calculate the growth rate of return, NPV and PVR for the project using a 6 year evaluation life.

3. A loader is being considered to tram coal from a stockpile to a coal load-out facility. The cost of the machine is estimated to be $900,000 with an estimated salvage of $225,000 at the end of 7 years from now. Operating costs are estimated to be $200,000 per year with major repairs of $150,000 and $100,000 required at the end of the 3rd and 5th years respectively. Given the required tram distance, it is estimated the machine can move 2,400 ton of coal per day, 250 days per year. For a desired minimum rate of return of 12%, calculate the present and annual cost of operating this machine over the next 7 years. Then calculate the break-even cost per ton of coal being trammed.

4. Rank these non-mutually exclusive alternatives for a 20% opportunity cost of capital. Values are given in thousands of dollars.

A)

	I=100	I=150				
C=100	C=200	C=250	I=300	I=300	I=300	I=300
0	1	2	3	4	5	6

B)

		I=200			
–	C=300	C=150	I=250	I=250	I=250
0	1	2	3	4	5

C)

C=200	I=170	C=200	I=350	I=350	I=350	C=100
0	1	2	3	4	5	6

5. A manager is trying to evaluate the economics of purchasing or leasing a natural gas processing facility. It may be purchased and installed on company land for $1,000,000 or leased for $250,000 per year with beginning of year lease payments. With either alternative, the annual revenue to the plant for natural gas liquids is expected to be $1,500,000 with $800,000 annual operating costs. The life of the plant is estimated to be 8 years. Net salvage value of the plant at the end of the 8th year is estimated to be $150,000 if you purchase. For a 15% minimum rate of return, determine whether the manager should purchase or lease the processing facility. Reinforce your economic conclusion by making a second evaluation using a different analysis.

6. Evaluate the economic potential of purchasing a gold property now (at year 0) for a $2 million mineral rights acquisition cost. Mining equipment costs of $3 million will be incurred at year 0. Mineral development costs of $1 million will be incurred at year 0, and mineral development costs of $1.5 million will be incurred at year 1. Production is expected to start in year 1 with 150,000 tons of gold ore. Production in years 2, 3, and 4 is estimated to be 250,000 tons per year. Gold ore reserves are estimated to be depleted at the end of year 4. Reclamation costs (treated as operating expenses) of $0.5 million will be incurred at year 5. Equipment will be sold at year 5 for $1 million. All gold ore is estimated to contain 0.1 ounce of gold per ton of ore, and metallurgical recovery is estimated to be 90%. The price of gold is forecast to be $300 per ounce in year 1, escalating 15% in year 2, 20% in year 3, and 10% in year 4. Operating costs are estimated to be $20 per ton of ore produced in year 1, escalating 8% per year thereafter. Make before-tax ROR, NPV, PVR, and Growth ROR analyses for a minimum ROR of 15%.

7. Consideration is currently being given to determine whether a D9N bulldozer should be purchased or leased for necessary service over the next five years. If the machine is purchased, the year 0 purchase price for the D9N is $750,000. Maintenance costs are estimated to be $50,000 at year 0, $100,000 at year 1 (with that amount increasing by 10.0% per year at years 2,3, and 4), and $70,000 at year 5. Major repairs of $180,000 at the end of year 2, and $160,000 at the end of year 4 are also estimated to be required. The end-of-year 5 salvage is estimated to be $50,000. The alternative to purchasing is to lease the machine for $82.50 per hour. It is assumed the machine will operate 18 hours per day, 26 days per month, 12 months per year. An $82.50 per hour lease rate applies for the first three years, then the lease cost is expected to increase by 10.0% to $90.75 per hour for years 4 and 5. The hourly lease rate includes all maintenance and repair costs. Allocate the value of the lease payments for the first 6 months to year 0. Allocate months 7 through 18 lease payments at year 1 and so forth (with months 43 through 54 at year 4) and allocate the final six months of payments (55 through 60) at month 60 to best account for the time value of money. Assume the before-tax minimum rate of return is 20%. Calculate the before-tax present worth costs for each alternative and the incremental net present value (NPV) to determine which of these two alternatives is the economic choice. Then, determine the lease cost per hour that would make leasing break-even with purchasing.

8. Make the same analyses asked for in Auxiliary Problem #7 on an after-tax basis. Assume that if you purchase, the machine will be depreciated over 7 years using modified ACRS depreciation with the half-year convention, beginning in year one. Expense all maintenance and repair costs in the year incurred assuming other income exists to utilize all deductions in the year they are realized. Write off the remaining book value at the end of year 5. If the machine is leased, assume it is an operating lease so all lease payments will be 100% deductible in the year they are realized. The effective income tax rate is estimated to be 38.0%. Assume the after-tax minimum DCFROR is 20.0%. Calculate the after-tax present worth costs for each alternative and the incremental after-tax NPV to determine which of these two alternatives is the economic choice. Then, determine the lease cost per hour that would make leasing break-even with purchasing.

9. Development of a natural gas property is projected to involve production, costs and prices as follows with costs expressed in thousands of dollars and production and price in units as noted. Mcf = Thousand Cubic Feet, MMcf = Million Cubic Feet and M$ = Thousands of Dollars.

Year	0	1	2	3	4
Production, (MMcf/Yr)		300	700	500	150
Price, $/Mcf		2.00	2.25	2.50	$2.75
Royalties, 15% of Revenues		15%	15%	15%	15%
Intangible Well Cost, M$	600	300			
Tangible Well Cost, M$		400			
Tangible Pipeline Cost, M$		200			
Mineral Acquisition Cost, M$	100				
Operating Costs, M$		60	70	80	90

A) Calculate the annual before-tax cash flow, then calculate ROR, NPV, PVR and Growth ROR for a 15% minimum ROR, assuming the investor has a 100% working interest in the property and salvage is zero.

B) Assume this project is in a U.S. wilderness area so a $600,000 reclamation cost must be incurred at year 5, then calculate a valid project ROR.

10. A mutually exclusive alternative variation of the development described in Auxiliary Problem #9A is to delay the start of development until four years after year 0 to take advantage of sharply escalating natural gas prices expected to occur four to eight years from now. The four year development delay would make the start of new development year 0 equal to year 4 in problem #9A. Assume the mineral rights acquisition cost is incurred at year 0 and all other costs given in problem #9A will escalate 5% per year over the four year delay period and that year 5 to 8 production rates for the delayed project will be the same as in years 1 to 4 of problem #9. The natural gas selling price of $2.75 per Mcf in year 4 of problem #9A is estimated to escalate 20% per year over the following four years. Is it better to develop now for the development scenario described in problem #9A, or to delay the development for four years as described in this problem statement? Use the analysis method of your choice for a minimum rate of return of 15%.

11. Two used machines can be acquired for $60,000 per machine to provide necessary service for the next two years. The salvage of these machines is estimated to be $20,000 per machine at year two when the old machines will be replaced with one new machine capable of providing the same total service. The new machine would cost $350,000 at year 2. Instead of buying the old machines and replacing them at year 2, a new machine can be purchased today at year 0 for a cost of $300,000 to provide the necessary service. Service with either the old or new machines is needed for the next four years, so a four year evaluation life should be used. It is estimated that purchasing a new machine at year 0 will give it a salvage value of $80,000 at year 4 while purchasing a new machine at year 2 will give it a salvage value of $170,000 at year 4. Operating costs per machine with the used machines are estimated to be $60,000 at year 1 and $70,000 at year 2. Operating costs with a new machine purchased at year 0 are estimated to be $75,000 at year 1, $80,000 at year 2, $85,000 at year 3 and $90,000 at year 4. Operating costs with a new machine purchased at year 2 are estimated to be $80,000 at year 3 and $85,000 at year 4. Assuming a minimum discount rate of 15%, use present worth cost analysis to determine the most economical alternative for providing the necessary service. Then determine the four equal end of year revenues at years 1 through 4 for each alternative that would cover the cost of service and give the investor a 15% ROR.

12. Two alternative choices exist for you to invest $100,000 as shown on the following time diagrams.

    A) C=$100,000 _____ - _____ - _____ - L=$627,500
             0   1   2 7

    B) C=$100,000   I=$44,190   I=$44,190 ..... I=$44,190   L=0
             0   1   2 7

    Assuming a minimum ROR of 15%, determine the economically better choice using A) ROR Analysis, B) NPV Analysis, C) PVR Analysis, D) Growth ROR Analysis and E) Future Value Analysis. Discuss the consistency (or lack of consistency) of results with the different methods of analysis.

13. Investment of $100,000 is projected to generate increasing annual production that gives today's dollar net revenues of $30,000 in year 1, $40,000 in year 2 and $50,000 in year 3 with a $40,000 salvage value at year 3. Net revenues and salvage are projected to escalate 8% in year 1, 6% in year 2 and 4% in year 3. Calculate the escalated dollar ROR and NPV for a minimum escalated dollar ROR of 20%. Then calculate the equivalent constant dollar project ROR and NPV assuming inflation will be 8% in year 1, 10% in year 2 and 12% in year 3.

14. A chemical company wants you to analyze whether it is better economically to sell patent rights to a new chemical process for $300,000 cash now at year 0 or whether it would be better to keep the patent rights and develop them using one of two development scenarios for which projected costs (C) and incomes (I) are given on the following diagrams. All dollar values shown are in thousands of dollars.

                    I=$100   I=$420   I=$420
    A) C=$700   C=$300   C=$200 ..... C=$200
             0   1   2 9

                                I=$670   I=$670
    B) C=$500   C=$800   C=$250 ..... C=$250
             0   1   2 9

    Use ROR Analysis to determine whether it is better to sell or develop with the "A" or "B" scenario assuming the minimum ROR is 15%. Verify your results with NPV and PVR Analysis. Using any valid analysis, if the minimum ROR is raised to 25% what is your economic choice?

15. Evaluate the economics of using an ore conveyor system as an economic alternative to haul trucks using present worth cost analysis for a 15 year life and a minimum rate of return of 15%. Consider a cost of $16 million for an ore conveyor system in evaluation year 0 with operating costs of $2.5 million in year 1 and estimated to increase by an arithmetic gradient of $300,000 per year in each year after year 1 for the 15 year estimated mine life. Two major repairs costing $4 million and $6 million are estimated to be required at the end of evaluation years 5 and 10. Salvage value is estimated to be $7 million in evaluation year 15. The alternative to the conveyor system is to use 7 new haul trucks with a 170 ton capacity and a cost of $800,000 per truck in evaluation year 0. The haul trucks would have a 5 year life and salvage values of $100,000 each. Operating costs per truck are estimated to be $400,000 in evaluation year 1 and to increase by an arithmetic gradient of $60,000 per truck year through year 5. In 5 years the 7 trucks would be replaced with new trucks costing an estimated $1,400,00 per truck with salvage values of $150,00 per truck 5 years later in evaluation year 10. Operating costs per truck are estimated to be $550,000 in year 6 and to increase by an arithmetic gradient of $70,000 per truck for evaluation years 7 through 10. In 10 years the 7 trucks would be replaced again with new trucks costing $2,300,000 per truck with salvage of $200,000 per truck 5 years later in evaluation year 15. Operating costs per truck are estimated to be $700,000 in year 11 and to increase by an arithmetic gradient of $80,000 per truck for evaluation years 12 through 15. Verify your result with incremental rate of return.

16. Production of crude oil from a 10,000 foot deep north sea well that has L-80 carbon steel 5" tubing requires down-hole injection of chemicals to control tubing corrosion due to high temperatures and pressures and corrosive chlorides in the crude oil. It is proposed to replace the L-80 carbon steel tubing, which cost $8.50 per foot 1 year ago, with 13% chrome stainless steel tubing that would cost $30 per foot. 10,000 feet of tubing are needed and installation costs are estimated to be $80,000. Annual cost savings in chemicals, labor and chemical injection equipment are projected to be $100,000 in year 1 following the installation of the new tubing with savings escalating 7% per year in succeeding years. Use NPV Analysis for a 15% minimum ROR and 6 year evaluation life with a salvage value of 0 in year 6 to determine if installation of the 13% chrome tubing is economically desirable. Assume the existing L-80 carbon steel tubing has no salvage value at year 0. What physical use life will cause the 13% chrome tubing replacement investment to yield a 15% ROR?

17. An existing mineral operation is expected to generate annual net revenue (revenue minus operating costs) of $100 million per year at each of years 1, 2, 3, and 4. Purchase of mineral reserves contained in an adjacent property for $40 million now (time zero) is being considered with the expectation that $50 million would be spent on development and equipment at year 1, and another $55 million at year 2. This expansion would make the total project net revenue $100 million at year 1, $140 million at year 2, $150 million at year 3, $160 million at year 4, and $65 million in each of years 5 through 10. Equipment is projected to be replaced for a cost of $65 million at the end of year 6, and the salvage value at the end of year 10 is estimated at $40 million. Make before-tax NPV analysis to determine whether the project expansion is economically justifiable, given that the minimum rate of return is 15%. Verify your conclusion using before-tax ROR and PVR analyses.

```
Present -        R=100  R=100  R=100  R=100    -       -        - ........ -
         ─────────────────────────────────────────────────────────────────
         0        1      2      3      4       5       6       7 ....... 10

         R=100  R=140  R=150  R=160  R=65    R=65    R=65 ..... R=65
Expand C=40  C= 50  C= 55                          C=65                    L=40
         ─────────────────────────────────────────────────────────────────
         0        1      2      3      4       5       6       7 ....... 10
```

18. A mineral property is producing at a rate that will generate $5 million in annual net revenue (revenue minus operating costs) during the next year (assume end-of-year 1). Escalation of operating costs is expected to be offset by sales escalation in future years so that annual end-of-year net revenue will remain constant at $5 million each year until mineral reserves are depleted 10 years from now at the current production rate. Increase of the production rate is being considered by incurring a $2 million development and equipment cost now (year 0) and a $4 million equipment and development cost a year from now (year 1). These expansion costs would permit increasing mineral production to give projected total net revenues of $6 million at year 1 and $8 million per year at year 2 through 8 when reserves will be depleted at the increased production rate. Use net present value analysis to evaluate the economic desirability of the expansion investments for a minimum rate of return of 20%. Verify your results using rate of return analysis and PVR analysis.

```
Present   -       I=5    I=5 .............. I=5    I=5     I=5
         ───────────────────────────────────────────────────
         0        1      2 ................ 8      9       10

                  I=6
Expand   C=2     C=4    I=8 .............. I=8      -       -
         ───────────────────────────────────────────────────
         0        1      2 ................ 8      9       10
```

19. A chemical company has done research in recent years that has resulted in a new process patent. To acquire the patent rights an outside investor has offered to pay $2 million now and another $4 million in two equal deferred payments of $2 million each 4 and 5 years from now. The investor has an excellent credit rating and sufficient assets so that the offer seems financially solid. The company estimates that internal development of a new plant to implement the patent rights would cost $0.5 million now and $4 million a year from now to generate net income (revenue minus operating costs) of $1 million a year from now and $2 million per year 2 and 3 years from now. If the plant is developed internally it is projected that it would be sold for $6 million 3 years from now. Use ROR Analysis to determine if the economics favor internal development or selling, assuming other opportunities exist to invest capital at 15%. Then determine the single lump sum sale value that received now would make the economics of selling and developing equivalent.

20. A deep water-flood project has been on line for 2 years and problems with artificial lift equipment are becoming evident. Engineering calculations indicate that the producing wells are capable of 750 barrels of fluid per day (BFPD), but problems with the existing artificial lift system has limited production capacity to 400 BFPD per well. The project engineer has to decide whether to (1) reduce the injection rates to match the artificial lift capabilities, or (2) maintain injection and redesign the artificial lift equipment to lift larger volumes of fluid (750 BFPD per well). If injection is reduced the reserves will be recovered slower with the "reduced injection" schedule shown below. If the artificial lift system is modified the reserves can be accelerated and recovered according to the "modified lift" schedule. M = Thousand.

Year	Reduced Injection Oil Production (M Bbl)	Modified Lift Oil Production (M Bbl)
1	1200	1500
2	1300	1700
3	1500	2200
4	1700	2150
5	1400	1700
6	1300	1500
7	1200	1300
8	1100	750
9	1000	350
10	750	100
11	400	0

The year 0 cost of the up-graded artificial lift facility is estimated at $7 million (85% tangible) with operating costs of $1.5 million more a year relative to the current operation. Other known information follows: 1) working interest is 100%, 2) net interest is 80% and 3) oil price per barrel is $24.00 (assume escalation of incremental operating expenses exactly offsets escalation of incremental revenues). Is it economically preferable to reduce the injection rates or to redesign and modify the lift system if the minimum acceptable before-tax rate of return is 15%?

21. A mining company is evaluating whether it is economically desirable to pay $5 million now for a partially developed gold mine if another $3 million must be spent a year from now for further development with a 70% probability of success and if successful another $4 million must be spent 2 years from now with a 90% probability of this final investment giving a profitable producing gold mine that will generate profits of $4 million per year for 20 years of production starting 3 years from now, assuming a washout of income and operating costs escalation. Salvage value will be 0 at the end of the project and if failure occurs at years 1 or 2 assume net abandonment costs and salvage values will be 0. If the escalated dollar minimum ROR is 20% is the project economical?

22. A coal mining project has been on line for 2 years. Engineering mine plan calculations indicate that the present mine production can be increased to the accelerated coal mining production schedule shown below by changing the mine plan and acquiring additional new equipment. The project engineer has to decide whether to (1) maintain current production rates, or (2) accelerate production by purchasing additional mining equipment to increase coal production. M = Thousand.

Year	Present Production (M Tons)	Accelerated Production (M Tons)
1	1200	1500
2	1300	1700
3	1500	2200
4	1700	2150
5	1400	1700
6	1300	1500
7	1200	1300
8	1100	750
9	1000	350
10	750	100
11	400	0

The year 0 cost of the accelerated coal mining production equipment is estimated at $7 million with operating costs of $1.5 million more a year relative to the current operation. Other known information follows: 1) working interest is 100%, 2) net revenue interest after royalties is 80% and 3) coal price per ton is $24.00 (assume escalation of incremental operating expenses exactly offsets escalation of incremental revenues). Is it economically desirable to maintain present coal mining production rates or to accelerate coal mining production if the minimum acceptable before-tax rate of return is 15%?

23. C = Capital Cost, OC = Operating Cost, I = Income. Values are in dollars.

    A) C=25,000   I=8,000   I=8,500   -> gradient = +500/yr.   L=0
       ───
       0   1   2 9

                     I=8,000   I=18,000   I=18,00
    B) C=12,000   C=15,000   OC=10,000 .... OC=10,000
       ───
       0   1   2 10

                          C=21,000
                  I=18,000 I=19,000   I=22,000   I=22,000
    C) C=20,000 OC=10,000 OC=10,000 OC=10,000 .... OC=10,000
       ───
       0   1   2   3 11

If alternatives A, B, and C are mutually exclusive, which alternative (if any) would be the economic choice if the minimum acceptable rate of return is 20%. If alternative A, B, and C are non-mutually exclusive, rank them in their order of economic desirability using PVR.

24. A prospect consists of two parallel structures on opposite sides of a fault. Both structures are long and narrow and must be drilled separately. Structure A has two potentially productive zones while structure B has only one potentially productive zone. Total Area is 6400 acres, 65% in Structure A and 35% in Structure B. Zone 1 has a geologic chance factor (probability of success) of 9.0% in Structure A and 25% in Structure B. Zone 2, found only in Structure A, has a geologic chance factor of 5.0%. Zone 2 is 500 feet deeper than Zone 1.

Assume development can only occur in the following cases:

1) All zones are productive.
2) Zone 2 of Structure A and Zone 1 of Structure B are both productive.
3) Zones 1 and 2 of Structure A are productive.

Draw the decision tree for this problem and label each branch with the appropriate probability of occurrence.

25. Make expected NPV and expected PVR analysis of the following petroleum exploration and production investment situation assuming the minimum rate of return is 15%. Acquisition of mineral rights at time zero will cost $200,000 and exploration drilling at time zero is expected to cost $800,000 with a 20% probability of success. Exploration drilling failure will require incurring a $50,000 year 1 abandonment cost. If logs from the exploration well indicate success, well completion, producing equipment, tank battery and pipeline costs of $700,000 will be incurred at year 1 with an estimated 100% probability of successfully bringing the well into production. Year 1 net revenue (revenue minus operating expenses) of $300,000 and year 2 through 10 net revenue of $400,000 per year are projected to be realized over the well producing life with declining production assumed to be offset by increased selling prices of crude oil and natural gas to simplify the analysis calculations. If the exploration well is successful, 2 development wells will be drilled simultaneously at year 1 for an estimated cost of $600,000 per well and an 80% probability of success. Development drilling failure will require incurring a $50,000 per well year 2 abandonment cost. Successful wells will be completed at year 2 for a cost of $500,000 per well with year 2 development well net revenues of $300,000 per well and year 3 through 11 net revenues of $500,000 per well per year projected to be realized.

26. A gold project is currently under economic consideration. It is estimated that $1,000,000 would be spent on defining reserves and acquiring the rights and necessary permitting for the property in year 0. The acquisition cost would be followed by the investment of $5,000,000 in mine development, $7,000,000 in mine equipment, and $2,000,000 in working capital for spare parts and product inventories, etc. All three costs (development, equipment, and working capital) are allocated to the end of year 1. Working capital is assumed to be liquidated at the end of year 8 when the project is terminated. Treat the revenue from working capital as regular income at year 8.

    The property is expected to generate 6,000 tons of ore per day for 150 days per year starting in year 2. Mining is limited to 150 days per year due to weather considerations. The ore is expected to have an average grade of 0.05 ounces of gold per ton with an anticipated recovery rate of 0.85. Assume the average selling price of gold is $330 per ounce per year, and operating costs are $210 per ounce per year. Escalation of price and operating costs each year is a "washout," meaning that before-tax profits are constant each year at $120 per ounce ($330/oz minus $210/oz). In acquiring the property, the company has agreed to pay a 6.0% royalty on "net profits" until the project pays out. Net profits are defined as gross revenue less operating costs. After payout, the royalty changes to 30% of net profits for the remainder of the project. Payout of the cumulative, undiscounted year 0 and 1 capital costs of $15,000,000 is based on "undiscounted net profits minus the 6% royalty."

    Calculate the ROR, NPV, and PVR for the mine development investor and also for the royalty recipient, assuming the before-tax, escalated dollar minimum rate of return is 15.0%. Then determine what before-tax dollars could be invested in a reclamation cost at year 9 to give the development investor a 15% ROR.

27. Make the analysis asked for in Auxiliary Problem #26 on an after-tax basis. Assume the year 0 $1,000,000 acquisition cost will be deducted for tax purposes by cost depletion. The $7,000,000 year 1 equipment cost will be deducted by 7 year life MACRS depreciation starting in year 1 with the half-year convention. 70% of the year 1 mining development cost of $5,000,000 will be expensed at year 1, and the remaining 30% will be amortized over 60 months with a full 12 month deduction at year 1. Assume the effective income tax rate is 40%. Calculate the DCFROR, NPV, and PVR for the mine development investor and also for the royalty recipient, assuming the after-tax, escalated dollar minimum ROR is 15.0%. Then determine what before-tax dollars could be invested in a reclamation cost at year 9 to give the development investor a 15% after-tax DCFROR. Assume the cost would be 100% deductible at year 9. Finally, neglecting the reclamation cost and prior to incurring any year 0 costs, what is the before-tax acquisition cost (at year 0) to acquire the rights to develop this property that just gives the development investor a 15% after-tax DCFROR?

28. An investor has paid $100,000 for a machine today (time 0) that is estimated to have a 70% probability of successfully producing 5000 product units per year for each of the next 3 years, when the machine is estimated to be obsolete with a zero salvage value. The product price is the unknown to be calculated, so it is estimated to be $X per unit in year 1 escalated dollars and to increase 10% per year in year 2 and 6% in year 3. Total operating costs are estimated to be $8000 in year 1 escalated dollars and to increase by 15% in year 2 and 8% in year 3. The annual inflation rate is estimated to be 7%. What must be the year 1, 2 and 3 escalated dollar product selling price if the investor is to receive a 12% annually compounded constant dollar expected DCFROR on invested dollars? Use modified ACRS depreciation rates for a 5 year depreciation life starting depreciation in year 0 with the half year convention. Write off the remaining book value at the end of year 3. Other taxable income is assumed to exist against which to use year 0 negative taxable income. Assume a 40% income tax rate. Consider zero net cash flow to be realized the 30% of the time the project fails. This assumes that after-tax equipment dismantlement costs will exactly offset the tax write-off and salvage value benefits.

29. A non-mineral project has been analyzed to have the following cash investment after-tax cash flow stream:

-$800,000	+$400,000	+$500,000	+$550,000
0	1	2	3

Convert the cash investment cash flow to leveraged cash flow assuming $500,000 is borrowed at year 0 for 12% interest per year with the loan to be paid off with three uniform and equal mortgage payments at years 1, 2 and 3. Assume a 40% effective ordinary income tax rate.

A) Calculate the leveraged project DCFROR.
B) How much could be paid at year 0 to acquire the rights to develop the leveraged project and achieve a 25% leveraged DCFROR on equity dollars if the acquisition cost is amortizable over 3 years (years 1, 2 and 3)?

30. A proposed project has today's dollar costs and revenues as follows:

	Rev=300	Rev=300
C=200	OC=100	OC=100
0	1	2

For an escalated dollar minimum discount rate of 12%:

A) Calculate the project escalated dollar NPV for revenue escalation of 5% in year 1, and 6% in year 2, and cost escalation of 8% in year 1, and 10% in year 2.
B) Calculate the project constant dollar NPV assuming inflation will be 7% per year and escalation of costs and revenues is the same as in Case A. Remember you must adjust the escalated dollar minimum discount rate of 12% using text Equation 5-1 to calculate the equivalent constant dollar minimum discount rate for use in this constant dollar NPV analysis.
C) Calculate the project escalated dollar NPV assuming today's dollar values equal escalated dollar values. State the explicit cost and revenue escalation assumption built into this analysis.
D) Calculate the project constant dollar NPV assuming today's dollar values equal constant dollar values. State the explicit cost and revenue escalation assumption built into this analysis.

31. You are to determine the investment DCFROR that an investor who pays $400,000 for an office building at year 0 would realize on equity investment based on the following data. 90% of the acquisition cost will be for the building which goes into service in the first month of year 1 (business buildings are real property, depreciable straight line over 39 years). 10% of the acquisition cost is for land, deductible only against the terminal sale value estimated to be $500,000 at the end of year 2. Any sale gain would be taxed as individual ordinary income. $320,000 of the acquisition cost will be borrowed at year 0 at 10% annual interest with the loan set up to be paid off over 5 years with uniform and equal mortgage payments. Assume unpaid loan principal will be paid off at the end of year 2 when the property is sold. Revenues are projected to be $80,000 in year 1 and $85,000 in year 2 with operating costs of $30,000 in year 1 and $35,000 in year 2. The effective ordinary income tax rate is 30% and other income exists against which to use deductions in any year that negative taxable income exists.

A) Calculate the leveraged investment DCFROR.
B) Determine the maximum investment price that could be paid to give the investor a 15% leveraged DCFROR on his equity invested dollars assuming the investment is 10% land and 90% office building.
C) Calculate the cash investment DCFROR that corresponds to the leveraged DCFROR calculated in part A for the $400,000 investment price. Then determine the maximum investment price that would give the investor a 15.0% cash equity investment DCFROR if it is 10% land and 90% office building.

32. A project manager is evaluating whether it is economical to develop a project requiring expenditures at time zero of $20,000 for land, $30,000 for inventory working capital, $80,000 for a business building, $240,000 for equipment and $60,000 for vehicles. Starting in year 1 he estimates that production will generate annual end-of-year escalated revenue of $500,000 with escalated operating costs of $300,000. In the following years it is estimated that operating costs and revenue will both escalate at 10% per year. At the end of year 4, it is estimated that all the assets and working capital can be sold for an escalated terminal revenue of $600,000. Determine the investment DCFROR assuming a 40% effective income tax rate. Use straight line depreciation over 39 years for the building cost starting in year 1, assuming 12 months of service in year 1; MACRS depreciation for a 7 year life for the equipment cost starting at year 1 with the half-year convention; and MACRS depreciation for a 5 year life for the vehicle cost starting at year 1 with the half-year convention. Assume the terminal value gain is taxed as ordinary income. Take a write-off on all of the remaining tax book values at the end of year 4. For an after-tax escalated dollar minimum rate of return of 15%, determine NPV and PVR in addition to the previously requested DCFROR analysis.

33. A corporation has requested that you evaluate the economic potential of purchasing a gold property now (at year 0) for $2 million mineral rights acquisition cost. Mining equipment costs of $3 million will be incurred at year 0 and the equipment will be placed into service at year 0 when depreciation starts using modified ACRS 7 year life depreciation with the half year convention at year 0. Write-off the remaining book value at year 5. Mineral development costs of $1 million will be incurred at month 1 of year 0 and mineral development costs of $1.5 million will be incurred at month 1 of year 1. Production is projected to start in year 1 with the mining of 150,000 tons of gold ore, with uniform production of 250,000 tons of gold ore per year in each of years 2, 3 and 4. Gold ore reserves are estimated to be depleted at the end of year 4. Reclamation costs (treat as operating expenses) of $0.5 million in escalated dollars will be incurred at year 5 when escalated $1 million is projected to be realized from equipment salvage value. All gold ore is estimated to contain 0.1 ounce of gold per ton of ore and metallurgical recovery is estimated to be 90%. The price of gold is estimated to be $300 per ounce in year 1 and to escalate 15% in year 2, 20% in year 3 and 10% in year 4. Operating costs are estimated to be $20 per ton of ore produced in year 1 and to escalate 8% per year. Assume other income exists against which to use negative taxable income in any year. The effective income tax rate is 40%.

A) Calculate the cash investment DCFROR and NPV for a minimum escalated dollar DCFROR of 15%.

B) If it is considered likely that after acquiring the property and before spending money on development and equipment the company can generate a cash offer of $5 million for the property with the execution of the sale agreement and cash payment to be at year 1, is it economically better for the company to sell or keep and develop the property?

C) What sale value at year 1 makes the economics of selling break-even with development for the assumptions of part B?

D) If development is partially financed with $5 million borrowed at 10% annual interest at year 0 to be paid off with 4 equal mortgage payments at years 1 through 4, calculate the leveraged investment DCFROR and NPV for a leveraged minimum escalated dollar DCFROR of 15%.

E) What sale value at year 1 makes the economics of selling break-even with development using borrowed money for the sale assumptions of part B?

34. A pipeline to transport natural gas from a new gas well to an existing trunk line is estimated to cost $200,000 at year 0 with escalated dollar operating costs estimated to be $9,000 per year at each of production years 1 through 4. It is expected that the gas well will be shut-in at the end of year 4 and that the pipeline salvage value will be zero. Projected natural gas production to be handled by the pipeline follows:

Year	0	1	2	3	4
Average Annual Production (MMcf)		2,000	1,500	1,000	500

where MMcf equals million cubic feet and Mcf equals thousand cubic feet. The pipeline cost of $200,000 would be depreciated over a 7 year life using MACRS depreciation starting in year 1 with the half year convention. A write-off on remaining book value would be taken at year 4. The effective income tax rate is 40%. Calculate the uniform transportation price per Mcf of natural gas transported that would give the pipeline investor:

A) A 15% escalated dollar DCFROR on invested capital.

B) A 15% constant dollar DCFROR on invested capital for inflation of 8% per year over the project life.

35. A conveyor to transport coal (or mineral concentrate) from a loading point to a shipping facility is estimated to cost $200,000 at year 0 with escalated dollar operating costs estimated to be $9,000 per year at each of production years 1 through 4. It is expected that use of the conveyor will terminate at the end of year 4, and that the salvage value will be zero. Projected coal (or mineral concentrate) production to be handled by the conveyor follows:

Year	0	1	2	3	4
Average Annual Production (M tons)		2,000	1,500	1,000	500

where "M tons" = thousand tons.

The conveyor cost of $200,000 would be depreciated over a 7 year life using MACRS depreciation, starting in year 1 with the half-year convention. A write-off on remaining book value would be taken at year 4. The effective income tax rate is 40%. Calculate the uniform transportation price per ton of coal (or mineral concentrate) that would give the investor:

A) A 15% escalated dollar DCFROR on invested capital.

B) A 15% constant dollar DCFROR on invested capital for inflation of 8% per year over the project life.

NOTES ON D,D&A CALCULATIONS

Modified ACRS Depreciation Table 7-3, p. 327

Year	3	5	7	10
1	.3333	.2000	.1429	.1000
2	.4445	.3200	.2449	.1800
3	.1481	.1920	.1749	.1440
4	.0741	.1152	.1249	.1152
5		.1152	.0893	.0922
6		.0576	.0892	.0737
7			.0893	.0655
8			.0446	.0655
9				.0656
10				.0655
11				.0328

Regular Corporation, Mining Project
- Expense 70% of Development & Exploration, p. 312.
- Amortize 30% of Dev. & Explor Over 60 Months, p. 312.
- Take Larger of Percentage or Cost Depletion, p.330.
  Use Table 7-4, & 50% Limit on Percentage Depln, p. 333-4.

Integrated Petroleum Company Project
- Expense 70% of Intangible Drilling Costs, p. 313.
- Amortize 30% of IDC's Over 60 Months, p. 313.
- Only Take Cost Depletion, p. 330.

Non-Integrated Petroleum Company Project
- Expense 100% of Intangible Drilling Costs, p. 313.
- Take Larger of Percentage or Cost Depletion
  On First 1,000 Bbls/Day of Production, Table 7-4, p. 330.
- 100% Limit Applies to Qualifying Percentage Depletion
- Cost Depletion Only on Prod. Above 1,000 Bbl/Day

Percentage Depletion Rates in Table 7-5, Pg 334.

Cost Depletion, Pg 331.

$$(\text{Adjusted Basis})\left(\frac{\text{Units Removed \& Sold Each Yr.}}{\text{Total Reserves @ Beginning of Yr}}\right) = \text{Cost Depletion}$$

"Adjusted Basis" is reduced each year for "actual" depletion taken in preceding year.

SUMMARY WORKSHEET FOR CASH FLOW CALCULATIONS

PROBLEM # _____

Year	0	1	2	3	4	5	6	7
Production								
Selling Price $/Unit								
Gross Revenue								
- Royalties								
Net Revenue								
- Research / Develop / IDC's								
- Operating Expense								
- Depreciation								
- Amortization								
- Writeoff's on D, D & A								
Taxable Income Before Depl.								
- Limit (50% or 100%)								
- Percentage Depletion								
- Cost Depletion								
- Loss Forward								
Taxable Income								
- Tax @ ___ %								
+Tax Credits (If Applic.)								
= Net Income								
+ Depreciation Deduction								
+ Amortization Deduction								
+ Depletion Deduction								
+ Writeoff's on D, D & A								
+ Loss Forward Deduction								
- Capital Costs:								
- Depreciable Equip. Costs								
- Amortizable Costs								
- Mineral Rts. Acq. Costs								
- Land (Surface Rts)								
- Working Capital								
- Other								
= Cash Flow								
x(P/F 12%, n)	1.0000	.8929	.7972	.7118	.6355	.5674	.5066	.4523
= PW Cash Flow								
= Cum. CF (Yearly NPV)								

Table 7-4, Text Pg 333, (Not Applicable for Integrated Producer's & Independents Over 1,000 Bbls/Day)

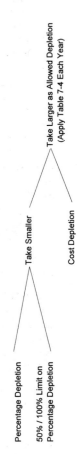

Percentage Depletion

50% / 100% Limit on Percentage Depletion

Take Smaller

Take Larger as Allowed Depletion (Apply Table 7-4 Each Year)

Cost Depletion

Modified ACRS Depreciation Table 7-3, p. 327

Year	3	5	7	10
1	.3333	.2000	.1429	.1000
2	.4445	.3200	.2449	.1800
3	.1481	.1920	.1749	.1440
4	.0741	.1152	.1249	.1152
5		.1152	.0893	.0922
6		.0576	.0892	.0737
7			.0893	.0655
8			.0446	.0655
9				.0656
10				.0655
11				.0328

Regular Corporation, Mining Project
- Expense 70% of Development & Exploration, p. 312.
- Amortize 30% of Dev. & Explor Over 60 Months, p. 312.
- Take Larger of Percentage or Cost Depletion, p.330.
Use Table 7-4, & 50% Limit on Percentage Depln, p. 333-4.

Integrated Petroleum Company Project
- Expense 70% of Intangible Drilling Costs, p. 313.
- Amortize 30% of IDC's Over 60 Months, p. 313.
- Only Take Cost Depletion, p. 330.

Non-Integrated Petroleum Company Project
- Expense 100% of Intangible Drilling Costs, p. 313.
- Take Larger of Percentage or Cost Depletion
On First 1,000 Bbls/Day of Production, Table 7-4, p. 330.
- 100% Limit Applies to Qualifying Percentage Depletion
- Cost Depletion Only on Prod. Above 1,000 Bbl/Day

Cost Depletion, Pg 331.

Percentage Depletion Rates in Table 7-5, Pg 334.

Cost Depletion:

$$(\text{Adjusted Basis})\left(\frac{\text{Units Removed \& Sold Each Yr.}}{\text{Total Reserves @ Beginning of Yr}}\right) = \text{Cost Depletion}$$

"Adjusted Basis" is reduced each year for "actual" depletion taken in preceding year.

Table 7-4, Text Pg 333, (Not Applicable for Integrated Producer's & Independents Over 1,000 Bbls/Day)

Percentage Depletion ↘
 → Take Smaller → 50% / 100% Limit on Percentage Depletion
Cost Depletion ↗

 → Take Larger as Allowed Depletion (Apply Table 7-4 Each Year)

Cost Depletion

SUMMARY WORKSHEET FOR CASH FLOW CALCULATIONS

PROBLEM #	0	1	2	3	4	5	6	7
Production								
Selling Price $/Unit								
Gross Revenue								
- Royalties								
Net Revenue								
- Research / Develop / IDC's								
- Operating Expense								
- Depreciation								
- Amortization								
- Writeoffs on D, D & A								
Taxable Income Before Depl.								
- Limit (50% or 100%)								
- Percentage Depletion								
- Cost Depletion								
- Loss Forward								
Taxable Income								
- Tax @ %								
+Tax Credits (If Applic.)								
= Net Income								
+ Depreciation Deduction								
+ Amortization Deduction								
+ Depletion Deduction								
+ Writeoff's on D, D & A								
+ Loss Forward Deduction								
- Capital Costs:								
- Depreciable Equip. Costs								
- Amortizable Costs								
- Mineral Rts. Acq. Costs								
- Land (Surface Rts)								
- Working Capital								
- Other								
= Cash Flow								
x(P/F 12%, n)	1.0000	.8929	.7972	.7118	.6355	.5674	.5066	.4523
= PW Cash Flow								
= Cum. CF (Yearly NPV)								